PHILOSOPHICAL WRITINGS

The text of this work is reprinted from
The Nelson Philosophical Texts

General Editor
RAYMOND KLIBANSKY

Emeritus Professor of Philosophy,
McGill University and University of Heidelberg
Fellow, Wolfson College, Oxford University

PHILOSOPHICAL WRITINGS

A Selection

JOHN DUNS SCOTUS

Translated, with Introduction and Notes, by
ALLAN WOLTER, O.F.M.

With a Foreword by
MARILYN MCCORD ADAMS

HACKETT PUBLISHING COMPANY
Indianapolis / Cambridge

JOHN DUNS SCOTUS: ca. 1266-1308

Cover design by Listenberger Design

For further information, please address

Hackett Publishing Company
P.O. Box 44937
Indianapolis, Indiana 46204

Library of Congress Cataloging-in-Publication Data

Duns Scotus, John, ca. 1266-1308.
    Duns Scotus, philosophical writings.

    "The text of this work is reprinted from the
Nelson Philosophical Texts"—T.p. verso.
    A reprint of the Nelson edition with Latin text
and English translation on facing pages with new
frwd, introd., and bib.
    Bibliopgraphy: p.
    Includes.
    1. God. 2. Soul. 3. Knowledge, Theory of
4. Metaphysics. I. Wolter, Allan Bernard,
1913-   . . II. Title.
B765.D72E58   1987   211   87-11990
ISBN 0-87220-019-1
ISBN 0-87220-018-3 (pbk.)

CONTENTS

PHILOSOPHICAL WRITINGS

FOREWORD TO THE SECOND EDITION

In 1977-78, the Center for Medieval and Renaissance Studies at UCLA offered to bring an expert on medieval philosophy to our department for a quarter. My first choice was Allan B. Wolter, the scholar who has done more than anyone else writing in English to render the philosophy of John Duns Scotus accessible and intelligible. Wolter's published research on Scotus is characterized by a rare balance of insight, philosophical penetration, and clarity of presentation. The body of his interpretive work is not only the place any new Scotus-scholar must start; it is an achievement that will be difficult to surpass.

However fine the secondary literature, responsible teaching of history of philosophy always introduces the students to the primary sources. And where medieval philosophy is concerned, this requires translations in most American schools and universities. Apart from medievalists, few philosophy faculty and only a tiny minority of students are proficient in Latin. And even those who made their way through Caesar in high school will find Scotus' Latin a challenge!

Wolter began applying his natural flair for translation to this problem in the mid 1950s. Assigned to teach scholastic philosophy to M.A. candidates in the New York Province, Wolter found there were no readings with which to work. Worse than that, the Vatican (modern critical) edition of Scotus' *Ordinatio* had just begun to appear. So Wolter turned to the Assisi manuscript (Codex

vii

Assisii, bibliotheca communalis 137) for his Latin text,
correcting obvious errors against other manuscripts. (It is
interesting to note that the Vatican edition, which has
since become available, differs very little from Wolter's
version, except that Wolter includes while Vatican foot-
notes interpolations obviously intended by Scotus.) Editing, translating, and making judicious selections as he
went, Wolter produced the present anthology for his
course. The decision to publish, first taken in 1958,
resulted in the 1962 issue of an English-Latin version in
The Nelson Philosophical Texts series, edited by Raymond Klibansky. An English-only paperback was published by Bobbs-Merrill in the Library of Liberal Arts
series in 1964. In reverting to the original English-Latin
format, the present re-publication of *Duns Scotus: Philosophical Writings* wins three advantages: (i) Scotus' philosophy is rendered into clear English; (ii) Wolter's original
Latin text is preserved for contrast with the Vatican edition; and (iii) students and faculty are provided with a
wonderful tool for learning to read Scotus' Latin.

In subject matter, the present volume constitutes an
introduction to Scotus' metaphysics and epistemology.
The first selection sets forth Scotus' vision of God as the
goal of any rational metaphysics whose subject is being
qua being. The second is a defense of his subtle position
on the possibility of univocal predication between God
and creatures. The third and fourth contain perhaps the
most elaborate and ingenious version of the cosmologi-
cal argument in the history of philosophy. The fifth
contains Scotus' rejection of scepticism and sets forth his
own version of Aristotelian reliabilism in epistemology.
The final selection includes Scotus' critique of Aquinas-
style proofs of the soul's incorporeality and immortality
along with Scotus' own, more guarded conclusions.

Wolter's subsequent translations combine with this
volume to fill out several advanced syllabi on Scotus'

philosophy. In 1966, Wolter rendered into English Scotus' elegant but difficult *De Primo Principio, A Treatise on
God as First Principle*, which re-appeared in a second
edition with Wolter's extensive and penetrating commentary in 1983 (Franciscan Herald Press, Chicago, Illinois).
In collaboration with Felix Alluntis, Wolter published
*John Duns Scotus: God and Creatures, The Quodlibetal Ques-
tions* (Princeton University Press, 1975; reprinted by
Catholic University of America Press, Washington, D.C.,
1981). Most recently, in *Duns Scotus on the Will and Morality* (Catholic University of America Press, Washington,
D.C. 1986), Wolter has opened up Scotus' action theory,
moral psychology, and ethics with a substantial and wide-
ranging selection of texts and comprehensive philosophical analysis.

Thanks to Wolter's contributions, both in research and
translation, it is now possible to teach the full range of
Scotus' thought to philosophy students at the graduate
and undergraduate level. I applaud Hackett's decision to
bring the present volume, the obvious staple for any
course on later medieval philosophy, back into print.

University of California,   MARILYN MCCORD ADAMS
  Los Angeles
  October 1986

PREFACE TO THE FIRST EDITION

In a volume of the present size, a compiler can give a broader if somewhat piecemeal view of a man's philosophy by limiting the length of the selections, or he may sacrifice comprehensiveness of subject matter in the interests of revealing his thinker at work. I have chosen the latter alternative, building the present selection around five key questions concerned with God and the human soul, the two philosophical topics of greatest interest to an *ex professo* theologian like Duns Scotus.

Following the Avicennian interpretation of Aristotelian metaphysics, like Albertus Magnus, Siger of Brabant, Aquinas and most scholastics of his day, Scotus envisioned God as the goal of any rational metaphysic whose subject is being *qua* being. The two selections dealing with the existence and unicity of God, then, form the core of his "first philosophy." They are introduced by a few short sections in which Scotus describes this "transcendental science" and the type of conclusion it purports to establish, followed by a question wherein the Subtle Doctor analyzes his philosophical concept of God in terms of his controversial thesis regarding the univocity of being. Of the two questions about the human soul, one touches on its spirituality and immortality, the other concerns its ability to attain certain knowledge.

Taken from Scotus' most important work, his *Ordinatio* (called more frequently, if less accurately, his *Oxford Commentary on the Sentences of Peter Lombard*), the key questions are presented in their entirety, except for certain minor

marginal notes in the manuscript text and—where Scotus has combined several questions into one—those portions not germane to the question selected. The manuscript (Codex Assisii, bibliotheca communalis 137) from which the Latin text is taken, represents an early fourteenth-century attempt at a critical edition of this work and is the basis of the Vatican edition now in progress. Where the text is obviously at fault, however, I have not hesitated to adopt a better manuscript reading for the translation.

The short bibliography makes no attempt to do justice to the flood of recent Scotistic literature, especially in foreign languages, but is limited to larger English monographs on specific aspects of Scotus' philosophy or to works like those of Father Copleston or Miss Sharp, wherein a fairly brief but comprehensive account of Scotus' general philosophical positions can be found.

May I take this occasion to express my indebtedness to the late Father Philotheus Boehner, o.f.m., and to Father Gaudens Mohan, o.f.m., of the Franciscan Institute, for help in preparing and checking the Latin text. I am deeply grateful also to Professor Raymond Klibansky for his part in bringing this volume to fruition, though I have not been able to accept all his suggestions. I take full responsibility both for the constitution of the text and for the translation.

The Franciscan Institute,   ALLAN B. WOLTER
St Bonaventure, N.Y.
1962

INTRODUCTION

The documentary evidence on the life of John Duns Scotus is scanty, comprising hardly more than half a dozen specifically chronological records. The most likely account of his birthplace is found in Scotist John (Mair) Major's history of his native Scotland, published in 1521, based on an even earlier tradition.

John Duns, that subtle doctor,...was a Scottish Briton, for he was born at Duns, a village eight miles distant from England, and separated from my own home by seven or eight leagues only. When he was no more than a boy, but had been already grounded in grammar, he was taken by two Scottish Minorite friars to Oxford, for at that time there existed no university in Scotland. By the favour of those friars he lived in the convent of the Minorites at Oxford, and he made his profession in the religion of Blessed Francis. As he was a man of the loftiest understanding and the keenest powers in debate, his designation of 'the subtle' was fully justified. At Oxford he made such progress that he left behind him for the admiration of after ages a monumental work upon the *Metaphysics* and four books of the *Sentences*. These writings of his are commonly called the English or Oxford work. When he was afterwards summoned by the Minorites of Paris to that city, he produced there another set of lectures on the *Sentences*, more compendious than that first edition, and at the same time more useful. These lectures we have but lately caused to be printed with metal types. In the end he went to Cologne, and there died while still a young man.[1]

---

1. *A History of Greater Britain as well England as Scotland Compiled from the Ancient Authorities by John Major, by name indeed a Scot, but by profession a Theologian*. Translated from the original Latin by Archibald Constable (Edinburgh, 1892), pp. 206-207.

xiii

The fact that in the manuscripts he is called both "John Duns" and "John of Duns" suggests that Duns is his family name as well as the place of his birth. In choosing 1966 for the International Congress to commemorate the seventh centenary of that event, and in raising a cairn near the Pavilion Lodge of the Duns castle on the outskirts of the town of Duns in Berwickshire and a statue of John in the town's Public Park, scholars honored a long tradition not only as to the site of his birth but approximately when it occurred. The more specific details of his parentage, his early schooling at Haddington and the story of his entry into the Franciscan order, however, as found in the so-called Tweedy transcription of the Chronicle of the Scottish Franciscans preserved in the eighteenth century *Monasticon Scoticanum* by Marianus Brockie, O.S.B., can no longer be trusted.[2]

More certain, however, is the record discovered by Longpré of Scotus' ordination to the priesthood by Oliver Sutton, Bishop of Lincoln, on March 17, 1291. Of the forty-eight priests ordained that day in the priory of St. Andrew, Northampton, five were Franciscans or Minorites, including "Fr. Johannes Dons."[3]

On July 26, 1300 we know for certain Scotus was at Oxford (in the diocese of Lincoln), for we find his name among the twenty-two friars of the Oxford convent whose names the English provincial, Hugh of Hartlepool, submitted to John Dalderby, Bishop of Lincoln, for

---

2. H. Docherty, "The Brockie Forgeries," *The Innes Review* 16 (1965), pp. 79-127; idem, "The Brockie MSS. and Duns Scotus," *De doctrina Ioannis Duns Scoti* (Acta Congressus Scotistici Internationalis Oxonii et Edimburgi 11-17 Sept. 1966 celebrati), I (Romae, 1968), pp. 329-60.

3. E. Longpré, O.F.M., L'ordination sacerdotale du bx. Jean Duns Scotus. Document du 17 mars 1291," *Archivum Franciscanum Historicum* 22 (1929), pp. 54-62.

faculties to hear confessions at the friars church in Oxford.[4]

The colophon of Codex 66 of Merton College, Oxford, contains this note by an early fourteenth-century hand: "This is from the *Ordinatio* of the Venerable Friar John Duns of the Order of Friars Minor, who flourished at Cambridge, Oxford and Paris, and died in Cologne."[5]

In the Worcester manuscript (F 69), one of the earliest of Scotus' Parisian lectures on the *Sentences*, is the remark that Scotus began commenting on the first book "at Paris in the year of the Lord 1302, the third having started," and that he commented on the fourth book "in the study at Paris in the year 1303." The phrase "the third having started" seems to be a reference to the autumn term (that began about October 9, 1302).[6] According to the "Gallican custom" the new year began on 25 March, the feast of the Annunciation. Scotus' presence in Paris at this time is confirmed by the fact that we find his name listed among those friars who on June 25, 1303 refused to support King Philip IV in his appeal to a general council against Pope Boniface VIII. The penalty for such opposition was exile from France within three days.[7]

Scotus was evidently back in Paris again by the end of 1304, for his former teacher, Gonsalvus of Spain, newly elected Minister General or head of the Franciscan Order, sent a letter from Ascoli in the March of Ancona on November 18, 1304 to William, guardian of the Fran-

---

4. A. G. Little, "Chronological Notes on the Life of Duns Scotus," *English Historical Review* 47 (1932), p. 572.

5. Ibid., p. 571.

6. Ibid., pp. 574-75.

7. Ibid., pp. 575-77.

ciscan convent at Paris.[8] In translation it reads as follows:

In reference to the promotion of Friar Giles of Ligny, about whom I have been informed by your letters, we ought, as the custom is, to make provision for another similar presentation. Since, according to the statutes of the Order and the statutes of your convent, the bachelor to be presented at this time should belong to some province other than the province of France, I assign to you Friar John Scotus, of whose laudable life, excellent knowledge, and most subtle ability, as well as his other remarkable qualities, I am fully informed, partly from long experience and partly from report which has been spread everywhere—to be presented primarily and in the regular course after the said Friar Giles. I enjoin you nevertheless that you make such presentation with due solemnity without much expense. If, however, you should be certain that the Chancellor be willing to license two of our friars at the same time, I desire that Friar Albert of Metz, if he shall be able to return to the convent, be promoted together with the said Friar John. In which case, I rule that Friar Albert on account of his seniority should incept first, Friar John incepting afterwards under him. Farewell in the Lord and pray for me. Given in the place of Ascoli of the province of the March of Ancona, xiv Kal. Dec. 1304.

The final mention of Scotus is found in the records of a provincial chapter at Cologne where he signed as "Fr. Johannes, lector Coloniae." The document gives permission for the erection of a convent and is dated *more Gallicorum* Feb. 20, 1307 (actually 1308).[9]

These documents, when viewed against the general historical background of the times, make it possible to construct the following more or less probable sketch of Scotus' life.

His family name was Duns. At the time Scotus was in Paris there were more than forty other friars in the Franciscan convent by the name of John. Here he

---

8. Ibid., pp. 577-78; Denifle-Chatelain, *Chartularium Universitatis Parisiensis*, II, p. 117.

9. Ibid., p. 582.

received the additional title of "Scotus" by reason of his nationality. At the time John Duns studied at Paris "Scotus" apparently was used exclusively in the sense of "a native of Scotland," and not, as in earlier times, to designate indiscriminately Irish or Scottish ancestry.

A popular tradition that goes back for centuries and was probably known to John Major claims that John's father was the younger son of the Duns of Grueldykes and lived on an estate adjoining the present town of Duns. The house where tradition maintains John was born stood near the more westerly lodge, now called the Pavilion Lodge, of Duns Castle. In the course of improvements made in 1790, the large stone marking the site of the house was built into the nearby dike and, according to local historians, was pointed out for generations. The stone cairn erected there on the occasion of the International Congress honoring his birth reads: "John Duns Scotus, the Subtle Doctor, and Member of the Franciscan Order, was born on this site in 1266. Wherever his distinguished name is uttered, he sheds luster on Duns and Scotland, the town and land which bore him. Erected by the Franciscan Order on the Seventh Centenary of his Birth, Sept. 1966."[10]

This probable date was arrived at because Bishop Sutton ordained at Northampton on both December 23, 1290 and March 17, 1291, and Callebaut argued that Scotus must have come of canonical age for ordination somewhere between these two dates. This would place his birth somewhere between December 23, 1265 and March 17, 1266. Fifteen was the earliest canonical age John could have entered the novitiate of the Franciscans. John Major's remark "when he was no more than a boy, but had been already grounded in grammar, he was

---

10. *Acta Ordinis Minorum* 85 (1966), p. 504.

taken by two Scottish Minorite friars to Oxford" suggests, in view of the custom of the times, that Scotus was taken into the convent as a *puer oblatus* or postulant, continuing his studies under some of the friars, until he was old enough to enter the Order. On this score, Callebaut places his entrance into the notiviate late in 1279 or early in 1280 and his solemn profession of vows a year later.[11]

Some manuscripts refer to Scotus as belonging to the English province, which is not strange if we recall the history of the Franciscans or Greyfriars in Scotland. Except for the short period of four years (1235-39) during which Bro. Elias as Minister General inflated the number of Franciscan provinces to 72, the Scottish friaries were never numerous enough to enjoy the status of an independent province, and for most of Scotus' lifetime they were under the jurisdiction of the northern English custody of Newscastle-on-Tyne.[12]

What happened between Scotus' entry into the Order and his ordination in 1291 is a matter of conjecture, as is also the period between 1291 and 1300 when he was again at Oxford. It is also problematical exactly when he studied or taught at Cambridge. Some have even argued for an earlier study period in Paris. Callebaut, for example, stressing the requirements of the University of Paris, claimed that Scotus must have spent at least four years in Paris some time shortly after 1292.[13] At the time he suggests, however, England was at war with France

---

11. A. Callebaut, O.F.M., "A propos du bx. J. D. S. de Littledean. Notes et recherches historiques de 1265 a 1292," *Archivum Franciscanum Historicum* 24 (1931), pp. 305-29.

12. R. M. Huber, O.F.M. CONV., *A Documented History of the Franciscan Order (1182-1517)* (Milwaukee and Washington, D.C., 1944) pp. 766-67.

13. A. Callebaut, O.F.M., "Le bx. J. D. S. étudiant à Paris vers 1293-6," *Archivum Franciscanum Historicum* 17 (1924), pp. 3-12.

and King Edward I had forbidden English students to cross the channel. Brampton gives a more plausible account of Scotus' continued career at Oxford, arguing that it began in October 1288 and ended in June 1301.[14] Scotus started his *Lectura* on the *Sentences* in the academic year that began in October 1298, and not in 1300 as previously thought. The following year (Oct. 1299 to June 1301) he lectured on Sacred Scripture. It was also during that last year as a bachelor that he would have taken part in the *Vesperies* of Friar Philip Bridlington (one of the public disputations connected with Philip's licensing as the Franciscan master of theology at Oxford.[15] That Thomas Sutton, the regent master of the Oxford Dominicans devoted an entire work to criticizing Bk. I of Scotus' commentary on the *Sentences* attests to Scotus' fame as well as his presence at Oxford at the turn of the century.[16]

Scotus never became a master at Oxford, however, for the long list of Franciscan bachelors before him waiting their turn to incept as well as John's considerable fame caused his superiors to send him to the more prestigious university of Paris when the opportunity arose. According to the Worcester manuscript we can infer that he must have arrived in Paris in time for the autumn term of 1302. Klibansky provides confirmation of Scotus' presence in

---

14. C. K. Brampton, "Duns Scotus at Oxford, 1288-1301," *Franciscan Studies* 24 (1964), pp. 5-20.

15. E. Longpré, O.F.M., "Philippe de Bridlington O.F.M. et le bx. Duns Scot," *Archivum Franciscanum Historicum* 22 (1929), pp. 587-88.

16. Thomas Anglicus (= Thomas von Sutton), *Liber propugnatorius super primum sententiarum contra Joannem Scotum* (Venedig 1523), reprint Frankfurt a. Main: Minerva G.M.B.H., 1966; cf. esp. fol. 100vb: "In ista quaestione [d. 26] ponit doctor iste quandam opinionem tanquam probabilem [scil. ponit personas divinas distingui per realitates absolutas]: quam cum ipse eam doceret Oxonie compulsus est publice revocare."

Paris during the scholastic year 1302-1303 and shows in all probability that he was present as a bachelor participant in the famous disputation between the Franciscan Master Gonsalvus and the Dominican Master Eckhart.[17]

Apparently Scotus' Parisian lectures that would have ended June 29, 1303 were interrupted by the decree of King Philip the Fair. The French monarch had quarreled with Pope Boniface VIII over the taxation of church property to support Philip's standing armies for his wars with England. When the Pope excommunicated the King, the latter appealed to a General Council of the Church to depose the Pope. He won over the French clergy, the universities and others to his cause. A great anti-papal demonstration took place on June 24. Mendicants of Paris marched in the procession. Berthold of St. Denis, Bishop of Orleans and ex-Chancellor of the University of Paris, together with two Dominicans and two Franciscans addressed the meeting. The following day royal commissioners examined each friar at the Franciscan convent to find out whether he was with or against the King. Some seventy friars, mostly French, sided with the King, while the rest (some eighty odd) remained loyal to the Pope. Among the latter we find the name of Scotus. According to royal orders, the Pope's partisans were to leave France within three days. Boniface countered with the Bull of August 15, 1303, in which he suspended the University's right to give degrees in theology, canon and civil law. This ban was withdrawn by Pope Benedict XI on April 2, 1304, and by April 18 the friars began to return.[18]

Where Scotus went during this exile is unknown. England, Bologna and Cologne have all been suggested. At

---

17. R. Klibansky, *Commentarium de Eckardi magisterio* (*Magistri Eckardi Opera Latina*, vol. 13, pp. xxx-xxxiii.

18. A. G. Little, *op. cit.*, p. 577.

any rate the exile was not long, for Scotus was back in Paris in 1304. If he returned by May he would, according to university regulations, begin commenting on Bk. IV of the *Sentences* on the third "legibile" day and complete his lectures by end of June. In the *Ordinatio* IV, dist. 25, q. 1 there is reference to a papal document of Benedict XI that Scotus says he himself saw, probably that issued in January 31, 1304, and in *Reportata parisiensia*, dist. 17 he cites Benedict's "new constitution *Inter cunctas*" issued February 17, 1304.[19]

There is some question as to the sequence in which Scotus commented on the four books of the *Sentences* at Paris, because of future tense references to Bks. II and III in Bk. IV. What is more, the difference among the "reportata" versions has suggested he may have commented twice on the *Sentences* at Paris, as others did, because of the great number of students there (three times that of Oxford).[20] To settle these questions further study of the manuscripts containing his Paris lectures is necessary. This much information on his teaching, however, seems certain. By the time Gonsalvus sent the Guardian at Paris instructions for his inception as the next master of theology, Scotus had completed or would shortly complete all the necessary requirements for promotion.

Probably his inception as master took place early in 1305. That the customary interval between the completion of the lectures on the *Sentences* and being licensed as master (four years according to university statutes) did not intervene was due probably to one of the many privileges granted to the friars. During his regency, we

---

19. Ibid.

20. F. Pelster, S.J., "Duns Skotus nach englishen Handschriften," *Franziskanische Studien* 10 (1923), pp. 11-15; Little, *op. cit.*, p. 578; Brampton, *op. cit.*, pp. 13-15.

know he conducted one solemn "quodlibetal disputation," probably during Advent of 1306 or Lent of 1307,[21] as well as an "ordinary disputation" with William Peter Godin, O.P., the Dominican master, on the question of whether matter is the principle of individuation.[22]

The fact that we have but one *Quodlibet* of Scotus argues that his regency was cut short by his departure for Cologne. The last record of his life indicates that he was in Cologne in February 1308, and if he had been teaching during the current semester, as the title "lector Coloniae" indicates, he must have begun at least by the autumn of 1307.

Various reasons have been assigned for his presence in Cologne. Callebaut and others have argued that the Minister General of the Friars sent him there to escape the consequences of his opposition to the King's action against the Knights Templars or that Scotus' departure was connected in some way with his defence of the doctrine of the Immaculate Conception against its Dominican adversaries. Longpré suggests a more prosaic reason and one perhaps nearer the truth, namely the common custom in the Order of sending the more brilliant lectors from one study house to another. At any rate, Scotus served a brief lectorship at Cologne. The traditional date of his death is November 8, 1308. His remains lie in the nave of the Minoritenkirche near the Cologne Cathedral, where he is venerated as a saint.

It is deplorable that Scotus' early death left almost every one of his major works in an unfinished state. But so great was his fame and following that his disciples made every effort to put his writings before the public.

---

21. P. Glorieux, *La littérature quodlibétique* II; Bibliotheque Thomiste 21 (Paris, 1935), p. 153.

22. Pelster, *op. cit.*, pp. 15-16.

With apparently more haste than prudence, they shuffled together earlier and later redactions, inserted parts to be deleted alongside their corrected substitutes and incorporated notes found in the margins or on scattered slips sandwiched between the pages of the master. It is only after decades of intense research by such men as Pelster, Pelzer, Longpré, Balić and others that some semblance of order has begun to emerge from the chaos. Not only have many treatises in the Wadding-Vivès *Opera omnia* been proved spurious, but even the certainly authentic writings appear in a new light. Today the following works are ascribed to Scotus.

THEOLOGICAL WORKS

1. *Commentaries on the Sentences*

Scotus commented several times on the *Sentences* of Peter Lombard. As John Major indicated, the two most important of these were the monumental Oxford work (*Opus oxoniense*, or *Ordinatio* as it is now called); the other was that of Paris (*Opus parisiense* or *Reportata parisiensia*), which John Major was instrumental in having printed. Modern research has not only revealed the existence of the original *Lectura* at Oxford, which is the basis of the *Ordinatio*, together with other unedited reports (e.g. one done at Cambridge), but has rediscovered the meaning of the terms *ordinatio* and *reportatio*. The original lecture of a master as copied down by one of his students or some scribe is known as a *reportatio*. If such a "reported version" is checked by the teacher himself it is referred to as a *reportatio examinata*. A *lectura* such as we have in the case of Scotus' Oxford and Cambridge periods is not strictly a *reportatio* but stems from the notes Scotus used for his

lectures. Almost invariably a lecturer would revise and enlarge his original lectures before presenting them for final publication and transmission to the booksellers. Such a redaction is known as an *ordinatio*, inasmuch as it represents a finished draft as ordered or arranged by the author himself. In most cases this was dictated to one or more secretaries provided for that purpose, so that often no autograph of its exists. Though Scotus had begun his *Ordinatio* based on his Oxford lectures before leaving England for Paris (as the date 1300, mentioned in question 2 of the Prologue would indicate), the reference in Bk. IV to the Bull of Benedict XI issued on 1304 suggests he was still at work on it in France.

In the original edition of this work I used the Latin text of the Assisi communal library, codex 137, because at the time I did the translation the text of Vatican critical edition was not available. Known now as Codex A, this manuscript is described in great detail by Balić in the introductory "De Ordinatione I. Duns Scot; disquisitio historico-critica," in the first volume of the Vatican edition of the *Opera omnia*. The scribe of Codex A evidently had access both to Scotus' original version (which he refers to as the "liber Scoti") as well as to a later version in which Scotus cancelled some portions and added others. And in the margin of his manuscript he tried to indicate these changes. The Vatican edition in an attempt to establish the original "liber Scoti" has relegated some of these later emendations found in Codex A to what it calls "interpolated texts," most of which can be found in *Reportatio* I A (which is the examined report of his later Paris lecture). Even though the selections II-V became available in the Vatican edition before our edition and translation reached the publication stage, since the number of interpolated texts turned out to be minimal, it seemed useful to retain the reading of Codex A, which for all practical purposes was identical with that of critical edition.

A third collection of questions on Bks. I and II of the *Sentences* goes by the name "Additiones magnae." Unlike the "small additions" consisting of a paragraph or so, these are a series of complete questions which represent an edited version of Scotus' Paris lectures with supplements from the "ordinatio" or revision of his Oxford lectures. They were made by William of Alnwick, Scotus' secretary, and seem to be an abridged version of a longer "reportatio" of the original Paris lectures. They are contained in Codex V (MS Vaticanus latinus 876, ff. 226ra-310vb) under the title "Lectura I parisiensis." The colophon to Bk. I reads: "Expliciunt magnae Additiones primi libri" followed by a list of the questions and "Expliciunt tituli quaestionum lecturae parisiensis super primum Sententiarum magistri Iohannis Duns, doctoris de Ordine Fratrum Minorum." After a question on the formalities, called the "Logica Scoti," are the questions on Bk. II. Sometimes only the title of the question is given with the exhortation "Hanc quaestionem quaere in ordinatione!" The colophon to Bk. II reads: "Expliciunt Additiones secundi libri magistri Ioannis de Duns, subtilis doctoris, extractae per magistrum Willelmum de Alnewyk, de Ordine Fratrum Minorum de lectura Parisiensi et Oxoniensi praedicti magistri Ioannis, cui propitietur Deus." The frequent references back to the *Ordinatio*, especially in Bk. II, suggests to me that Scotus had not only begun the prologue, but had completed a considerable portion of the "ordinatio" of his Oxford lectures before leaving for Paris, and that Alnwick intended this edited version of the Paris lectures as an update of what Scotus had done on his revision of Bks. I and II of the *Ordinatio*. Further study is necessary to substantiate this theory, but it would explain the fact, for example, that the treatment of the formal distinction in the Paris lectures seems to be a later and more fully developed account than that which he proposed in the *Ordinatio* I. The "examined report" of the Paris lectures

found in the version known as "Reportatio I A" should
obviously be given more weight than the "additiones
magnae" account, preferred by John Major and Wadding
and printed in their editions of Bk. I of the *Reportata
parisiensia*. But from an initial study of the few questions
of Rep. I A that Professor Adams and I have recently
published, it seems that Alnwick in his edited version of
these lectures was careful to retain not only the sense of
Scotus but often the very wording.[23]

2. Disputations

Scotus held several isolated disputations both as
bachelor and as master. He functioned in the former role
at the *Vesperies* of Philip of Bridlington, O.F.M. as well as in
the *disputatio in aula* on the occasion of Giles of Ligny's
promotion as master in Paris. The dispute with Peter
Godin, O.P. on the principle of individuation as well as the
Quaestio disputata de formalitatibus referred to by Adam
Wodam as *Logica Scoti* seem to be the work of Scotus as
master. More important than these isolated, and for the
most part, unedited, disputations are the *Quaestiones quodlibetales* and the *Collationes parisienses et oxonienses*. The
former comprise twenty-one questions that Scotus discussed as regent master in Paris, and represent one of the
latest and most mature of his works. The *Collationes*, on
the other hand, are much shorter disputed questions.
According to Balić they are forty-six in number, nineteen
of which were held in Paris and the rest in Oxford.[24] Little
and Pelster have pointed out that it was customary for

23. See A. B. Wolter and M. M. Adams, "Duns Scotus' Parisian Proof
for the Existence of God," *Franciscan Studies* XX (1982). pp. 249-321.

24. C. Balić, "De Collationibus Ioannis Duns Scoti, Doctoris Subtilis ac
Mariani," *Bogoslovski Vestnik*, 9 (1929), pp. 185-219.

students of logic, philosophy and theology to hold disputations every week or fortnight as a method of reviewing the material they had covered in their daily studies and suggest that those of Scotus "are private disputations of the students in the Franciscan house at Oxford [or Paris] in which the bachelor Duns Scotus, probably as master of students, took a leading part."[25] In addition to the incomplete collection edited by Wadding, C. R. S. Harris has edited five more questions.[26]

PHILOSOPHICAL WORKS

The *Tractatus de primo principio* is a short but important compendium of Scotus' natural theology. It seems to be one of his latest works and draws heavily on the *Ordinatio*. The Latin text is available in a modern critical edition done by M. Mueller, O.F.M. (Frieburg im Breisgau: Verlag Herder & Co., 1941). As one of the casualties of World War II, existing copies of this edition are limited. The text is reprinted respectively with a Spanish translation by Felix Alluntis, O.F.M. in *Obras del Doctor Sutil Juan Duns Escoto* (Madrid: Biblioteca de Auctores Christianos, 1960), pp. 595-710; with an Italian translation and commentary by Pietro Scapin, *Il Primo Principio degli esseri* (Padova: Liviana editrice, 1973); a German translation and commentary by Wolfgang Kluxen, *Johannes Duns Scotus: Abhandlung über das erste Prinzip* (Darmstadt: Wissenschaftliche Buchgesellschaft, 1974). A new edition and

---

25. A. G. Little and F. Pelster, *Oxford Theology and Theologians* (Oxford: Clarendon Press, 1934), p. 56.

26. C. R. S. Harris, *Duns Scotus*, v. 2 (Oxford: Clarendon Press, 1927), pp. 361-78.

English translation was done by Evan Roche, O.F.M., *The De Primo Principio of John Duns Scotus: A Revised Text and Translation* (St. Bonaventure, N.Y.: The Franciscan Institute, & Louvain, Belgium: E. Nauwelaerts, 1949). A. B. Wolter's *John Duns Scotus: A Treatise on God as First Principle* contains a new edition from which either the Mueller or Roche texts can be reconstructed (Chicago: Franciscan Herald Press, 1966); a second edition to which a paragraph by paragraph commentary on the text has been added was published by the same press in 1983.

Also authentic are the *Quaestiones subtilissimae in Metaphysicam Aristotelis*, although the last two books (X and XII) found in the Wadding and Vivès editions are spurious. Once believed to be an earlier work of Scotus, it seems to have been composed after the *Lectura*. The text of these questions as found in present editions is in a deplorable state. Fortunately, a team of editors from the Franciscan Institute at St. Bonaventure University is presently at work on a critical edition of this important text.

Somewhat less certain is the role Scotus played in regard to the *Quaestiones in libros Aristotelis De Anima*, which have traditionally been attributed to him. In addition to doctrinal discrepancies with the certainly authentic works, the Wadding edition contains passages found literally in Gonsalvus of Spain.

Less important for the history of Scotism are the logical writings found in the Wadding and Vivès editions. The following are generally accepted as genuine works of Scotus: *Quaestiones super Universalia Porphyrii*; *Quaestiones in librum Praedicamentorum*; *Quaestiones in I et II librum Perihermenias*; *Opus secundum sive octo quaestiones in duos libros Perihermenias*; *Quaestiones in libros Elenchorum*. There are still some difficulties connected with these works, however, so that perhaps the final word remains to be said.

Even more dubious are the *Theoremata*. Internal evi-

dence militates very strongly against their authenticity, though external reasons favor it. Even if Duns Scotus is definitely established as their author, the question of their literary genre and how they are to be interpreted remains to be determined, for this small tract seems to be simply notes or outlines of problems proposed as a disputation exercise, rather than a finished composition.[27]

The following philosophical works found in the Wadding and Vivès collections, however, are definitely spurious: *Grammatica speculativa* (Thomas of Erfurt); *Quaestiones in librum I et II priorum Analyticorum Aristotelis*; *Quaestiones in librum I et II posteriorum Analyticorum*; *Expositio et quaestiones in VIII libros Physicorum Aristotelis*; *Meteorologicorum libri quatuor*; *Expositio in XII libros Metaphysicorum Aristotelis seu Metaphysica textualis* (Antonius Andreas); *Conclusiones utilissimae ex libris Metaphysicorum Aristotelis collectae, Quaestiones dipsutatae de rerum principio* (Vital du Four); *Quaestiones miscellaneae de formalitatibus* (except the first question which contains the "Logica Scoti"); *De cognitione Dei tractatus imperfectus*, and *Tractatus de perfectione statuum*.

EDITIONS AND TRANSLATIONS

The first volumes of the new critical Vatican edition beginning with the *Ordinatio* appeared in 1950.[28] The

---

27. A. B. Wolter, "The Theologism of Duns Scotus," *Franciscan Studies* 7 (1947), pp. 257-73, 367-98; idem, *John Duns Scotus: A Treatise on God as First Principle,* 2d ed. (Chicago: Forum Books, Franciscan Herald Press, 1983), pp. xiv-xvi.

28. *Doctoris Subtilis et Mariani, Ioannis Duns Scoti, Ordinis Fratrum Minorum, opera omnia* (Civitas Vaticana: typis Polyglottis Vaticanis, 1950 --).

enormous difficulty of editing this most important of Scotus' writings is evidenced by the fact that after some thirty odd years only the first of the four books of the *Sentences*, together with three distinctions from the second book, have been completed. In addition, however, the Commission has published the hitherto unedited original *Lectura* of Bk. I and the first part of Bk. II on which the *Ordinatio* revision was based. For the greater portion of Scotus' writings, therefore, scholars must still have recourse to twelve volumes of the Luke Wadding edition.[29] In addition to the text, these contain notes, summaries and commentaries by famous Scotists. The Vivès edition in twenty-four volumes is practically a reprint of that of Wadding without the latter's indices.[30]

Of the single works, in addition to the aforementioned editions of the *De primo principio*, the first two books of the *Opus oxoniense* were edited by M. Fernandez Garcia, O.F.M. under the title *Commentaria oxoniensia* (Ad Claras Aquas [Quaracchi]: ex typographia Collegii S. Bonaventurae, 1913-14) and a photoreprint of the Wadding edition of the *Quaestiones quodlibetales* was done by the Franciscan Institute (St. Bonaventure, N.Y., 1950).

In addition to the English translations of the *De primo principio* mentioned earlier, Scotus' other major work, his magisterial *Quodlibet*, is available in English translation together with an introduction, notes and a glossary of technical terms by Felix Alluntis, O.F.M. and Allan B. Wolter, O.F.M., *Duns Scotus: God and Creatures: The Quodlibetal Questions* (Princeton: Princeton University Press, 1975), paperback ed. Washington, D.C.: The Catholic University of America Press, 1981.

---

29. *R. P. F. Joannis Duns Scoti, Doctor Subtilis, opera omnia* (Lugduni: sumptibus Laurentii Durand, 1639).

30. *Joannis Duns Scotus, Doctor Subtilis, Ordinis Minorum, opera omnia* (Parisiis: apud Ludovicum Vivès, 1891-95).

SELECT BIBLIOGRAPHY

The best bibliography to date is that prepared for the Scotistic Commission by Odulfus Schaefer, O.F.M., *Bibliographia de vita, operibus et doctrina Iohannis Duns Scoti Doctoris Subtilis ac Mariani saeculorum XIX-XX*, Romae: Orbis Catholicus, Herder, 1955. It was updated by Schaefer in "Conspectus brevis bibliographiae Scotisticae recentioris," *Acta Ordinis Fratrum Minorum* 85 (1966) pp. 531-550 and Servus Gieben, O.F.M. CAP., "Bibliographia Scotistica recentior, *Laurentianum* 6 (1965) pp. 1-31.

Bettoni, E., O.F.M., *Duns Scotus: The Basic Principles of his Philosophy*, translated and edited B. Bonansea, O.F.M. Washington, D.C., Catholic University of America, 1961, reprint by Greenwood Press, Westport, Conn. forthcoming.

Campbell, B. J., O.F.M., *The Problem of One or Plural Substantial Forms in Man as Found in the Works of St. Thomas Aquinas and John Duns Scotus*, Philadelphia: University of Pennsylvania, 1940.

Copleston, F. C., S.J., *A History of Philosophy*, vol. II (Medieval Philosophy from Augustine to Scotus), Westminster, MD: The Newman Press, 1950.

Day, S. J., O.F.M., *Intuitive Cognition: A Key to the Significance of the Later Scholastics*, St. Bonaventure, N.Y.: Franciscan Institute, 1947; see also A. B. Wolter, "Duns Scotus on Intuition, Memory and Our Knowledge of Individuals," *History of Philosophy in the Making*, ed. L. J. Thro, S.J. (Washington, D.C.: University Press of America, 1982), pp. 81-104.

Effler, R. R., O.F.M., *John Duns Scotus and the Principle "Omne Quod Movetur ab Alio Movetur,"* St. Bonaventure, N.Y.: Franciscan Institute, 1962.

Gilson, E., *The Spirit of Medieval Philosophy*, trans. A. H. C. Downes, London: Sheed and Ward, 1936.

Grajewski, M. J., O.F.M., *The Formal Distinction of Duns Scotus*, Washington, D.C.: Catholic University of America, 1944; for Ockham's analysis and critique see M. M. Adams, "Ockham on Identity and Distinction," *Franciscan Studies* 36 (1976), pp. 5-74.

Miklem, N., *Reason and Revelation: A Question from Duns Scotus*, Edinburgh: Nelson, 1953; see also A. B. Wolter, "Duns Scotus and the Necessity of Revealed Knowledge, Prologue to the *Ordinatio* of John Duns Scotus," *Franciscan Studies* 11, nn. 3-4 (Sept. - Dec. 1951), pp. 231-72.

Ryan, J. K. and Bonansea, B. M., *John Duns Scotus, 1265-1965.* (Studies in Philosophy and the History of Philosophy, vol. 3). Washington, D.C.: The Catholic University of America Press, 1965.

Saint-Maurice, Beraud de, *John Duns Scotus: A Teacher for our Times*, trans. C. Duffy, O.F.M., St. Bonaventure, N.Y.: Franciscan Institute, 1955.

Sharp, D. E., *Franciscan Philosophy at Oxford in the Thirteenth Century*, Oxford: University Press, 1930.

Vier, P. C., O.F.M., *Evidence and its Function According to John Duns Scotus*, St. Bonaventure, N.Y.: Franciscan Institute, 1951.

Wolter, A. B. "Duns Scotus, John," *The Encyclopedia of Philosophy*, ed. Paul Edwards (New York: Macmillan and Free Press, 1967), vol. 2, pp. 427-36.

_____, *The Transcendentals and their Function in the Metaphysics of Duns Scotus*, St. Bonaventure, N.Y.: The Franciscan Institute, 1946.

_____, *Duns Scotus on the Will and Morality*, Washington, D.C.: Catholic University Press, 1986.

The series "Studia Scholastico-Scotistica" published by the Societas Internationalis Scotistica contains the papers given at the International Scotistic Congresses held every five years beginning with the year 1966; to date they contain *De doctrina Ioannis Duns Scoti*, vols. 1-4 (Romae, 1968); *Deus et Homo ad mentem I. Duns Scoti*, vol. 5 (Romae, 1972); *Regnum Hominis et Regnum Dei*, vols. 6-7 (Romae, 1978); *Homo et Mundus*, vol. 8 (Romae: 1984).

I

CONCERNING METAPHYSICS

Summary

1. Metaphysics, the science of the transcendentals
2. Concept and articulation of the transcendental
3. Primacy of "being" among the other transcendentals
4. On the deduction of the attributes of "being"
5. Being as the subject and God as the goal of metaphysics

[I. DE METAPHYSICA]

[1. METAPHYSICA, UT SCIENTIA TRANSCENDENTIUM] *

Necesse est esse aliquam scientiam universalem, quae per se consideret illa transcendentia, et hanc scientiam vocamus metaphysicam, quae dicitur a meta, quod est trans, et physis scientia, quasi transcendens scientia, quia est de transcendentibus.

[2. DE TRANSCENDENTIS NOTIONE EJUSQUE DIVISIONE] †

Sed tunc est dubium, qualia sunt illa praedicata, quae dicuntur de Deo [formaliter], ut sapiens, bonus, etc. Respondeo : ens prius dividitur in infinitum et finitum quam in decem praedicamenta, quia alterum istorum, scilicet [ens] finitum, est commune ad decem genera. Ergo quaecumque conveniunt enti ut indifferens ad finitum et infinitum, vel ut est proprium enti infinito, conveniunt sibi non ut determinatur ad genus sed ut prius, et per consequens, ut est transcendens et est extra omne genus. Quaecumque sunt communia Deo et creaturae, sunt talia quae conveniunt enti ut est indifferens ad finitum et infinitum ; ut enim conveniunt Deo sunt infinita, ut creaturae sunt finita. Ergo [illa] per prius conveniunt enti quam ens dividatur in decem genera, et per consequens quodcumque tale est transcendens.

Sed tunc est aliud dubium, quomodo ponitur sa-

---

* *Quaestiones subtilissimae in Metaphysicam Aristotelis*, prol., n. 5 (Vivès, VOL. VII, 5^a).

† *Opus oxoniense*, I, dist. VIII, q. iii (Assisi 137, f. 50v^a; cf. Vatican ed., VOL. IV, 205-207).

[I. CONCERNING METAPHYSICS]

[1. METAPHYSICS, THE SCIENCE OF THE TRANSCENDENTALS]

There must necessarily exist some universal science which considers the transcendentals as such. This science we call "metaphysics", from "meta", which means "beyond", and "the science of nature".[1] It is, as it were, the transcending science, because it is concerned with the transcendentals.

[2. CONCEPT AND ARTICULATION OF THE TRANSCENDENTAL]

Now a doubt arises as to what kind of predicates are those which are predicated formally of God, for instance, "wise", "good", and the like. I answer that before "being" is divided into the ten categories, it is divided into infinite and finite. For the latter, namely finite being, is common to the ten genera. Whatever pertains to "being", then, in so far as it remains indifferent to finite and infinite, or as proper to the Infinite Being, does not belong to it as determined to a genus, but prior to any such determination, and therefore as transcendental and outside any genus. Whatever [predicates] are common to God and creatures are of such kind, pertaining as they do to being in its indifference to what is infinite and finite. For in so far as they pertain to God they are infinite, whereas in so far as they belong to creatures they are finite. They belong to "being", then, prior to the division into the ten genera. Anything of this kind, consequently, is transcendental.

But then another doubt arises. How can wisdom be

pientia transcendens, cum non sit communis omnibus entibus, [et transcendentia videntur communia omnibus]. Respondeo, sicut de ratione [generis] generalissimi non est habere sub se plures species, sed non habere aliud supraveniens genus sicut hoc praedicamentum Quando, quia non habet supraveniens genus, est generalissimum, licet paucas habeat species aut nullas, ita transcendens quodcumque nullum habet genus sub quo contineatur. Unde de ratione transcendentis est non habere praedicatum supraveniens nisi ens. Sed quod ipsum sit commune ad multa inferiora, hoc accidit. Hoc patet ex alio : quia ens non tantum habet passiones simplices convertibiles, sicut unum, verum, et bonum, sed habet aliquas passiones ubi opposita distinguuntur contra se, sicut necesse esse vel possibile, actus vel potentia, et hujusmodi.

Sicut autem passiones convertibiles sunt transcendentes quia consequuntur ens inquantum non determinatur ad aliquod genus, ita passiones disjunctae sunt transcendentes ; et utrumque membrum illius disjuncti est transcendens, quia neutrum determinat suum determinabile ad certum genus ; et tamen unum membrum illius disjuncti formaliter est speciale non conveniens nisi uni enti, sicut necesse esse in ista divisione necesse esse vel possibile esse, et infinitum in ista divisione finitum vel infinitum, et sic de aliis.

Ita etiam potest sapientia esse transcendens et quodcumque aliud quod est commune Deo et creaturae, licet aliquod tale dicatur de solo Deo, aliquod autem de Deo et aliqua creatura. Non oportet autem transcendens ut transcendens dici de quocumque ente, nisi sit convertibile cum primo transcendente, scilicet ente.

considered a transcendental if it is not common to all beings, for transcendentals seem to be common to all? I answer that just as it is not of the nature of a supreme genus to have many species contained under it, but it is of its nature not to have any genus over and above it (the category of "when", for instance, is a supreme genus since it has no genus over and above it, although it has few, if any, species contained under it), so also whatever is not contained under any genus is transcendental. Hence, not to have any predicate above it except "being" pertains to the very notion of a transcendental. That it be common to many inferior notions, however, is purely incidental. This is evident too from the fact that "being" possesses not only attributes which are coextensive with it, such as "one", "true" and "good", but also attributes which are opposed to one another such as "possible-or-necessary", "act-or-potency", and suchlike.

But if the coextensive attributes are transcendental because they pertain to "being" as not determined to a definite genus, then the disjunctive attributes are transcendental too. And both members of the disjunction are transcendental since neither determines its determinable element to a definite genus. Nevertheless, one member of the disjunction is proper and pertains formally to one being alone, for instance, "necessary" in the disjunction "necessary-or-possible", or "infinite" in the disjunction "finite-or-infinite", and so also with the others.

And so "wisdom", or anything else, for that matter, which is common to God and creatures, can be transcendental. A transcendental, however, may also be predicated of God alone, or again it may be predicated about God and some creature. It is not necessary, then, that a transcendental as transcendental be predicated of every being, unless it be coextensive with the first of the transcendentals, namely "being".

[3. DE PRIMITATE ENTIS RESPECTU CAETERORUM
TRANSCENDENTIUM] *

Dico quod ex istis quatuor rationibus sequitur, cum nihil possit esse communius ente, et ens non possit esse commune univocum dictum in quid de omnibus per se intelligibilibus, quia non de differentiis ultimis, nec de passionibus suis, sequitur quod nihil est primum objectum intellectus nostri propter communitatem ipsius in quid ad omne per se intelligibile.

Et tamen hoc non obstante, dico quod primum objectum intellectus nostri est ens, quia in ipso concurrit duplex primitas, scilicet communitatis et virtualitatis. Nam omne per se intelligibile aut includit essentialiter rationem entis, vel continetur virtualiter, vel essentialiter in includente essentialiter rationem entis. Omnia enim genera et species et individua et omnes partes essentiales generum et ens increatum includunt ens quidditative. Omnes autem differentiae ultimae includuntur in aliquibus istorum essentialiter. Omnes autem passiones entis includuntur in ente et in suis inferioribus virtualiter.

Igitur illa, quibus ens non est univocum dictum in quid, includuntur in illis quibus ens est sic univocum. Et ita patet quod ens habet primitatem communitatis ad prima intelligibilia, hoc est, ad conceptus quidditativos generum et specierum et individuorum et partium essentialium omnium istorum et entis increati, et habet primitatem virtualitatis ad omnia intelligibilia inclusa in primis intelligibilibus, hoc est, ad conceptus qualitativos differentiarum et passionum propriarum.

Quod autem supposui, communitatem entis dicti in quid ad omnes conceptus quidditativos praedictos, hoc

* *Opus oxoniense*, I, dist. III, q. iii (Assisi 137, f. 28v^b-29r^b; cf. Vatican ed., VOL. III, 85-93).

[3. PRIMACY OF "BEING" AMONG THE
OTHER TRANSCENDENTALS]

And I say that . . . since nothing can be more
common than "being", and that "being" cannot be
predicated univocally and *in quid* [2] of all that is of itself
intelligible (because it cannot be predicated in this way
of the ultimate differences [3] or of its attributes),[4] it
follows that we have no object of the intellect that is
primary by reason of a commonness *in quid* in regard to
all that is of itself intelligible.

And yet, notwithstanding, I say that "being" is the
first object of the intellect, because in it a twofold primacy
concurs, namely, a primacy of commonness and of
virtuality.[5] For whatever is of itself intelligible either
includes essentially the notion of "being" or is contained
virtually or essentially in something else which does
include "being" essentially. For all genera, species,
individuals, and the essential parts of genera, and the
Uncreated Being all include "being" quidditatively. All
the ultimate differences are included essentially in some
of these. All the attributes of "being" are virtually
included in "being" and in those things which come
under "being".

Hence, all to which "being" is not univocal *in quid* are
included in those to which "being" is univocal in this
way. And so it is clear that "being" has a primacy of
commonness in regard to the primary intelligibles, that
is, to the quidditative concepts of the genera, species,
individuals, and all their essential parts, and to the
Uncreated Being. It has a virtual primacy in regard to
the intelligible elements included in the first intelligibles,
that is, in regard to the qualifying concepts of the ultimate
differences and proper attributes.

My supposition that "being" is predicated commonly
in quid of all the aforementioned quidditative concepts

probatur de omnibus illis, duabus rationibus positis in prima quaestione hujus distinctionis ad probandum communitatem entis ad ens creatum et increatum, quod ut pateat, pertracto eas aliqualiter.

Primam sic : de quocumque enim praedictorum conceptuum quidditativorum contingit intellectum certum esse ipsum esse ens, dubitando de differentiis contrahentibus ens ad talem conceptum. Et ita conceptus entis, ut convenit illi conceptui, est alius a conceptibus illis inferioribus de quibus intellectus est dubius ; ita alius quod inclusus in utroque inferiori conceptu, nam differentiae illae contrahentes praesupponunt eumdem conceptum entis communem quem contrahunt.

Secundam rationem pertracto sic, sicut argutum est quod Deus non est cognoscibilis a nobis naturaliter nisi ens sit univocum creato et increato, ita potest argui de substantia et accidente ; cum enim substantia non immutet immediate intellectum nostrum ad aliquam intellectionem sui, sed tantum accidens sensibile, sequitur quod nullum conceptum quidditativum poterimus habere de ea nisi aliquis talis possit abstrahi a conceptu accidentis. Sed nullus talis quidditativus, abstrahibilis a conceptu accidentis est nisi conceptus entis.

Quoad autem est suppositum de substantia, quod non immutat intellectum nostrum immediate ad actum circa se, hoc probatur : quia quidquid praesens immutat intellectum illius absentia potest naturaliter cognosci ab intellectu, quando non immutatur, sicut apparet secundo *De anima*,* quod visus est tenebrae perceptivus, quando scilicet lux non est praesens, et ideo tunc visus non immutatur. Igitur si intellectus naturaliter immutatur a substantia immediate ad actum circa ipsam, sequeretur quod quando substantia non esset praesens, posset

---

* II, cap. x (420ª, 23).

is established by the two arguments used in the initial question to prove that being is predicated commonly of created and uncreated being [Cf. pp. 20–3]. That what I have supposed may be evident, I now explain these reasons a little.

I explain the first reason thus. Of each of the aforementioned concepts, the intellect can be certain that it is a being and still be in doubt about the differences which delimit "being" to the concept in question. And so the concept of being, in so far as it agrees with the concept in question, is other than the dubious concepts which come under it. But it is other in such a way that it is included in both of the concepts which come under it, for these limiting differences presuppose the same concept of being which they limit.

The second reason I explain as follows : We argued that God cannot be known naturally unless being is univocal to the created and uncreated. We can argue in the same way of substance and accident, for substance does not immediately move our intellect to know the substance itself, but only the sensible accident does so. From this it follows that we can have no quidditative concept of substance except such as could be abstracted from the concept of an accident. But the only quidditative concept of this kind that can be abstracted from that of an accident is the concept of being.

Our assumption that substance does not immediately move our intellect to know the substance itself, we prove thus : If something moves the intellect when it is present, then whenever the intellect is not so moved, it will be able to know naturally that this object is absent. This is clear from the De anima, BK. II,* according to which the sense of sight can perceive darkness when, presumably, light is not present, and the sense, in consequence, is not moved. Therefore, if substance immediately moved the intellect naturally to know the substance itself, it would follow that when a substance was absent, the intellect

cognosci non esse praesens, et ita naturaliter posset cognosci in hostia altaris consecrata non esse substantiam panis, quod est manifeste falsum. Nullus igitur conceptus quidditativus habetur naturaliter de substantia immediate causatus a substantia, sed tantum causatus vel abstractus primo ab accidente, et illud non est nisi conceptus entis.

Per idem concluditur etiam propositum de partibus essentialibus substantiae. Si enim materia non immutat intellectum ad actum circa ipsam, nec forma substantialis, quaero quis conceptus simplex in intellectu habebitur de materia vel forma ? Si dicas quod aliquis conceptus relativus, puta partis, vel conceptus per accidens, puta alicujus proprietatis materiae vel formae, quaero quis est conceptus quidditativus, cui iste per accidens vel relativus attribuitur ? Et si nullus quidditativus [habetur, nihil erit, cui attribuatur iste conceptus per accidens, nullus autem quidditativus] potest haberi nisi impressus vel abstractus ab illo quod movet intellectum, puta ab accidente, et ille erit conceptus entis. Et ita nihil cognoscetur de partibus essentialibus substantiae, nisi ens sit commune univocum eis et accidentibus.

Istae rationes non includunt univocationem entis *in quid* ad differentias ultimas et passiones.

De prima, ostenditur quia aut intellectus est certus de aliquo tali quod sit ens, dubitando utrum sit hoc vel illud, tamen non est certus quod sit ens quidditative sed quasi predicatione per accidens.

Vel aliter, et melius : quilibet talis conceptus est simpliciter simplex, et ideo non potest secundum aliquid concipi et secundum aliquid ignorari, sicut patet per Philosophum nono *Metaphysicae*, in fine,* de conceptibus

---

* ix, cap. ix (1051^b, 25).

could know that it was not present. Hence, it could know naturally that the substance of bread does not exist in the Consecrated Victim of the Altar, which is clearly false.[6] Naturally, then, we have no quidditative concept of substance caused immediately by substance itself. Our only quidditative concept thereof is that caused by, or first abstracted from, an accident, and this is none other than the concept of being.

By the same token, our conclusion holds for the essential parts of substance. For if neither matter nor form move the intellect to an act of knowledge about themselves, I ask "What simple concept shall we have of matter or form?" If you say that it is some relative concept, for instance, of some part, or that it is an incidental concept, for instance, of some property of matter or form, then I ask "What is the quidditative concept to which this incidental or relative concept is attributed?" And if there is no quidditative concept, there will be nothing to which this incidental concept may be attributed. But the only quidditative concept possible is caused by, or abstracted from, that which does move the intellect, viz. an accident. And this will be the concept of being. Consequently, nothing is known of the essential parts of substance unless "being" is univocal, common to them and to the accidents.

These reasons do not imply that "being" is predicated *in quid* of the ultimate differences and attributes.

The first does not, for the intellect [according to the argument] is certain that some such thing is a being while it doubts whether it is this being or that. The intellect, however, is certain that it [viz. an ultimate difference or attribute] is not being quidditatively, but it is as it were "being" by way of accidental predication.

Or another and better way. Every such concept is irreducibly simple [7] and therefore one part of it cannot be conceived while another part remains unknown, as is evident from the statement of the Philosopher (in

simpliciter simplicibus, quod non est circa eos deceptio, sicut est circa quidditatem complexorum ; quod non est intelligendum quasi intellectus simplex decipiatur formaliter circa intellectionem quidditatis, quia in intellectione simplici non est verum vel falsum, sed circa quidditatem compositam potest intellectus simplex virtualiter decipi. Si enim ista ratio est in se falsa, tunc includit virtualiter propositionem falsam ; quod autem est simpliciter simplex, non includit virtualiter proximo nec formaliter propositionem falsam, et ideo circa ipsam non est deceptio. Vel enim totaliter attingitur vel non attingitur, et tunc omnino ignoratur. De nullo igitur simpliciter simplici conceptu potest esse certitudo secundum aliquid ejus et dubitatio secundum aliud.

Per hoc etiam patet ad secundam rationem supra positam, quia tale simpliciter simplex omnino est ignotum nisi secundum se totum concipiatur.

Tertio etiam modo potest responderi ad primam rationem, quod ille conceptus de quo est certitudo, est alius ab illis de quibus est dubitatio, et si ille certus idem salvatur cum alterutro illorum dubiorum, vere est univocus, ut cum alterutro illorum accipitur. Sed non oportet quod insit utrique illorum in quid, sed ut sic, vel est univocus eis ut determinabilis ad determinantes, vel ut denominabilis ad denominantes. Unde breviter, ens est univocum in omnibus, sed conceptibus non simpliciter simplicibus est univocus in quid dictus de eis ; simpliciter simplicibus est univocus ut determinabilis vel ut denominabilis, non autem ut dictum de eis in quid, quia hoc includit contradictionem.

Ex his apparet quomodo in ente concurrat duplex

Metaphysics, BK. IX, near the end) that there is no deception regarding irreducibly simple concepts as there is regarding the quiddity of what is complex. This is not to be understood as though the simple intellect [8] is formally deceived regarding the knowledge of quiddities, for in simple intellection there is neither truth nor falsity. In regard to a quiddity that is composed, however, the simple intellect can be virtually deceived. For if such a notion is false in itself, then it includes virtually a false proposition. But what is irreducibly simple includes a false proposition neither virtually nor formally, and therefore there is no deception in its regard. Either it is grasped totally or not at all, in which case it remains completely unknown. Of no irreducibly simple concept, therefore, can we be certain of one part and doubtful about another.

From this, it is clear also as far as the second reason stated above is concerned, that what is so irreducibly simple remains completely unknown unless it is grasped fully as it is in itself.

A third reply is possible regarding the first reason. This concept of which we are certain is other than those of which we are in doubt. Now if this same element of which we are certain is preserved with both of the doubtful concepts, it is truly univocal in the sense that it is grasped with both of them. It is not necessary, however, that it be contained in both of them *in quid*, but it may either be contained *in quid* or be univocal to them as determinable is univocal to determinant, or as what can be denominated to what denominates. To put it briefly, then, "being" is univocal for all. But for concepts that are not irreducibly simple, it is predicated of them univocally *in quid* ; for concepts irreducibly simple, it is univocal as something determinable or denominable, but it is not univocal in the sense that it is predicated of them *in quid*, for that would be a contradiction.

And so it is clear how in "being" there concurs a two-

primitas, videlicet primitas communicabilitatis in quid ad omnes conceptus non simpliciter simplices, et primitas virtualitatis in se vel in suis inferioribus ad omnes conceptus simpliciter simplices.

[4. DE ENTIS PASSIONUM DEDUCTIONE] *

Quantum ad primum dico quod istud disjunctum necessarium vel possibile est passio entis circumloquens passionem convertibilem, sicut sunt talia multa illimitata entibus. Passiones autem entis convertibiles, ut communius, immediate dicuntur de ente, quia ens habet conceptum simpliciter simplicem, et ideo non potest esse medium inter ipsum et suam passionem, quia neutrius est definitio quae possit esse medium. Si etiam est aliqua passio entis non prima, difficile est videre per quam priorem, ut per medium, possit concludi de ente, quia nec facile est videre ordinem passionum entis. Nec si ille ordo cognosceretur, viderentur propositiones sumptae ab eis pro praemissis esse multum evidentiores conclusionibus. In passionibus autem disjunctis, licet illud totum disjunctum non possit demonstrari de ente, tamen communiter supposito illo extremo quod est minus nobile de aliquo ente, potest concludi illud extremum quod est nobilius de aliquo ente. Sicut sequitur : si aliquod ens est finitum, ergo aliquod ens est infinitum ; et si aliquod est contingens, ergo aliquod ens est necessarium, quia in talibus non posset enti particulariter inesse imperfectius extremum nisi alicui enti inesset perfectius extremum a quo dependeret.

Sed nec isto modo videtur posse ostendi extremum

---

* *Opus oxoniense*, I, dist. xxxix, q. i (Assisi 137, f. 91r^b–91v^a ; cf. Vivès, VOL. X, 625^a–626^a).

fold primacy, namely, a primacy of commonness *in quid* in regard to all concepts that are not irreducibly simple and a primacy of virtuality in itself or in its inferiors regarding all concepts which are irreducibly simple.

[4. ON THE DEDUCTION OF THE ATTRIBUTES OF "BEING"]

I say that this disjunction "necessary-or-possible", like the countless other such found among beings, is an attribute of "being" that is equivalent to a coextensive attribute. But the coextensive attributes, as something more common, are affirmed immediately of "being", because "being" is an irreducibly simple concept and consequently no middle term can exist between "being" and its attribute, for neither has a definition that might serve as a middle term. Also, if there is some attribute of "being" that is not immediate, it is difficult to see what prior attribute could be used as a middle term to link it with "being", for it is not easy to discern any order among the attributes of "being". And even if we knew of such an order among them, any propositions about them we might use as premises seem scarcely more evident than the conclusions. In the disjunctive attributes, however, while the entire disjunction cannot be demonstrated from "being", nevertheless as a universal rule by positing the less perfect extreme of some being we can conclude that the more perfect extreme is realised in some other being. Thus it follows that if some being is finite, then some being is infinite. And if some being is contingent, then some being is necessary. For in such cases it is not possible for the more imperfect extreme of the disjunction to be existentially predicated of "being", particularly taken, unless the more perfect extreme be existentially verified of some other being upon which it depends.

But we see that the less perfect member of such a

imperfectius talis disjunctionis ; non enim si perfectius
est in aliquo ente, ex hoc necesse est imperfectius esse in
alio ente ; et hoc nisi illa extrema disjuncta essent corre-
lativa, sicut causa et causatum. Ideo igitur non potest
ostendi de ente per aliquod prius medium hoc disjunctum, necessarium vel contingens. Nec etiam ista
pars disjuncti quae est contingens posset ostendi de
aliquo, supposito necessario de aliquo, et ideo videtur
ista : Aliquod ens est contingens, esse vera prima et non
demonstrabilis propter quid. Unde Philosophus * arguens
contra necessitatem futurorum, non deducit ad aliquid
impossibilius hypothesi, sed ad aliquod impossibile nobis
manifestius, scilicet quod non oportet consiliari. Et ideo
negantes talia manifesta indigent poena vel scientia vel
sensu, quia secundum Avicennam primo *Metaphysicae* † :
Negantes primum principium sunt vapulandi vel exponendi igni, quousque concedant quod non est idem
comburi et non comburi, vapulari et non vapulari. Ita
etiam isti, qui negant aliquod ens contingens, exponendi
sunt tormentis, quousque concedant quod possibile est
eos non torqueri.

[5.   ENS UT SUBJECTUM ET DEUS UT FINIS METAPHYSICAE]‡

Hic tria videnda primo si primus et supremus habitus
naturaliter acquisitus perficiens intellectum viatoris
cujusmodi est habitus metaphysicae, habeat Deum pro
primo objecto?...
De primo est controversia inter Avicennam et Aver-

---

* *De interpretatione*, cap. ix (18^b, 26–35).
† Aristotle, *Topica*, I, cap. xi (105^a, 4–5).
++ Reportatio I A, prol. q. iii, art. i (Vienna, Oesterreichische Natio-
nalbibliothek, cod. lat. 1453, f. 8va-b).

disjunction cannot be established in this fashion, for if the more perfect exists in some being, there is no necessity on this score that the less perfect should exist in some other being, unless, of course, the two extremes of the disjunction should happen to be correlatives, such as "cause" and "caused". Consequently, this disjunction "necessary-or-contingent", cannot be established of "being" through some prior medium. Neither could the contingent part of the disjunction be established of anything on the supposition that something necessary exists. The proposition : "Some being is contingent", therefore, seems to be a primary truth and is not demonstrable by an *a priori* demonstration, which gives the reason for the fact.[9] That is why the Philosopher, in arguing against the theory that future events are necessary, makes no attempt to deduce from it something even more impossible than the hypothesis, but he deduces from it an impossibility that is more apparent to us, namely, that there would be no need to deliberate [about the future]. And therefore, those who deny such manifest things need punishment or knowledge or sense, for as Avicenna puts it (*Metaphysics* 1) † : "Those who deny a first principle should be beaten or exposed to fire until they concede that to burn and not to burn, or to be beaten and not to be beaten, are not identical". And so too, those who deny that some being is contingent should be exposed to torments until they concede that it is possible for them not to be tormented.

[5. BEING AS THE SUBJECT AND GOD AS THE GOAL
OF METAPHYSICS]‡

Here we must first see whether metaphysics as the first and highest of the naturally acquired habits perfecting man's intellect in this present life has God as its first object...

On this point there is a controversy between Avicenna

roem. Posuit enim Avicenna quod Deus non est subjectum esse in metaphysica, sed aliquid aliud ut ens, quia nulla scientia probat suum subjectum esse; metaphysicus probat Deum esse et substantias separatas esse; ergo etc. Averroes reprehendit Avicennam in commento ultimo I *Physicorum*; supposita majori Avicennae, quod nulla scientia probat suum subjectum esse, quae est communis utrique, capit quod Deus est subjectum in metaphysica et quod Deum esse non probatur in metaphysica sed in physica, quia nullum genus substantiarum separatarum potest probari esse nisi per motum, quod pertinet ad physicam.

Sed Avicenna bene dicit et Averroes valde male. Et accipio propositionem utriusque communem, scilicet: "Nulla scientia probat suum objectum esse," quae vera est propter primitatem subiecti ad scientiam, quia si esset posterius, posset ipsum probari esse in illa scientia in qua habet rationem posterioris et non objecti adaequati. Sed majorem primitatem habet subjectum respectu scientiae posterioris quam prioris; ergo si scientia prima non potest probare suum subjectum esse, quia est subjectum primum, ergo multo magis nec scientia posterior; ergo si metaphysica non potest probare Deum esse, multo magis nec physica. Probatio minoris, quia duplicem primitatem habet subjectum prioris scientiae ad posteriorem respectu scientiae prioris. Item, si Deum esse est demonstratum in physica et suppositum tamquam subjectum in metaphysica, ergo conclusio in physica est simpliciter principium, quia principium in scientia est ex subiecto ejus et per consequens physica erit simpliciter prior metaphysicae; quae omnia sunt absurda.

Item, ex omni proprietate manifesta in effectu potest concludi causam esse, si talis proprietas non ponitur in esse nisi solum a tali causa vel a tali causalitate. Sed non solum hujusmodi proprietates quae considerantur in physica, ut motum esse, manifeste concludunt causam esse moventem, sed etiam proprietates consideratae in

and Averroes. Avicenna claims that not God, but something else, such as being, is the subject of metaphysics. For no science proves the existence of its own subject, yet the metaphysician proves that God exists. In his final comment on Bk. I of the *Physics*, Averroes attacks Avicenna, using the same major premise admitted by both that no science proves the existence of its subject. God is the subject of metaphysics and his existence is not proved there but in physics, for it is only by means of motion that any sort of pure spirit can be proved to exist, and motion pertains to the science of physics.

Avicenna has spoken well, however, and Averroes very badly and against him I use the basic proposition they both hold, namely: "No science proves the existense of its subject." This is true, because of the priority a subject has with respect to the science. For if it were posterior, its subject could be proved in a lower science, where it would be conceived under some inferior aspect inadequate for its role as the object [of the higher science]. But a subject enjoys a greater priority over a lower science than over its own higher science. If the highest science, therefore, cannot establish the existence of its subject, since this is first or highest, still less can an inferior science do so.

The minor is proved because of the double primacy the subject of a higher science has in regard to a lower science's relationship to a prior science. Also, if God's existence is something demonstrated in physics and presupposed in metaphysics as subject, then—to put it simply—a conclusion in physics is the starting point of metaphysics, for any science starts with its subject. Hence, physics will be prior to metaphysics—all of which is absurd.

Also, if any property can exist only in virtue of such and such a cause, from every such property that appears in an effect, we can infer the existence of its cause. Now it is not just such properties of the effect considered in physics, such as that something is moved, that leads one to con-

metaphysica, ut ens posterius, ens possibile, ens finitum, prout sunt in effectu, concludunt de causa primitatem simpliciter, actualitatem et infinitatem, et hujusmodi, ex quibus potest demonstrari esse de primo ente potius quam ex ratione motus.

Dico ergo ad quaestionem quantum pertinet ad istam articulum quod Deus non est subjectum in metaphysica, quia ut supra probatum in prima quaestione* de Deo, potest tantum esse una scientia, quae non est metaphysica. Quod probo sic: De omni subjecto scientiae subalternatae praecognoscitur ex sensibus an est vel si est, ut patet de subjecto perspectivae. Licet enim linea visualis, quae est subjectum in perspectiva, possit demonstrari tamquam conclusio geometriae, tamen si est subjectum alicujus scientiae subalternatae, de eo oportet statim esse notum si est, sine ulteriori inquisitione ex sensu vel experientia, scilicet quod sibi non repugnat esse; sicut enim principia statim sciuntur apprehensis terminis, et cum subjectum sit causa principii et per consequens prius eo in entitate et cognoscibilitate, ita cum subjectum non sit posterius suo principio nec ignotius, opertet ipsum esse statim notum ex sensibus si est; sed nulla ratio propria conceptibilis de Deo potest statim esse nobis nota si est; ergo nulla notitia viatoris acquisita naturaliter a nobis potest esse de Deo sub aliqua ratione ejus propria. Minor patet, quia prima ratio propria de Deo quam concipimus est quod sit primum ens; sed primum ens non est primo notum ex sensibus, sed oportet prius concipere possibilitatem unionis terminorum, et antequam sciamus hanc compositionem esse possibilem, oportet quod aliquod ens demonstretur esse primum. Concedo ergo cum Avicenna quod Deus non est subjectum in metaphysica; nec

---

* q. 1, art. iv.

clude to the existence of a moving cause, but the same is true of properties considered in metaphysics. If an effect represents something posterior, possible, or finite, such properties imply their cause enjoys an unqualified primacy, actuality, infinity and the like. It is from properties of this sort rather than from notion of motion that the existence of a first being can be demonstrated.

So far as this article is concerned, then, I say that God is not the subject of metaphysics, for as we proved earlier in the first question* there can be but one science about God as first subject, and this is not metaphysics. And I prove this in the following way. The senses tell us whether or not any subject of a subordinate science exists, as is clear in the case of optics. For although a visible line, which is the subject of optics, could be demonstrated as a conclusion of geometry, nevertheless if it is the subject of some subordinate science, one needs to know immediately, without any further experience or investigation by the senses, whether or not it can be, namely, that there is nothing absurd about its existence. Just as principles are grasped immediately once the terms are apprehended through the medium of the senses, so too the existence of the subject must be known immediately from the senses. For the subject is not posterior or less known than the principle, since the subject is its cause, and hence prior to the principle in entity and knowability. But no knowledge acquired naturally in this life represents any characteristics of God that is proper to him. The minor is evident, for the first proper notion we have about God is that he is the first being. "First being," however, is not something initially known from the senses, for we must first ascertain that the combination of these two terms makes sense. Before we can know this combination represents something possible, we need to demonstrate that some being is first.

Hence, I concede with Avicenna that God is not the subject of metaphysics. Nor is this contradicted by the

obviat dictum Averroris I *Posteriorum*,+ nec illud I *Metaphysicae*, # quod metaphyica est circa causas altissimas, quia loquitur sicut consuevit I *Priorem*,** cum dicitur: "Primum oportet dicere circa quid et de quo, quoniam circa demonstrationem et de disciplina demonstrativa, i.e., universali scientia demonstrandi. Unde "circa" notat proprie circumstantiam causae finalis, sicut ly "de" circumstantiam causae materialis; unde metaphysica est circa causas altissimas finaliter ad quas terminatur ipsius speculatio.

+ Aristotelis, *Analytica posteriora*, I, cap. 1 (71a10-12).
# I, cap. ii, *passim*.
** *Analytica priora*, I, cap. i (24a, 10ff).

dictum of Averroes [about prior knowledge of the existence of the subject] (from the *Posterior Analytics*, Bk. I),+ nor the statement that metaphysics is concerned with the highest causes (from *Metaphysics*, Bk. I).# For the Philosopher speaks there as he did in the *Prior Analytics* I,** where he says: "First we need to determine what this is concerned with and is about, for it is concerned with demonstration and is about the demonstrative branch of learning, i.e. it is about the general science of demonstrating". Hence, "concerned with" denotes properly the circumstance of the final cause, just as the word "about" designates the circumstance of the material cause. Consequently, metaphysics is concerned with the highest causes as its goal, and ends with the theoretical knowledge of them.

II
MAN'S NATURAL KNOWLEDGE
OF GOD

Summary of the Argument

QUESTION : Is the intellect of man in this life able to know God naturally ?

PRO ET CONTRA

BODY OF THE QUESTION

Preliminary observations

The opinion of Henry of Ghent

Scotus's own opinion

> *First statement :* It is possible to have a quidditative concept of God
>
> *Second statement :* God is conceived not only analogously, but also univocally
>
> *Third statement :* God's essence is not known intuitively by man in this life
>
> *Fourth statement :* Man can have many proper concepts of God
>
> *Fifth statement :* We know God through the intelligible species of creatures

REPLY TO THE ARGUMENTS AT THE BEGINNING

Reply to Henry's arguments

[II. COGNITIO NATURALIS DE DEO] *

Circa tertiam distinctionem quaero primo de cognoscibilitate Dei. Et quaero primo : *Utrum Deus sit naturaliter cognoscibilis ab intellectu viatoris.*

[Pro et Contra]

Arguo quod non :

Philosophus III *De anima* † dicit : Phantasmata se habent ad intellectum sicut sensibilia ad sensum. Sed sensus non sentit nisi sensibile, ergo intellectus nihil intelligit nisi cujus phantasma potest per sensus apprehendere. Deus autem non habet phantasma nec est aliquid phantasma nec est aliquid phantasibile ; ergo, etc.

Item II *Metaphysicae* ‡ : sicut oculus noctuae ad lucem solis, sic et intellectus noster ad ea quae sunt manifestissima naturae ; sed ibi est impossibilitas ; ergo et hic.

Item I *Physicorum* ** : Infinitum inquantum infinitum est ignotum. Et II *Metaphysicae* †† : Infinita non contingit cognoscere ; ergo nec infinitum, quia eadem videtur esse improportio intellectus finiti ad infinitum et ad infinita, quia aequalis excessus vel non minor.

Item Gregorius *Super Ezechielem* ‡‡ : Quantumcumque

---

* *Opus oxoniense*, I, dist. III, q. i (Assisi 137, f. 25r^a-27r^b; cf. Vatican ed., VOL. III, 1-48).
† III, cap vii (431^a, 14).   ‡ II, cap. i (993^b, 9).
** I, cap. iv (187^b, 8).   †† II, cap. ii (994^b, 22).
‡‡ *Sermons on Ezechiel*, I, hom. viii, n. 30 (Migne, P.L., LXXVI, 868).

[II. MAN'S NATURAL KNOWLEDGE OF GOD]

Concerning the third distinction I ask first whether it is possible to know God. And I ask first : *whether the intellect of man in this life is able to know God naturally.*

[Pro et Contra]

I argue that it cannot [1] :

[Arg. I]. The Philosopher in *De anima*, BK. III, † says : "Sense images are related to the intellect in the same way as sense objects are related to the senses". But the senses perceive only what is sensible. Therefore the intellect is unable to grasp anything whose sense image cannot be known by the senses. Of God there is no sense image. Neither is He such that He could be perceived by such a sense faculty. Therefore, etc.

[Arg. II]. Again, according to *Metaphysics*, BK. II ‡ : "As the eyes of bats are to the blaze of day, so is our intellect to the things which are by nature most evident". But if it is impossible to know such things, it is impossible to know God.

[Arg. III]. Also, according to *Physics*, BK. I ** : "The infinite as infinite is unknowable". And according to the *Metaphysics*, BK, II †† : "It is not possible to know an infinite [number] of things". Therefore, neither can the Infinite Being be known, since an infinite number and an Infinite Being would seem to be equally disproportionate to our intellect ; for an Infinite Being exceeds the powers of our intellect in the same measure as, or certainly to no less a degree than, does the infinite in number.

[Arg. IV]. Gregory, also, in his commentary on Ezechiel says ‡‡ : "No matter how far our mind may have

mens nostra in contemplatione profecerit Dei, non ad illud quod ipse est, sed ad illud quod sub ipso est attingit.

Contra :

v *Metaphysicae* * : Metaphysica est theologia de Deo et circa divina principaliter, ergo etc. Et in actu ejus,† scilicet in consideratione actuali substantiarum separatarum ponit felicitatem humanam.

[Corpus Quaestionis]

[*Notiones Praeviae*]

In prima quaestione non est distinguendum quod Deus possit cognosci negative vel affirmative, quia negatio non cognoscitur nisi pre affirmationem : II *Perihermenias,* in fine,‡ et IV *Metaphysicae.*** Patet etiam quod nullas negationes cognoscimus de Deo nisi per affirmationes per quas removemus alia incompossibilia ab illis affirmationibus.

Negationes etiam non summe amamus.

Similiter etiam aut negatio concipitur praecise aut ut dicta de aliquo. Si praecise concipitur negatio, ut non lapis, hoc aeque convenit nihilo sicut Deo, quia pura negatio dicitur de ente et de non ente. Igitur in hoc non magis intelligitur Deus quam nihil vel chimera. Si intelligitur ut negatio dicta de aliquo, tunc quaero illum conceptum subtractum de quo intelligitur ista negatio esse vera. Aut erit conceptus affirmativus aut negativus. Si est affirmativus, habetur propositum. Si negativus, quaero ut prius. Aut negatio concipitur praecise aut ut

---

* v, cap. vii (1064^a, 36).
† *Ethica Nicomachea*, x, cap. viii.
‡ *De interpretatione*, cap. xiii (22^a, 33) ; cf. also cap. xiv *in fine.*
** IV, cap. ii (1004^a, 10–16).

progressed in the contemplation of God, it does not attain to what He is, but to what is beneath Him''.

To the contrary :

According to *Metaphysics*, BK. V * : "Metaphysics is a theology of God and is primarily concerned with the divine". And [Aristotle] places man's happiness in the actual possession of such knowledge, that is to say, in the actual speculation about the pure spirits.

[Body of the Question]

[Preliminary Observations]

In this first question there is no need to make the distinction that we cannot know what God is : we can only know what He is not.[2] For every denial is intelligible only in terms of some affirmation. ‡ ** It is also clear that we can know negations of God only by means of affirmations ; for if we deny anything of God, it is because we wish to do away with something inconsistent with what we have already affirmed.

Neither are negations the object of our greatest love.

Furthermore, if something is negated, either the negation is considered simply in itself or as predicated of something. If a negation, such as "not-stone", is considered simply in itself, it is as characteristic of nothing as it is of God, for a pure negation is predicated of both what is and what is not a being. Consequently, what we know through such a negation is no more God than it is a chimera or nothing at all. If the negation is understood as modifying something, then I inquire after the underlying notion of which the negation is understood to be true. It will be either an affirmative or a negative notion. If it is affirmative, we have what we seek. If it is negative, I inquire as I did before. Either the negation is conceived simply in itself or as predicated of something.

dicta de aliquo. Si primo modo, hoc aeque convenit nihilo sicut Deo. Si ut dicta de aliquo, sicut prius ; et quantumcumque procederetur in negationibus, vel non intelligeretur Deus magis quam nihil vel stabitur in aliquo affirmativo conceptu qui est primus.

Nec secundo est distinguendum de cognitione quia [*read* quid] est et si est, quia in proposito quaero conceptum simplicem de quo cognoscatur esse per actum intellectus componentis et dividentis. Numquam enim cognosco de aliquo si est, nisi habeam aliquem conceptum illius extremi de quo cognosco esse ; et de illo conceptu quaeritur hic.

Nec tertio oportet distinguere si est, ut est quaestio de veritate propositionis vel ut est quaestio de esse Dei, quia si potest esse, quaero de veritate propositionis in qua est esse tamquam praedicatum de subjecto ; ad concipiendum veritatem illius quaestionis vel propositionis, oportet praeconcipere terminos illius quaestionis, et de conceptu simplici illius subjecti si est possibilis est nunc quaestio.

Nec quarto valet distinguere de conceptu naturali et supernaturali, quia quaeritur de naturali.

Nec quinto valet distinguere de naturaliter loquendo de natura absolute vel de natura pro statu isto, quia quaeritur praecise de cognitione pro statu isto.

Nec sexto valet distinguere de cognitione Dei in creatura vel in se, quia si cognitio habeatur per creaturam ita quod cognitio discursiva incipiat a creatura, quaero in quo termino sistitur ista cognitio. Si in Deo in se, habeo propositum, quia illum conceptum Dei in se quaero. Si non sistitur in Deo in se, sed in creatura,

If the first be true, then the negation applies to nothing as well as to God. If it is conceived as predicated of something, then I argue as before. And no matter how far we proceed with negations, either what we know is no more God than nothing is, or we will arrive at some affirmative concept which is the first concept of all.

In the second place, there is no point in distinguishing between a knowledge of His essence and a knowledge of His existence,[3] for I intend to seek a simple concept of which existence may be affirmed or denied by a judgment of the intellect. For I never know anything to exist unless I first have some concept of that of which existence is affirmed. And this is what we seek here.

Thirdly, in regard to God's existence there is no need to distinguish between the question of the truth of the proposition and the question of His existence.[4] For before there can be any question of the truth of a proposition wherein existence is predicated of a subject, it is necessary first of all to conceive the terms of this proposition. Now the question is this: "Is it possible to have a concept of the subject [of this proposition : 'God exists'] by natural means?"

Fourthly, the distinction between a natural and supernatural concept is out of place, because we are interested here only in the former.[5]

Fifthly, in regard to the natural, there is no necessity for a distinction between "nature, absolutely speaking" and "nature, in our present state", for we are interested only in the latter.[6]

Sixthly, the distinction between knowing God in Himself and knowing Him in a creature is not to the point.[7] For if our knowledge comes through a creature in the sense that the reasoning process begins with what can be known from a creature, then I ask "What do we know at the conclusion of this process?" If it is God Himself, then I have what I seek, for I am looking for a concept of God Himself. If it is not God, but a creature,

tunc idem erit terminus et principium discursus, et ita
nulla notitia habebitur de Deo ; saltem non est intellectus
in ultimo discursus termino quam diu sistit in aliquo
objecto quod est principium discurrendi...

Est ergo mens quaestionis ista : Utrum aliquem
conceptum simplicem possit intellectus viatoris habere
in quo conceptu simplici concipiatur Deus.

[Opinio Henrici]

Ad hoc dicit quidam doctor sic loquendo : De cognitione
actus distingui potest ex parte objecti et potest cognosci
per se vel per accidens, in particulari vel in universali.

Realiter per accidens non cognoscitur Deus, quia quidquid de ipso cognoscitur est ipse, tamen cognoscendo
aliquod attributum ejus cognoscimus quasi per accidens
quid est. Unde de attributis dicit Damascenus libro
primo, capitulo 4 * : Non naturam dicunt Dei, sed quae
circa naturam.

In universali etiam, puta in generali attributo, cognoscitur ; non quidem in universali secundum praedica-
tionem quod dicatur de ipso in quo nullum est velle [sic !
universale], quia quidditas illa est de se singularis, sed in
universali quod tantum analogice commune est sibi et
creaturae, tamen quasi unum a nobis concipitur propter
proximitatem conceptuum, licet sint diversi conceptus.

---

* Migne, P.G., xciv, 800.

then the beginning and conclusion of the reasoning process are identical, and therefore I have no knowledge of God at all—or at least God is not grasped at the end of the reasoning process so long as the mind does not get beyond the object that served as the initial point of the argument.

The meaning of the question, then, is this : "Is it possible by natural means for man's intellect in the present life to have a simple concept in which concept God is grasped?"

[*The Opinion of Henry of Ghent*]

A certain teacher [8] answers the question in this way : An act of knowledge can be distinguished in terms of its object, and on this score we can distinguish : (*a*) a knowledge of a thing through the thing itself ; (*b*) a knowledge of the thing through something incidental to it ; (*c*) a knowledge of the thing in particular ; and (*d*) a knowledge of the thing in general.

In reality there is no knowledge of God *through something incidental to Him*, for whatever is known of God is God Himself. Nevertheless, we do know what God is in a *quasi-incidental* manner when we know some one of His attributes. Hence, Damascene says * that the attributes "do not bespeak the nature of God, but something about the nature".

God is also known *in a general way*, that is, through some universal attribute. Not indeed that any attribute, universal by way of predication, is affirmed of Him in whom nothing is universal, for His essence is singular of its very nature. He is known, however, in a "universal" that is only analogically common to Himself and to a creature. This universal is conceived by us as though it were one notion, because of the close resemblance of the concepts it contains, although the latter in reality are diverse.

In particulari non cognoscitur ex creaturis, quia creatura est peregrina similitudo ejus, sic quia tantum conformis ei quo ad alia attributa quae non sunt illa natura in particulari. Ergo cum nihil ducat in cognitione alterius nisi sub ratione similis, sequitur, etc.

Item in universali tripliciter cognoscitur : generalissime, generalius, generaliter.

Generalissime tres habet gradus : cognoscendo enim quodcumque ens, ut hoc ens est, indistinctissime concipitur [Deus quia concipitur] ens quasi pars conceptus, et est primus gradus ; et amovendo hoc et concipiendo ens est secundus gradus. Jam enim ut conceptum, non ut pars, concipitur commune analogum Deo et creaturae. Quod si distinguatur conceptus entis qui Deo convenit, puta concipiendo ens indeterminatum negative, id est non determinabile, a conceptu entis qui convenit analogice, quod est ens indeterminatum privative, jam est tertius gradus. Primo modo indeterminatum abstrahitur, ut forma ab omni materia ut in se subsistens et [im]participabilis. Secundo modo indeterminatum est velle [*sic !*] vel universale abstractum a particularibus quod est actu participatum in illis.

Post istos tres gradus generalissime concipiendi concipitur Deus generalius concipiendo quodcumque attributum non simpliciter ut prius, sed cum praeeminentia summa.

Generaliter autem concipitur concipiendo quodcumque

God is not known *in particular* from creatures, because a creature bears only an external likeness to Him, since it resembles Him only in those attributes which do not constitute Him as this particular nature. Now since one thing can be known through another only by reason of the similarity existing between the two, it follows that God is not known in particular through creatures.

Furthermore, there are three ways in which we may have a general knowledge of God : (*a*) in a *most* general way, (*b*) in a *less* general way, and (*c*) in the *least* general manner.

(*a*) The *most* general knowledge we have of God comprises three stages. To know any being as "this being" is already to conceive God in a very indistinct way ; for "being" is included, as it were, as part of the concept. This is the first step. The second step consists in removing the "this" and conceiving simply "being". For "being", in so far as it is a concept and not simply a part of a concept, is already conceived as analogically common to God and creature. We are in the third stage, if the concept of "being" which pertains to God is distinguished from the concept of "being" which pertains analogically to creatures, if, for instance, God is conceived as a being that is *negatively* undetermined, that is, incapable of being determined, while a creature is conceived as a being that is *privatively* undetermined.[9] In the first instance, "undetermined" is conceived abstractly as something self-subsistent and incapable of being participated in, like a form that lacks all matter. In the second, "undetermined" is a universal abstracted from particulars and not actually shared by them.[10]

(*b*) In addition to these three stages of most general knowledge, God is grasped in a *less general* and more specific way, when any given attribute is conceived not in an unqualified manner as before, but as existing in the highest degree of perfection possible to such an attribute.

(*c*) God is known in the *least general manner*, however,

attributum esse idem cum suo primo attributo, scilicet esse, propter simplicitatem.

Nec per speciem propriam cognoscitur, quia nihil est eo simplicius, sed ad modum aestimativae per speciem aliquam alienam ex creaturis. Et hoc omnibus tribus modis praedictis...

[*Opinio Scoti*]

Respondeo aliter ad primam quaestionem et in quibusdam, scilicet in quinque, contradicam positioni praedictae. Rationes meae positionis ostendent oppositum hujus positionis...

[*Prima Sententia*]. Dico ergo primo quod non tantum haberi potest conceptus naturaliter in quo quasi per accidens concipitur Deus, puta in aliquod attributo, sed etiam aliquis conceptus in quo per se et quidditative concipiatur Deus.

Probo : quia concipiendo sapientem concipitur proprietas, secundum eum, vel quasi proprietas in actu secundo perficiens naturam. Ergo intelligendo sapientem oportet prius intelligere aliquod quid, quia cum intelligo istud quasi proprietatem inesse, et ita ante conceptus omnium passionum vel quasi passionum, oportet quaerere conceptum quidditativum cui intelligantur ista attribui ; et iste conceptus alius erat quidditativus de Deo, quia in nullo alio potest esse status.

[*Secunda Sententia*]. Secundo dico quod non tantum in conceptu analogo conceptui creaturae concipitur Deus, scilicet qui omnino sit alius ab illo qui de creatura dicitur, sed in conceptu aliquo univoco sibi et creaturae.

when the mind, on the basis of God's simplicity, identifies any of His other attributes with His primary attribute, namely, *being* itself.

Since nothing is simpler than God, He is known not through a species proper to Him, but, in a manner reminiscent of the operation of the estimative power through a species, alien to Him, derived from creatures. And this holds for all three of the aforementioned ways of knowing God.

[Scotus's own opinion]

My answer to the first question is different. I shall contradict the preceding view on five points. The reasons I give for my position will refute the other.

[First Statement]. In the first place, then, I say that it is naturally possible to have not only a concept in which God is known incidentally, as it were—for instance, under the aspect of some attribute—but also one in which He is conceived by Himself and quidditatively.

This I prove as follows. According to [Henry of Ghent], by conceiving "wise" we grasp a property or quasi-property which perfects the nature after the manner of a secondary act. In order to conceive "wise", therefore, it is necessary to have a conception of some prior subject, because I understand this property to be verified existentially. And so we must look beyond all our ideas of attributes or quasi-attributes, in order to find a quidditative concept to which the former may be attributed. This other concept will be a quidditative notion of God, for our quest for a quasi-subject will not cease with any other kind of concept.

[Second Statement]. Secondly, I say that God is conceived not only in a concept analogous to the concept of a creature, that is, one which is wholly other than that which is predicated of creatures, but even in some concept univocal to Himself and to a creature.

Et ne fiat contentio de nomine univocationis, univocum conceptum dico qui ita est unus quod ejus unitas sufficit ad contradictionem affirmando et negando ipsum de eodem, sufficit etiam pro medio syllogistico, ut extrema unita in medio sic uno sine fallacia aequivocationis concludantur inter se uniri et univocationem sic intellectam probo quadrupliciter.

[Arg. 1]. Primo sic : omnis intellectus certus de uno conceptu et dubius de diversis habet conceptum de quo est certus alium a conceptibus de quibus est dubius, subjectum includit praedicatum. Sed intellectus viatoris potest esse certus de Deo quod sit ens dubitando de ente finito vel infinito, creato vel increato ; ergo conceptus entis de Deo est alius a conceptu isto et illo, et ita neuter ex se, et in utroque illorum includitur, igitur univocus.

Probatio majoris : quia nullus idem conceptus est certus et dubius ; ergo vel alius, quod est propositum, vel nullus, et nunc non erit certitudo de aliquo conceptu.

Probatio minoris : Quilibet Philosophus fuit certus illud quod posuit primum principium esse ens, puta unus de igne et alius de aqua, certus erat quod erat ens. Non autem fuit certus quod esset ens creatum vel increatum, primum vel non primum. Non enim erat certus quod erat primum, quia tunc fuisset certus de falso, et falsum non est scibile ; nec quod erat ens non primum, quia tunc non posuissent oppositum.

Confirmatur etiam : nam aliquis videns Philosophos

And lest there be a dispute about the name "univocation", I designate that concept univocal which possesses
sufficient unity in itself, so that to affirm and deny it of
one and the same thing would be a contradiction. It
also has sufficient unity to serve as the middle term of a
syllogism, so that wherever two extremes are united by a
middle term that is one in this way, we may conclude to
the union of the two extremes among themselves. Univocation in this sense I prove by the following four arguments.

[Arg. 1]. The first is this. Every intellect that is
certain about one concept, but dubious about others has,
in addition to the concepts about which it is in doubt,
another concept of which it is certain. (The subject
includes the predicate.) Now, in this life already, a man
can be certain in his mind that God is a being and still
be in doubt whether He is a finite or an infinite being, a
created or an uncreated being. Consequently, the concept of "being" as affirmed of God is different from the
other two concepts but is included in both of them and
therefore is univocal.

Proof of the major. One and the same concept cannot
be both certain and dubious. Therefore, either there is
another concept (which is our contention), or there is
no concept at all, and consequently no certitude about
any concept.

I prove the minor. Every philosopher was certain that
what he postulated as a first principle was a being ; for
instance, one was certain that fire was a being, another
that water was a being. Yet he was not certain whether
it was a created or an uncreated being, whether it was
first or not first. He could not be certain that it was
the first being, for then he would have been certain
about something false, and what is false is not strictly
knowable.[11] Neither was he certain that it was not
first ; for then he would not have claimed the opposite.
This reason is confirmed as follows : Someone

discordare, potest esse certus de quocumque quod Deus [*read* quilibet] posuit primum principium esse ens, et tamen propter contrarietatem opinionum eorum, potuit dubitare utrum sit hoc ens vel illud. Et tali dubitanti, si fieret demonstratio concludens vel destruens aliquem conceptum inferiorem, puta quod ignis non erit ens primum, sed aliquid ens posterius primo ente, non destrueretur ille conceptus primus sibi certus quem habuit de ente, sed salvaretur in illo conceptu particulari probato de igne ; et per hoc probatur propositio supposita in ultima consequentia rationis, quae fuit quod ille conceptus certus quae est ex se neuter dubiorum in utroque istorum salvatur.

Quod si non cures de auctoritate illa accepta de diversitate opinionum philosophantium, sed dicas quod quilibet habet duos conceptus in intellectu suo propinquos, qui propter propinquitatem analogiae videntur esse unus conceptus. Contra hoc videtur esse quod tunc ex ista evasione videretur destructa omnis via probandi unitatem alicujus conceptus univocam. Si enim dicis hominem habere unum conceptum ad Socratem et Platonem, negabitur tibi et dicetur quod sunt duo, sed videntur unus propter magnam similitudinem.

Praeterea, illi duo conceptus sunt simpliciter simplices, ergo non intelligibiles nisi distincte et totaliter, ergo si nunc non videntur duo, nec post.

Item, aut concipiuntur ut omnino disparati et mirum quomodo videntur unus, aut ut comparati secundum analogiam aut secundum similitudinem vel distinctionem,

perceiving the disagreement among philosophers can still be certain that any of the things that they have acclaimed as the first principle is a being. Nevertheless, in view of the contrariety of opinions, he could be in doubt whether this or that being is primary. Now if we could demonstrate for such an individual the truth or falsity of one of these alternatives, for example that fire is not the first being, but is posterior to the first being, we would not destroy his first certain notion of it as a being, but this notion would survive in the particular conception which we had proven about fire. And this also proves the proposition stated as the final conclusion of the argument, namely that this certain concept, since as such it is neither of the doubtful notions, is preserved in both of them.

You may not recognise the force of this argument based on the diversity of opinion among the philosophisers, but insist that each has in his mind two concepts closely resembling each other. Yet because of the very closeness of the analogy, they seem to be one concept. The following consideration, however, may be urged against this. By such an evasion all possibility of proving the unity of any univocal concept would be destroyed. For if you say that "man" is one concept applicable to both Socrates and Plato, some one will deny it, asserting that there are two concepts, but they seem to be one because of their great similarity.

Furthermore, these two concepts are irreducibly simple. Unless, therefore, they are known distinctly and *in toto*, they cannot be known at all. Consequently, if these concepts are not perceived as two concepts now, they will not be perceived as two later on.

Again, either these two concepts are conceived as opposed to each other, and then it is strange how they are perceived as one. Or they are compared according to analogy, or according to similarity or distinction, in which case they are conceived as distinct either prior to

et tunc simul vel prius concipiuntur ut distincti, ergo non videntur unus.

Item, ponendo duos conceptus, ponis duo objecta formalia cognita, quomodo sunt duo cognita formalia et non ut distincta.

Praeterea, si intelligeret singularia sub propriis rationibus quamvis conceptus duorum ejusdem speciei essent similimi, non est dubium tamen, quin multo similiores quam isti duo in proposito, quia isti duo differunt specie, adhuc intellectus bene distingueret inter tales conceptus singularium...

[Arg. II]. Secundo principaliter arguo sic : Nullus conceptus realis causatur in intellectu viatoris naturaliter nisi ab his quae sunt naturaliter motiva intellectus nostri. Sed illa sunt phantasma vel objectum relucens in phantasmate et intellectus agens, ergo nullus conceptus simplex naturaliter fit in intellectu nostro modo nisi qui potest fieri virtute istorum, sed conceptus qui non esset univocus objecto relucenti in phantasmate, sed omnino alius prior ad quem ille habeat analogiam, non potest fieri virtute intellectus agentis et phantasmatis, ergo talis conceptus alius analogus qui ponitur naturaliter in intellectu viatoris numquam erit et ita non poterit haberi naturaliter aliquis conceptus de Deo, quod est falsum.

Probatio assumpti : Objectum quodcumque sive relucens in phantasmate sive in specie intelligibili cum intellectu agente vel possibili cooperante secundum ultimum suae virtutis facit sicut effectum sibi adaequatum conceptum suum proprium et conceptum omnium essentialiter vel virtualiter inclusorum in eo. Sed ille alius conceptus, qui ponitur analogus, non est essen-

or simultaneously with the comparison, and therefore they are not perceived as one concept.

Likewise, in postulating two concepts, you assume that two formal objects are known. How then can two formal objects be known and not be known as distinct?

Furthermore, if singulars were known under their proper notions even though the concepts of two of the same species were so very much alike, the intellect would still readily distinguish the concept of one singular from the other. And yet there is no doubt that such concepts are even more alike than the two concepts in question [viz. of God and of a creature], for the latter differ specifically.

[Arg. II]. My second principal argument is this. In the present life no concept representing reality is formed naturally in the mind except by reason of those factors which naturally motivate the intellect. Now these factors are the active intellect, and either the sense image or the object revealed in the sense image.[12] No simple concept, then, is produced naturally in our mind except that which can arise in virtue of these factors. Now, no concept could arise in virtue of the active intellect and the sense image that is not univocal but only analogous with, or wholly other than, what is revealed in the sense image. In the present life, since no other such analogous concept could arise in the intellect naturally, it would be simply impossible to have any natural concept of God whatsoever. But this is false.

Proof of the assumption. With the co-operation of the active and possible intellect, any object revealed in the sense image or existing as an intelligible species at the very most can produce in the intellect as its adequate effect (a) a proper concept of itself and (b) a concept of all that is essentially or virtually included in it. Now this concept which they postulate to be analogous is neither a proper concept of the object in the sense image nor is it a proper concept of anything virtually or essentially

tialiter nec virtualiter inclusus in isto, nec etiam est iste, ergo iste non fiet ab aliquo tali movente.

Et confirmatur ratio, quia objectum praeter conceptum suum proprium adaequatum et inclusum in ipso altero duorum modorum praedictorum nihil potest cognosci ex isto objecto nisi per discursum, sed discursus praesupponit cognitionem istius simplicitatis ad quod discurritur.

Formetur igitur ratio sic : quia nullum objectum facit conceptum simplicem proprium in isto intellectu conceptum simplicem proprium alterius objecti nisi contineat illud aliud objectum essentialiter vel virtualiter, objectum autem creatum non continet increatum essentialiter vel virtualiter, et hoc sub ea ratione sub qua sibi attribuuntur, ut posterius essentialiter attribuitur priori essentialiter, quia contra rationem posterioris essentialiter est includere virtualiter suum prius et patet quod objectum creatum non essentialiter continet increatum secundum aliquid omnino sibi proprium et non commune, ergo non facit conceptum simplicem et proprium enti increato...

[Arg. III]. Tertio arguitur sic : Conceptus proprius alicujus subjecti est sufficiens ratio concludendi de illo subjecto omnia conceptibilia quae sibi necessario insunt. Nullum autem conceptum habemus de Deo per quem sufficienter possumus cognoscere omnia concepta a nobis quae necessario sibi insunt. Patet de Trinitate, et aliis creditis necessariis ; ergo, etc.

Major probatur, quia immediatam quamlibet cognoscimus, inquantum terminos cognoscimus. Igitur patet major de omni illo conceptibili quod immediate inest conceptui subjecti, quod si insit mediate, fiet idem

included in it.[13]   Consequently, it cannot arise by any such moving factor.

And this argument is confirmed by the fact that except through a reasoning process the mind can know nothing from this object besides the proper and adequate concept of the object itself and whatever is included therein in one of the two aforementioned ways.   But such a reasoning process presupposes a knowledge of the simple thing towards which one reasons.

Consequently, the argument may be formulated as follows : No object will produce a simple and proper concept of itself and a simple and proper concept of another object, unless it contains this second object essentially or virtually.   No created object, however, contains the "Uncreated" essentially or virtually—at least in the way that the two are actually related, namely as what is by nature secondary is related to what is by nature prior.   For it is contrary to the very notion of what is essentially secondary to include virtually what is prior to it.   It is also obvious that the created does not contain, as part of its essence, something that is not merely common, but is exclusively proper to the 'Uncreated".   Therefore, it produces no simple and proper concept of the "Uncreated" at all.

[Arg. III].   The third argument is this.   The proper concept of any subject provides sufficient ground for concluding to everything conceivable which necessarily inheres in that subject.   We have no concept of God, however, that enables us to know every necessary attribute which we conceive of Him, as is evident from the fact of the Trinity, and the other necessary attributes that we know of Him by faith.   Therefore, etc.

Proof of the major.   We know any immediate proposition in so far as we know its terms.   Consequently, the major clearly holds for every concept that is immediately verified existentially of the subject-concept.   If it is a question of a notion that is only mediately verified, our

argumentum de medio comparato ad idem subjectum, et ubicumque stabitur, habetur propositum de immediatis, et ultra per illas scientur mediatae.

[Arg. IV]. Item, quarto potest sic argui. Aut aliqua perfectio simpliciter habet rationem communem Deo et creaturae, et habetur propositum, aut non, sed tantum propriam creaturae, et tunc ratio ejus non conveniet formaliter Deo, quod est inconveniens. Aut habet rationem omnino propriam Deo, et tunc sequitur quod nihil attribuendum est Deo, quia est perfectio simpliciter. Nam hoc nihil est aliud dicere, nisi quod quia ratio ejus ut convenit Deo, dicit perfectionem simpliciter, ideo ipsum ponitur in Deo, et ita peribit doctrina Anselmi *Monologion*,* ubi vult quod praetermissis relationibus in omnibus aliis quidquid est simpliciter melius ipsum quam non ipsum, attribuendum est Deo, sicut quodcumque non tale, est amovendum ab ipso. Primo ergo secundum ipsum aliquid cognoscitur esse tale et secundo attribuitur Deo. Ergo non est tale praecise ut in Deo.

Hoc etiam confirmatur quia tunc nulla perfectio simpliciter esset in creatura. Consequentia patet, quia nullius talis perfectionis etiam conceptus aliquis convenit creaturae nisi conceptus analogicus ex hypothesi. Talis secundum se, quia analogicus, est imperfectus et in nullo est ejus ratio melior non ipso, quia alias secundum illam rationem analogicam poneretur in Deo.

Confirmatur etiam haec quarto ratio sic : Omnis

---

* Cap. XV (Migne, P.L., CLVIII, 162-3).

argument will continue to apply to the middle term in reference to the subject-concept until we have what we are seeking—some immediate propositions. Through these immediate truths, then, the mediate truths will be known.

[Arg. IV]. A fourth argument can also be adduced. Either some pure perfection [14] has a common meaning as applied to God and creatures (which is our contention), or not. If not, it is either because its meaning does not apply formally to God at all (which is inadmissible), or else it has a meaning that is wholly proper to God, in which case nothing need be attributed to God because it is a pure perfection. For such an assumption is equivalent to saying that the meaning of such a perfection in so far as it applied to God, is a pure perfection and therefore is affirmed of God. But this is to bring to nought what Anselm teaches in the *Monologion*,* namely that, with regard to everything except relations, whatever is unconditionally better than something which is not it, must be attributed to God, even as everything not of this kind [i.e. everything that is not better than anything positive that is incompatible with it] must be denied of Him. According to Anselm, then, we first know something to be a pure perfection and secondly we attribute this perfection to God. Therefore, it is not a pure perfection precisely in so far as it is in God.

This is also confirmed by the fact that otherwise no pure perfection would exist in creatures. The consequence is evident, for in this hypothesis only such concepts as express such pure perfections analogously can be applied to a creature. But such a notion in itself is imperfect since it is only analogous to the pure perfection. And therefore, nothing is any better for having this analogous perfection than it would be if it did not have it, for otherwise such a perfection would be affirmed of God.

This fourth reason is also confirmed as follows. Every

inquisitio metaphysica de Deo sic procedit, considerando formalem rationem alicujus et auferendo ab illa ratione formali imperfectionem quam habet in creaturis et reservando illam rationem formalem et attribuendo sibi omnino summam perfectionem et sic attribuendo illud Deo. Exemplum de formali ratione sapientiae vel intellectus vel voluntatis. Consideratur enim in se et secundum se, et ex hoc quod ista ratio non concludit formaliter imperfectionem aliquam nec limitationem, removetur ab ipsa imperfectiones quae concomitantur eam in creaturis et reservata eadem ratione sapientiae et voluntatis attribuuntur ista Deo perfectissime, ergo omnis inquisitio de Deo supponit intellectum habere conceptum eundem univocum quem accepit ex creaturis.

Quod si dicas alia est formalis ratio eorum quae conveniunt Deo, ex hoc sequitur inconveniens, quod ex nulla ratione propria eorum prout sunt in creaturis possunt concludi de Deo, quia omnino alia et alia ratio illorum est et istorum. Immo non magis concludetur quod Deus est sapiens formaliter ex ratione sapientiae quam apprehendimus ex creaturis quam quod Deus est formaliter lapis. Potest enim conceptus aliquis alius a conceptu lapidis creati formari ad quem conceptum lapidis ut est idea in Deo habet iste lapis attributionem, et ita formaliter diceretur Deus est lapis secundum istum conceptum analogicum vel analogum, sicut sapiens secundum illum conceptum analogum.

Qualis autem sit univocatio entis, ad quanta et ad quae dicetur magis in quaestione de primo objecto intellectus.*

[*Tertia Sententia*]. Tertio dico quod Deus non cog-

---

* *Opus oxoniense*, 1, dist. iii, q. iii.

metaphysical inquiry about God proceeds in this fashion :
the formal notion of something is considered ; the imperfection associated with this notion in creatures is
removed, and then, retaining this same formal notion,
we ascribe to it the ultimate degree of perfection and
then attribute it to God. Take, for example, the formal
notion of "wisdom" or "intellect" or "will". Such a
notion is considered first of all simply in itself and
absolutely. Because this notion includes formally no
imperfection nor limitation, the imperfections associated
with it in creatures are removed. Retaining this same
notion of "wisdom" and "will", we attribute these to God
—but in a most perfect degree. Consequently, every
inquiry regarding God is based upon the supposition that
the intellect has the same univocal concept which it
obtained from creatures.

If you maintain that this is not true, but that the formal
concept of what pertains to God is another notion, a
disconcerting consequence ensues ; namely that from the
proper notion of anything found in creatures nothing at
all can be inferred about God, for the notion of what is
in each is wholly different. We would have no more
reason to conclude that God is formally wise from the
notion of wisdom derived from creatures than we would
have reason to conclude that God is formally a stone.
For it is possible to form another notion of a stone to
which the notion of a created stone bears some relation,
for instance, stone as an idea in God. And so we could
say formally, "God is a stone", according to this analogous concept, just as we say, "He is wise", according to
another analogous concept.

What kind of univocation is ascribed to being and how
far and to what it extends, will all be discussed more at
length in a subsequent question on the primary object
of the intellect.[15]

[*Third Statement*]. Thirdly, I say that God is not known
naturally by anyone in the present life in a proper and

noscitur naturaliter a viatore in particulari et proprie, hoc est, sub ratione hujus essentiae ut haec et in se.

Sed ratio illa posita ad hoc in praecedenti opinione non concludit. Cum enim arguitur quod non cognoscitur aliquid nisi per simile, aut intelligit per simile de similitudine univocationis aut imitationis. Si primo modo, igitur nihil cognoscitur de Deo secundum illam opinionem, quia in nullo habet similitudinem univocationis secundum illum modum. Si secundo modo, et creaturae non tantum imitantur illam essentiam sub ratione generalis attributi, sed etiam essentiam hanc ut est haec essentia sive ut nuda in se est existens, secundum eum ; sic enim magis est idea vel exemplar quoniam sub ratione generalis attributi ; ergo propter talem similitudinem posset creatura esse principium cognoscendi essentiam divinam in se et in particulari.

Est ergo alia ratio hujus quaestionis, videlicet quod Deus ut haec essentia in se non cognoscitur naturaliter a nobis, quia sub ratione talis cognoscibilis est objectum voluntarium non naturale nisi respectu sui intellectus tantum, et ideo a nullo intellectu creato potest sub ratione hujus essentiae ut haec est naturaliter cognosci. Nec aliqua essentia naturaliter cognoscibilis a nobis sufficienter ostendit hanc essentiam ut haec, nec per similitudinem univocationis nec imitationis. Univocatio enim non est nisi in generalibus rationibus, imitatio etiam deficit, quia imperfecta, quia creatura imperfecte eum imitatur.

Utrum autem sit alia ratio hujus impossibilitatis, videlicet propter rationem primi objecti, sicut alii ponunt, de hoc in quaestione de primo objecto.*

[*Quarta Sententia*]. Quarto dico quod ad multos con-

---

* *Opus oxoniense*, i, dist. iii, q. iii.

particular manner ; that is to say, we do not know Him in His essence itself precisely as this essence.

But the reason given for this in the preceding opinion is not conclusive. For, when [Henry] argues that one thing can be known from another only by reason of what is similar, we can only understand this likeness to be one of univocation or of imitation. If the first is meant, then nothing is known about God, for according to this opinion there is no likeness of univocation between God and creatures whereby He might be known by us. If the second is meant, then creatures would not imitate God's essence merely under the aspect of some general attribute, but also precisely as "this essence", unveiled and as it exists in itself, for in this way it is more an idea or exemplar than if it were conceived under some general attribute. By reason of this similarity, therefore, a creature, according to him, could be a principle of knowing the divine essence in itself and in particular.

There is, however, another reason for this conclusion that God Himself as this essence is not an object of natural knowledge for us ; for if He be known in this way by any intellect other than His own, it is as a voluntary and not as a natural object.[16] Therefore He cannot be known naturally by any created intellect precisely as "this essence". Neither is there any essence naturally knowable to us that would suffice to reveal "this essence" as "this essence" whether by reason of a likeness of univocation or of imitation. For there is univocation only where general notions are concerned. Imitation too is deficient because it is imperfect, for creatures only imperfectly imitate Him.

Whether there is another reason for the impossibility of such knowledge based on the nature of the primary object of the intellect, which some claim to be the quiddity of a material thing, will be discussed in the question on the primary object of the intellect.

[Fourth Statement]. Fourthly, I say that we can arrive

ceptus proprios Deo possumus pervenire qui non conveniunt creaturis. Cujusmodi sunt conceptus omnium
perfectionum simpliciter in summo, et perfectissimus
conceptus in quo quasi in quadam descriptione perfectissime cognoscimus Deum est concipiendo omnes perfectiones simpliciter et in summo.   Tamen conceptus
perfectior simul et simplicior nobis possibilis est conceptus
entis infiniti. Iste enim est simplicior quam conceptus
entis boni, entis veri, vel aliorum similium, quia infinitum
non est quasi attributum vel passio entis, sive ejus de quo
dicitur, sed dicit modum intrinsecum illius entitatis, ita
quod cum dico infinitum ens, non habeo conceptum
quasi per accidens ex subjecto et passione, sed conceptum
per se subjecti in certo gradu perfectionis, scilicet infinitatis, sicut albedo intensa non dicit conceptum per accidens sicut albedo visibilis ; immo intensio dicit gradum
intrinsecum albedinis in se et ita patet simplicitas hujus
conceptus ens infinitum.

Probatur perfectio istius conceptus, tum quia iste
conceptus inter omnes nobis conceptibiles conceptus
virtualiter plura includit, sicut enim ens includit virtualiter verum et bonum in se, ita ens infinitum includit
verum infinitum et bonum infinitum et omnem perfectionem simpliciter sub ratione infiniti.   Tum quia
demonstratione quia ultimo concluditur esse de ente
infinito, sicut apparet ex quaestione prima secundae
distinctionis.   Illa autem sunt perfectiora quae ultimo
cognoscuntur demonstratione quia ex eis, quia propter
eorum remotionem a creaturis difficilimum est ea ex
creaturis concludere.

Si dicis de summo bono vel summo ente quod istud

at many concepts proper to God in the sense that they do not apply to creatures. Such are the concepts of all the pure perfections when taken in the highest degree. And the most perfect concept of all, by which we know God most perfectly, as it were, in a descriptive sort of way, is obtained by conceiving all the pure perfections and each in the highest degree. Now a less perfect but simpler concept is possible to us, namely the concept of an infinite being. For this is simpler than the concept of "good being" or "true being" or other similar concepts, since infinite is not a quasi-attribute or property of "being" or of that of which it is predicated. Rather it signifies an intrinsic mode of that entity, so that when I say "Infinite Being", I do not have a concept composed accidentally, as it were, of a subject and its attribute. What I do have is a concept of what is essentially one, namely of a subject with a certain grade of perfection—infinity. It is like "intense whiteness", which is not a notion that is accidentally composed, such as "visible whiteness" would be, for the intensity is an intrinsic grade of whiteness itself. Thus the simplicity of this concept "Infinite Being" is evident.

Now the perfection of this concept is proved first from the fact that it virtually includes more than any other concept we can conceive. As "being" virtually includes the "good" and the "true", so "Infinite Being" includes the "infinitely good", the "infinitely true", and all pure perfections under the aspect of infinity. It is also proved from this fact. With a demonstration of fact,[17] the existence of an Infinite Being, or the fact that something has infinite being, is the last conclusion to be established. This is clear from Dist. II, q. i.[18] The more perfect, however, are the last to be established by a demonstration of fact which begins with creatures. For their very remoteness from creatures makes knowledge of them from creatures most difficult of attainment.

But if you say that "highest good" or "Highest Being"

dicit modum intrinsecum entis et includit virtualiter alios conceptus : respondeo, quod si summum intelligatur comparative, sic dicit respectum ad extra, sed infinitum dicit conceptum ad se. Si autem intelligas absolute summum, hoc est, quod ex natura rei non posset excedi, perfectio illa expressius concipitur in ratione infiniti entis. Non enim summum bonum indicat in se utrum sit infinitum vel finitum.

Ex hoc apparet improbatio illius quod dicitur in praecedenti opinione, quod perfectissimum est cognoscere attributa reducendo illa in esse divinum propter simplicitatem divinam. Cognitio enim esse divini sub ratione infiniti est perfectior cognitione ejus sub ratione simplicitatis, quia simplicitas communicatur creaturis, infinitas autem non secundum modum quo convenit Deo.

[*Quinta Sententia*]. Quinto dico quod ista quae cognoscuntur de Deo cognoscuntur per species creaturarum, quia sive universalius et minus universale cognoscantur per eandem speciem minus universalis sive utrumque habeat speciem sui intelligibilem. Si propriam saltem illud quod potest imprimere speciem minus universalis in intellectu potest etiam causare speciem cujuscumque universalioris et ita creaturae quae imprimunt proprias species in intellectu possunt etiam imprimere species transcendentium quae communiter conveniunt eis et Deo. Et tunc intellectus propria virtute potest uti multis speciebus simul ad concipiendum illa simul quorum sunt istae species, puta specie boni et specie summi et specie actus ad concipiendum aliquid summum bonum et actualissimum, quod apparet per locum a minori. Imaginativa enim potest uti speciebus diversorum

expresses an intrinsic mode of being and includes other concepts virtually, I reply that if "highest" be taken in a comparative sense, then it includes a relation to something extrinsic to the being, whereas "infinite" is an absolute concept. But if "highest" is understood in an absolute sense, i.e. as meaning that the very nature of the thing is such that it cannot be exceeded, then this perfection is conceived even more expressly in the notion of an infinite being, because "highest good" does not indicate as such whether it is infinite or finite.

This obviously refutes the assertion made in the previous opinion [of Henry], namely that the most perfect knowledge we have of God is to know His attributes as identified with the divine being in virtue of His simplicity. A knowledge of the divine being as infinite is, however, more perfect than a knowledge of Him as simple, for simplicity is shared with creatures, whereas infinity, as God possesses it, is not.

[*Fifth Statement*]. In the fifth place, I say that what we know of God is known through intelligible species of creatures. Whether the more universal and less universal have each their own proper intelligible species, or whether both are known through one and the same species, namely that which is less universal, this in any case is true. Whatever can imprint or cause a species of what is less universal, can also cause any species of that which is more universal. Thus it is that creatures which impress their own proper species on the intellect can also impress the species of the transcendentals which are common to themselves and to God.[19] Then, the intellect in virtue of its own power can make use of many such species simultaneously, in order to conceive at one time those things of which these are the species. For instance, it can use the species of "good", the species of "highest", the species of "act", to conceive the "highest good which is pure act". This is clear from an instance of the dialectical rule *a minori*,[20] for the imagination is able to use

sensibilium ad imaginandum compositum ex illis diversis, sicut apparet imaginando montem aureum.

Ex hoc apparet improbatio illius quod dicitur in praecedenti opinione de illa suffosione, quia suffodiendo numquam illud quod non subest suffosioni invenitur per suffosionem. Non autem subest conceptui creaturae aliquis conceptus vel species repraesentans aliquid proprium Deo quod sit omnino alterius rationis ab eo quod convenit creaturae, ut probatum est per secundam rationem in secundo articulo. Ergo per suffosionem nullus talis conceptus invenitur.

Et quod adducitur simile de aestimativa, dico quod videtur adduci falsum ad confirmationem alterius falsi, quia si maneat ovis in eadem natura et in eodem affectu naturali ad agnum, imitaretur [read mutaretur] tamen ut esset similis lupo per miraculum in omnibus accidentibus sensibilibus, puta colore, figura et sono et caeteris hujus-modi, agnus fugeret ovem sic mutatam sicut fugeret lupum. Et tamen in ove sic mutata non esset intentio nocivi, sed convenientis. Ergo aestimativa agni non suffoderet ad inveniendum intentionem convenientis sub speciebus sensibilibus, si praecise ita moveretur secundum appetitum sensitivum sicut accidentia sensibilia move-rent.

Si dicas quod ibi intentio convenientis non multiplicat se quia non sunt talia accidentia convenientia tali intentioni, et intentio convenientis non multiplicatur sine accidentibus convenientibus, hoc nihil est, quia si agnus fugeret lupum propter perceptionem nocivi con-ceptam ab aestimativa et illa non multiplicatur cum accidentibus istis sensibilibus quia non est cum eis

the species of different things perceptible to the senses and thus imagine a composite of these different elements, as is apparent, for instance, when we imagine a gold mountain.

This obviously refutes the assertion made in the previous opinion regarding the process whereby the intellect burrows beneath the concept of creatures. For by such a process, we can unearth only what lies beneath the surface. In the concept of a creature, however, no notion or species will be found to represent something proper to God which is wholly different in nature from anything pertaining to a creature, as we have proved in the second reason for the second statement. Consequently, we shall never discover such a concept by this burrowing process.

And as to the analogy of the estimative power, I would say that he seems to adduce one false instance to confirm another. For if a sheep were to remain the same in nature and to retain its natural affection towards a lamb, and yet by some miracle were to be changed accidentally so as to resemble a wolf in all its sensible manifestations, for instance in its colour, its shape, its cries, and all the rest of it, a lamb would flee from such a sheep just as it would flee from a wolf. And still such a sheep has only friendly, and not harmful, intentions towards the lamb. Consequently, the estimative power would not dig beneath the sense images to discover the friendliness, if it were moved according to the sense appetite in the precise way that the sensible appearances move it.

It does not help at all to say that this friendliness is not conveyed sensibly in such a case, since the external manifestations do not agree with the intent in question, and that it is only when the two agree that the friendly intent will be conveyed in a perceptible manner. For if the lamb flees from the wolf only because, by its estimative power, it perceives something inimical, and in the present case the intention [of friendliness] is not transmitted perceptibly where the sensible manifestations are

[in]tentio casu, ergo haec est suffosio agni ad intentionem nocivi, quae nulla est, aut si hic non fugit propter suffossionem, ergo nec alias.

[Ad Argumenta Principalia]

Ad argumenta istius quaestionis :

Ad primum dico quod illa comparatio debet intelligi quantum ad primam motionem intellectus ab objecto, ibi enim phantasma cum intellectu agente habent vicem objecti primi moventis, sed non debet intelligi quantum ad omnem actum sequentem primam motionem. Potest enim intellectus abstrahere omne objectum inclusum in objecto primo movente, et considerare illud abstractum non considerando illud a quo abstrahit et considerando istud abstractum sic considerat commune sensibili et insensibili, quia in illo consideratur insensibile in universali sicut et sensibile, et potest considerare illud abstractum et aliud abstractum in quo sit proprium alteri, scilicet insensibili ; sed sensus non est abstractivus, et ideo in omni actu tam primo quam secundo requirit objectum aliquod proprium movens quomodo non se habet phantasma ad intellectum.

Ad secundum dico quod Commentator exponit illud simile Philosophi de difficili et non de impossibili, et ratio sua est quia tunc natura fecisset otiose illas substantias abstractas intelligibiles, et non possibiles intelligi ab aliquo intellectu. Sed ista ratio ejus non valet ; tum

those [of a wolf], it follows that the lamb unearths a non-existent intention of enmity ; or if the lamb does not flee in virtue of what it discovers by such a burrowing process in the present instance, then neither does it do so in other cases.

[Reply to the Arguments at the Beginning]

As to the arguments at the beginning of this question :

To the first,[21] I reply that the Philosopher's comparison applies to the initial movement of the intellect by the object, for in this case the sense images together with the active intellect function in the role of primary moving object. It must not be understood, however, of all the actions which follow this initial movement. For the intellect can abstract any object which is included in that which produces the initial movement. It is able to consider the former without considering that from which it was abstracted. Now when the intellect considers something that has been abstracted in this way, it grasps what is common to both sensible and insensible. In its consideration the intellect can unite a second abstract notion with the first so that the latter becomes proper to something else, namely to the insensible, for in the abstracted are considered both the insensible (in the universal) as well as the sensible. The sense faculty, however, is incapable of making abstractions. Therefore, in all its acts, whether they be primary or secondary, it requires some object to first put it in motion. But this is not the way that the sense image is related to the intellect.

To the second,[22] I reply that the Commentator restricts this comparison of the Philosopher to what is difficult, but not impossible, to know. And his reason is that otherwise nature would have made these separate substances intelligible in vain, for no intellect would be able to know them. But this reason is invalid, first of all,

quia non est finis istarum substantiarum inquantum intelligibiles sunt ut intelligantur ab intellectu nostro, et ideo si hoc non conveniret eis, non propter hoc essent frustra intelligibiles ; tum quia non sequitur : non sunt intelligibiles ab intellectu nostro, ergo a nullo, possent enim intelligi a seipsis, et ideo est ibi fallacia consequentis. Unde licet multipliciter posset exponi auctoritas Philosophi, dico quod oculus noctuae non habet cognitionem nisi intuitivam et naturalem, et quantum ad istas duas conditiones potest exponi auctoritas Philosophi de impossibilitate, quia sicut est impossibile illi oculo intuitive considerare objectum istud, sic intellectui nostro est impossibile naturaliter et etiam intuitive cognoscere Deum.

Ad tertium, dico quod infinitum potentiale est ignotum quia unumquodque est cognoscibile inquantum est in actu. Non tamen est ignotum sequitur [*read* sic] quod repugnet sibi intelligi ab intellectu infinito, sed non potest infinitum cognosci ab aliquo intellectu cognoscente ipsum secundum modum suae infinitatis. Modus enim suae infinitatis est accipiendo alterum post alterum, et intellectus qui cognosceret hoc modo alterum post alterum, cognosceret semper finitum et numquam infinitum, intellectus tamen infinitus potest cognoscere totum illud simul, non partem post partem. Cum etiam arguitur de secundo *Metaphysicae* de infinitis et infinito, dico quod non est simile quia cognitio objectorum infinitorum numeraliter concluderet infinitatem potentiae cognoscentis, sicut patuit in quaestione prima secundae distinctionis argumento secundo ad infinitatem, quia videlicet ibi pluralitas ex parte objecti con-

because we cannot say that the sole purpose or reason for the intelligibility of these substances is that we may know them. Consequently, even if we could know nothing about them, we still could not say they are intelligible to no purpose. Secondly, it does not follow that just because these substances are unintelligible to our minds, they are unintelligible to all minds, for they could be intelligible to themselves. Therefore, we have the fallacy of affirming the consequent.[23] Wherefore I say that even though there are many ways in which this citation of the Philosopher could be explained, still the eye of the bat has only a natural and intuitive knowledge. And on the basis of these two characteristics the Philosopher's words can be explained even in terms of impossibility. For just as it is impossible for the eye of the bat to consider such an object naturally and intuitively, so it is also impossible for our intellect to possess a natural and intuitive knowledge of God.[24]

To the third,[25] I reply that the potentially infinite is unknown, because only to the extent that something is in act it is knowable. But it is not so unknown that it would be impossible for an infinite intellect to know it. Nevertheless the [potentially] infinite cannot be known by an intellect which proceeds to know it in the way that it is infinite. For it is infinite only in so far as the mind in considering only one thing after another never comes to an end. Now the mind which considers only one thing after another in this way always considers something finite and never something infinite. An infinite intellect, however, can know the whole thing at once, and not simply one part after another. And to the argument from *Metaphysics*, BK. II, concerning infinite numbers and the "Infinite", I reply that there is no parity between the two, for a knowledge of an infinite number of objects would imply that the faculty of knowledge itself is infinite (as is clear from q. i of dist. II regarding the infinity of God),[26] since one can infer a greater power of

cludit majoritatem virtutis in intellectu, sed intellectio alicujus infiniti non concludit infinitatem, quia non oportet actum habere talem modum realem, qualem habet objectum, quia actus sub ratione finiti potest esse ad objectum sub ratione infiniti nisi esset actus comprehensivus, et concedo quod talem actum circa objectum infinitum non habemus nec possibile est habere.

Ad Gregorium dico quod non debet intelligi quod contemplatio sistat sub Deo in aliqua creatura, quia hoc esset frui utendis, quod esset summa perversitas secundum Augustinum *LXXXIII Quaestionum*, quaestione xxx.* Sed conceptus illius essentiae sub ratione entis est imperfectior conceptu illius essentiae ut haec essentia est, et quia est imperfectior, ideo inferior in intelligibilitate, contemplatio autem de lege communi stat in tali conceptu communi, et ideo stat in aliquo conceptu qui est minoris intelligibilitatis quam Deus in se, ut est haec essentia. Et ideo debet intelligi ad aliquid quod est sub Deo, hoc est ad aliquid sub ratione intelligibilis cujus intelligibilitas est inferior intelligibilitate Dei in se, ut haec essentia singularis.

[*Ad Argumenta pro Opinione Henrici*]

Ad argumenta pro prima opinione, cum arguitur quod Deus non potest intelligi in aliquo conceptu communi sibi et creaturis univoce, quia est singularitas quaedam : consequentia non valet. Socrates enim inquantum Socrates est singularis et tamen a Socrate plura possunt abstrahi praedicata, et ideo singularitas alicujus non

---

* Migne, P. L., XL, 20.

intellect from a greater number of objects known. But a knowledge of something infinite does not imply that the act of knowledge itself is infinite unless it be an act which fully comprehends the object, for it is not necessary that the act and object should have the same mode of reality, since an act which by nature is finite can be related to an object which by nature is infinite. I admit, however, that we neither have, nor can have, such a comprehensive act of knowledge in regard to an infinite object.

To the [fourth] argument,[27] [that] of Gregory, I reply that we should not think that contemplation terminates in some creature beneath God, for this would be to enjoy as an end what is to be used as a means. According to Augustine,* this would be the greatest perversion. But the concept of God's essence under the aspect of "being" is less perfect than the concept of the same essence as "this essence". Because it is less perfect, it falls below the latter concept in intelligibility. But the contemplation that is characteristic of the ordinary dispensation rests with just such an [imperfect or] common concept, and hence with one of inferior intelligibility to God Himself considered as this essence. Consequently "to what is beneath God" must be understood in terms of being intelligible, [that is to say it refers to a concept] whose intelligibility is less than that of God considered in Himself as this singular essence.

[A Reply to the Arguments in Support of Henry]

To the arguments for the first opinion [28] I reply that when it is argued that God by reason of His unique singularity cannot be known through some concept univocally common to Himself and creatures, the consequence is invalid. For Socrates, in so far as he is Socrates, is singular. Nevertheless several predicates can be abstracted from Socrates. Consequently, the singularity

impedit, quin ab eo quod singulare est, possit abstrahi aliquis conceptus communis. Et licet quidquid ibi in re sit singulare ex se in existendo ita quod nihil contrahit aliud ibi ad singularitatem, tamen illud idem potest concipi ut hoc in re, vel quodammodo indistincte, et ita ut singulare vel commune.

Quod dicit pro illa opinione de cognitione per accidens, non oportet improbare, quia quasi per accidens cognoscitur in attributo, sed non praecise sicut probatum est.

of a thing is no impediment to the abstraction of a common concept. Though in reality everything in God, since it exists of itself, is singular, so that one thing does not contract another to singularity, nevertheless one and the same thing can be conceived indistinctly or as "this thing existing in reality", and thus it can be conceived either as common or as singular.

There is no need to refute what he says regarding an incidental knowledge of God, because God is known in a quasi-incidental manner in an attribute. However, this is not the sole way He can be known, as has been proved above.

III

THE EXISTENCE OF GOD

Summary of the Argument

[III. DE ESSE DEI] *

Circa secundam distinctionem quaero primo de his quae pertinent ad unitatem Dei, et primo, *utrum in entibus sit aliquid existens actu infinitum.*

[Pro et Contra]

Quod non, sic arguitur :

Si unum contrariorum esset actu infinitum, nihil sibi contrarium esset in natura ; ergo si aliquod bonum sit actu infinitum, nihil mali esset in universo. Respondetur quod major est vera de contrariis formaliter ; sed nihil malum contrariatur Deo formaliter. Contra : sive formaliter sive virtualiter contrarietur, si est infinitum, nihil patitur contrarium sui effectus, quia propter infinitam virtutem destruet omne incompossibile suo effectui ; ergo est major vera de contrario virtualiter, sicut formaliter. Exemplum : si sol esset infinite calidus virtualiter, nihil relinqueret frigidum in universo sicut nec si esset infinite calidus formaliter.

Item, corpus infinitum nullum aliud secum compatitur ; sicut nec ens infinitum aliquod aliud ens cum eo. Probatio consequentiae : tum quia sicut repugnat dimensio dimensioni, ita videtur actualitas actualitati repugnare ; tum quia sicut corpus aliud ab infinito, faceret cum illo aliquid majus infinito, ita ens aliud ab infinito videtur facere aliquid majus infinito.

Praeterea, quod ita est hic, quod non alibi, est

---

* *Opus oxoniense*, I, dist. II, q. i (Assisi 137, f. 14r^b-18r^b; cf. Vatican ed., VOL. II, 124-125, 148-221).

[III. THE EXISTENCE OF GOD]

First I inquire about those things which pertain to the unicity of God, and *I ask first whether in the realm of beings something exists which is actually infinite?*

[Pro et Contra]

To prove that no such thing exists the following arguments are cited [1] :

[Arg. I].   If one of two contraries were actually infinite, then nothing contrary to it would exist in nature ; therefore if some good were actually infinite, nothing evil would exist in the universe.   One answer given to this objection is that the major is true only of formal contraries, and evil is not formally contrary to God.[2] To the contrary :   It makes no difference whether contrariety be virtual or formal.   If something is infinite, it will not tolerate anything contrary to its effect, since by reason of its infinite power, it will destroy anything incompatible with its effect.   Therefore, the major is just as true of virtual contraries as it is of formal contraries. For example :   if the sun were infinitely hot either virtually or formally, in either case it would leave nothing cold in the universe.

[Arg. II].   Again, just as an infinite body would not permit the coexistence of another body, even so an infinite being would not tolerate the coexistence of any other being.   Proof of the consequence : Actuality seems to be opposed to actuality in the same way as dimension is opposed to dimension.   Furthermore, if a being other than the infinite could exist, it would seem to increase the infinite just as to add another body to an infinite body would produce something greater than the infinite.

[Arg. III].   Furthermore, anything present in this

infinitum respectu ubi ; et quod nunc est ita, quod non alias, est finitum respectu quando, et sic de singulis. Quod ita agit hoc, quod non aliud, est finitum quantum ad actionem ; ergo quod est ita hoc aliquid, quod non aliud, est finitum secundum entitatem. Deus est summe hoc, quia ex se singularitas ; ergo non est infinitus.

Item, VIII *Physicorum*,* virtus infinita, si esset, moveret in non-tempore ; nulla virtus potest movere in non-tempore ; quia si sic, motus esset in instanti ; ergo nulla est infinita.

Contra :

Ibidem Philosophus VIII *Physicorum* † probat primum movens esse potentiae infinitae, quia movet motu infinito ; sed haec conclusio non potest intelligi tantum de infinitate durationis, quia propter infinitatem potentiae probat quod non possit esse in magnitudine ; non repugnat autem magnitudini, secundum eum, quod in eo sit potentia infinita secundum durationem, sicut poneret de caelo.

Item, in Psalmo ‡ : Magnus Dominus et laudabilis nimis.

Item, Damascenus, lib. I, cap. iv ** : Est pelagus, etc.

[Corpus Quaestionis]

Ad primam quaestionem sic procedo, quia de ente infinito sic non potest demonstrari esse demonstratione propter quid quantum ad nos, licet ex natura terminorum

---

* VIII, cap. x (266^a, 24–266^b, 6).   † loc. cit. (266^b, 6).
‡ Ps. xlvii. 2 ; cxliv. 3.
** *De fide orthodoxa*, I, cap. ix (Migne, P.G., XCIV, 835).

place in such a way that it is nowhere else, is limited with regard to its whereabouts. What exists at just this moment and no other, is finite with regard to temporal duration. And so on with the single categories. Whatever does just this and nothing else, is finite in its action. Therefore, whatever is just this thing and no other, is limited in its entity. Now God above all is a "this", for He is singularity of His very nature. Therefore, God is not infinite.

[Arg. iv]. Again, according to *Physics*, bk. viii,* if an infinite force existed it would move or act instantaneously ; but no force can move things instantaneously, for if it could movement would take place in an instant. Consequently, nothing is infinite.

To the contrary :

[Arg. i]. In the same place in *Physics*, bk. viii,† the Philosopher proves that the First Mover is infinite in power because He moves with an infinite movement. But this conclusion cannot be understood of power that is infinite only in duration. The reason why it cannot is this. Aristotle proves that because this power [of the First Mover] is infinite, it cannot reside in a [finite] magnitude. But it is not contradictory, according to him, that a power infinite merely in duration should reside in a [finite] magnitude, for he assumes this to be the case with the heavens.[3]

[Arg. ii]. Also, in the Book of Psalms ‡ : "Great is the Lord and exceedingly to be praised".

[Arg. iii]. Also, in the fourth chapter of the first book of Damascene ** : "He is a sea [of infinite perfections]".

[Body of the Question]

My reason for proceeding as I do in this first question is this. Although the proposition "An infinite being

propositio est demonstrabilis propter quid. Sed quantum ad nos bene propositio est demonstrabilis quia ex creaturis. Proprietates autem infiniti entis relativae ad creaturas immediatius se habent ad illa quae sunt media in demonstratione quia quam proprietates absolutae, ita quod de illis proprietatibus relativis concludi potest immediatius esse per ista quae sunt media in tali demonstratione quam de proprietatibus absolutis ; nam immediate ex esse unius relativi sequitur esse sui correlativi. Ideo, primo declarabo esse de proprietatibus relativis entis infiniti, quae sunt primitas et causalitas. Et secundo declarabo esse de infinito ente, quia illae relativae proprietates soli enti infinito conveniunt. Et ita erunt duo articuli principales.

[*Articulus Primus. De Proprietatibus Relativis*]

Quantum ad primum, dico : proprietates relativae entis infiniti ad creaturas aut sunt proprietates causalitatis aut eminentiae. Causalitatis duplicis, aut efficientis aut finis. Quod additur de causa exemplari non est aliud genus causae ab efficiente, quia tunc essent quinque genera causarum ; unde causa exemplaris est quoddam efficiens, quia est agens per intellectum distinctum contra agens per naturam ; de quo alias.

In primo articulo principali, tria principaliter ostendam : primo ergo ostendam quod aliquid est in effectu inter entia quod est simpliciter primum omni primitate quae non includit aliquam imperfectionem. Pars enim est imperfectior toto et tamen prior ; pars enim participat entitatem totius et non est ipsum totum. Aliae autem sunt primitates quae non includunt aliquam

exists" can, by the very nature of its terms, be demon-strated by a demonstration of the reasoned fact,[4] we are not able to demonstrate it in this way. Nevertheless, we can demonstrate the proposition by a demonstration of fact beginning with creatures. However, those properties of the infinite being which refer to creatures are related more closely than the absolute properties to what we must use as middle terms in a demonstration of fact, so that in virtue of such a demonstration the relative properties are established prior to the absolute properties, for the existence of one term of the relation implies immediately that of its correlative. Consequently, I shall show first the existence of such relative properties of the infinite being as primacy and causality. Secondly, from these I shall show that an infinite being exists, because these relative properties pertain exclusively to a being that is infinite. And so there will be two principal articles.

[*Article I. Relative Properties of God*]

As to the first article, I say that the properties of the infinite being which refer to creatures are either of causality or of pre-eminence. Those of causality in turn are twofold, the properties of efficient and final causality. What is added about the exemplar does not involve another cause different in kind from the efficient, for then there would be five kinds of causes. Wherefore, the exemplar cause is a certain kind of efficient cause, namely an intelligent agent in contradistinction to a natural agent ; but more of this elsewhere.[5]

In the first main article, I shall set forth three principal points : *first*, in the realm of beings something actually exists which is simply first by every primacy that includes no imperfection. For a part, though prior to, is less perfect than, the whole, since the part shares in the unity of the whole and yet is not the whole itself. Other

imperfectionem ; ut primitas eminentiae et triplicis causalis independentiae ; scilicet efficientis, formalis vel exemplaris, et finalis. Primitas autem eminentiae non est primitas causalitatis ; non enim ex hoc quod unum ens praeeminet alteri est causa illius, nam primum et summum in quolibet genere praeeminet alteri posteriori in illo genere, et tamen non est causa illius. Primitas etiam exemplaris non distinguitur a primitate efficientiae, quia principium exemplans alia in esse intelligibili non est nisi principium efficiens per intellectum ; sicut enim naturale efficiens non distinguit efficiens sed continetur sub eo, sic nec exemplaris distinguitur ab efficiente. Sunt ergo duae causalitates contra se distinctae, scilicet causae efficientis et finalis. Et omnes illae primitates quas attribuimus Deo, nullam imperfectionem includunt. Unde primo ostendam quod est aliquid in effectu inter entia simpliciter primum secundum efficientiam et aliquid est quod etiam est simpliciter primum secundum rationem finis, et aliquid quod est simpliciter primum secundum eminentiam. Secundo ostendo quod illud quod est primum secundum unam rationem primitatis, idem est primum secundum alias primitates. Et tertio ostendo quod illa triplex primitas uni soli naturae convenit, ita quod non pluribus naturis differentibus specie vel quidditative. Et ita in primo articulo principali erunt tres articuli partiales.

[*Pars Prima. De Triplici Primitate*]. Primus articulus illorum includit tres conclusiones principales per triplicem primitatem. Quaelibet autem illarum trium conclusionum habet tres ex quibus dependet. Prima est quod aliquid sit primum. Secunda est quod illud est incausabile. Tertia est quod illud actu existit in entibus. Itaque in primo articulo sunt novem conclusiones, sed tres principales.

primacies, however, include no imperfection. Such is the primacy of pre-eminence and of independence in regard to the three kinds of causes, viz. efficient, formal or exemplar, and final. The primacy of pre-eminence, however, is not a primacy of causality. For just because one thing is more perfect than another, it does not follow that the former is the cause of the latter ; for the first and most perfect in any given genus is more perfect than any other of its kind and yet is not the cause of the others.[6] Neither is the primacy of exemplarity to be differentiated from that of efficiency, for the principle which copies what exists in thought is nothing else than an intelligent efficient cause. For just as a natural efficient cause [7] is not considered as distinct from efficient cause but rather as a subdivision thereof, so also the exemplar cause. Consequently, we have but two causalities distinct from one another, that of the efficient cause and that of the final cause. And none of these primacies which we attribute to God include any imperfection. Wherefore, I shall show that in the realm of beings something indeed exists which is simply first according to efficiency, and also that something exists which is simply first in the order of ends, and that something exists which is simply first by reason of pre-eminence. Secondly, I shall show that what is first in virtue of one kind of primacy is also first in virtue of the others. And thirdly, I shall show that this triple primacy pertains to but one nature, so as not to be found in several specifically or essentially different natures. This first article, then, will contain three subordinate parts.

[*Part I. The Triple Primacy*]. This first part comprises three principal conclusions corresponding respectively to the threefold primacy. Each of these three conclusions in turn depends upon three others : (1) Something is first, (2) It cannot be caused, (3) It actually exists in the realm of beings. And so the first part contains nine conclusions, three of which are principal.

[*a. De Primitate Efficientis*]. Prima autem conclusio istarum novem est ista, quod aliquod effectivum sit simpliciter primum, ita quod nec sit effectibile nec virtute alterius a se effectivum. Probatio : quia aliquod ens est effectibile ; aut ergo a se aut a nihilo vel ab aliquo alio. Non a nihilo, quia nullius est causa illud quod nihil est. Nec a se, quia nulla res est quae seipsam faciat vel gignat, I *De Trinitate.** Ergo ab alio. Illud aliud sit A. Si est A primum hoc modo exposito, propositum habeo. Si non est primum, ergo est posterius effectivum, quia effectibile ab alio vel a virtute alterius effec[ti]vum, quia si negetur negatio, ponitur affirmatio. Detur illud alterum et sit B de quo arguitur sicut de A argutum est. Et ita aut proceditur in infinitum quorum quodlibet respectu prioris erit secundum ; aut statur in aliquo non habente prius. Infinitas autem impossibilis est in ascendendo. Ergo, primitas necessaria, quia non habens prius, nullo priore se est posterius, nam circulum in causis esse est inconveniens.

Contra istam rationem sic instatur primo quod petat stare in causis ; secundo quod procedit ex contingentibus et ita non fit demonstratio. Secundum probatur, quia praemissae accipiunt esse de aliquo causato et omne causatum contingenter est. Similiter, procedit ex contingentibus quia ex rationibus productis et producti qui tantum sunt termini contingentes. Primum confirmatur per hoc quod secundum philosophantes infinitas est ascendendo, sicut ponunt exemplum de generationibus infinitis, quorum nullum est primum sed quodlibet

---

* *De Trinitate*, I, cap. i (Migne, P.L., XLII, 820).

[*a. The Primacy of Efficient Causality*]. Now the first of these nine conclusions is this : *Among beings which can produce an effect one is simply first*, in the sense that it neither can be produced by an efficient cause nor does it exercise its efficient causality in virtue of anything other than itself. Proof : Some being can be produced. Therefore, it is either produced by itself or by nothing or by something other than itself. Now it cannot be produced by nothing, for what is nothing causes nothing. Neither can it be produced by itself, for as Augustine points out in his work *De Trinitate*, BK. I,* nothing ever makes itself or begets itself. Therefore it can only be produced by another. Now let this other be called *A*. If *A* is first in the way we have described, then I have what I seek to prove. But if it is not first, then it is some posterior agent—either because it can be produced by something else or because it is able to produce its effect only in virtue of something other than itself. To deny the negation is to assert the affirmation. Let us assume that this being is not first and call it *B*. Then we can argue of *B* as we did of *A*. And so we shall either go on *ad infinitum* so that each thing in reference to what precedes it in the series will be second ; or we shall reach something that has nothing prior to it. However, an infinity in the ascending order [8] is impossible ; hence a primacy is necessary because whatever has nothing prior to itself is posterior to nothing prior, for a circle in causes is inadmissible.

Against this argument, it is objected, first, that the argument assumes an end in the series of causes ; secondly, that it begins with contingent propositions and hence is not a demonstration. This second objection is argued in this way. The premises assume the existence of something that has been caused, and everything caused exists contingently. The first objection is confirmed from the admission of those who philosophise that an infinity is possible in an ascending order, as for instance, when they assume infinite generations, where no single one is

secundum, quia secundum eos, non est inconveniens procedere in infinitum in productionibus ejusdem rationis ubi nullum est primum sed quodlibet secundum, et tamen hoc ab eis sine circulo ponitur.

Ad primam instantiam primo excludendam dico quod philosophi non posuerunt infinitatem possibilem in causis essentialiter ordinatis, sed tantum in accidentaliter ordinatis, sicut patet per Avicennam sexto *Metaphysicae*, cap. v, ubi loquitur de infinitate individuorum in specie. Et ad propositum melius ostendendum sciendum quae sunt causae essentialiter et accidentaliter ordinatae, ubi notandum quod aliud est loqui de causis per se et per accidens ; et aliud est loqui de causis per se sive essentialiter et accidentialiter ordinatis, nam in prima est tantum operatio unius ad unum, scilicet causae ad causatum, et est causa per se quae secundum naturam propriam, et non secundum aliquid sibi accidens, causat ut subjectum est causa per se respectu suae propriae passionis et in aliis ut album disgregat et aedificator aedificat ; sed causa per accidens econverso ut Polycletus aedificat. In secundo est comparatio duarum causarum inter se in quantum ab eis est causatum.

Et differunt causae per se sive essentialiter ordinatae a causis per accidens sive accidentaliter ordinatis in tribus. Prima differentia est, quod in per se ordinatis secunda in quantum causa dependet a prima ; in per accidens non, licet in esse vel aliquo modo alio dependeat. Filius enim licet secundum esse dependeat a patre, non

first but each is second to some other. For they find nothing inconvenient about proceeding to infinity with productions of the same kind, where nothing is first and every member [of the series] is second [to some other member]. And still they assume no circle in causes.

To exclude this first objection, I say that the philosophers do not assume the possibility of an infinity in causes essentially ordered, but only in causes accidentally ordered, as is evident from Avicenna's *Metaphysics*, BK. VI, c. v, where he speaks of an infinity of individuals in a species. To understand better what we have in mind, one should know that some causes are essentially ordered and others accidentally ordered. Here it should be noted that it is one thing to speak of incidental causes (*causae per accidens*) as contrasted with those which are intended by their nature to produce a given effect (*causae per se*). It is quite another to speak of causes which are ordered to one another essentially or of themselves (*per se*) and those which are ordered only accidentally (*per accidens*). For in the first instance we have merely a comparison one-to-one, namely of the cause to that which is caused. A *per se* cause is one which causes a given effect by reason of its very nature and not by reason of something incidental to it. For instance, the subject is a *per se* cause of its proper attributes. Other such instances are "white dilating" [9] or "a builder building". On the contrary, "Polycletus building" would be an incidental cause.[10] In the second instance, two causes are compared with each other in so far as they are causes of the same thing.

Per se or essentially ordered causes differ from accidentally ordered causes in three respects. The first difference is that in essentially ordered causes, the second depends upon the first precisely in its act of causation. In accidentally ordered causes this is not the case, although the second may depend upon the first for its existence or in some other way. Thus a son depends upon his father for

tamen in causando, quia patre mortuo potest agere sicut ipso vivo. Differentia secunda est, quod in per se ordinatis est causalitas alterius rationis et alterius ordinis, quia superior est perfectior ; in accidentaliter autem ordinatis non. Et differentia haec sumitur ex prima ; nam nulla causa a causa ejusdem rationis dependet essentialiter in causando, quia in causatione alicujus sufficit unum unius rationis. Tertia est, quod omnes causae essentialiter et per se ordinatae simul necessario requiruntur ad causandum, alioquin aliqua causalitas essentialis et per se deesset effectui ; in accidentaliter autem ordinatis non est sic, quia non requiritur simultas eorum in causando, quia quaelibet habet suam perfectam causalitatem sine alia respectu sui effectus. Sufficit enim quod successive causet una post aliam.

Ex his ostenditur propositum, scilicet quod infinitas essentialiter ordinatorum est impossibilis. Similiter secunda infinitas accidentaliter ordinatorum est impossibilis, nisi ponatur status in ordinatis essentialiter. Ergo omni modo est impossibilis infinitas in essentialiter ordinatis. Si etiam negetur ordo essentialis, adhuc infinitas est impossibilis. Ergo omni modo est aliquod primum necessario et simpliciter effectivum. Istarum trium propositionum assumptarum, propter brevitatem, prima dicatur A, secunda B, tertia C.

Probatio illarum, primo A, scilicet quod essentialiter ordinatorum infinitas est impossibilis. Probo tum quia in causis essentialiter ordinatis ubi ponit adversarius infinitatem secunda in quantum causat, dependet a prima, ex prima differentia. Si igitur essent causae

existence but is not dependent upon him in exercising his own causality, since he can act just as well whether his father be living or dead. The second difference is that in essentially ordered causes the causality is of another nature and order, inasmuch as the higher cause is more perfect. Such is not the case, however, with accidentally ordered causes. This second difference is a consequence of the first, since no cause in the exercise of its causality is essentially dependent upon a cause of the same nature as itself, for to produce anything one cause of a given kind suffices. The third difference is that all *per se* and essentially ordered causes are simultaneously required to cause the effect, for otherwise some causality essential to the effect would be wanting. In accidentally ordered causes this is not so, because there is no need of simultaneity in causing inasmuch as each possesses independently of the others the perfection of causality with regard to its own effect. For it is enough that one cause after the other exercises causality successively.

From all this we propose to show that an infinity of essentially ordered causes is impossible ; secondly, that an infinity of accidentally ordered causes is also impossible unless we admit a terminus in an essentially ordered series ; therefore an infinity in essentially ordered causes is impossible in any case ; thirdly, even if we deny the existence of an essential order, an infinity of causes is still impossible. Consequently, in every instance, of necessity some first being able to cause exists. For the sake of brevity, let us call the first of these three assumptions *A*, the second *B* and the third *C*.

Proof of the first of these propositions, *A* (namely that an infinity of essentially ordered causes is impossible) : I prove this first, because in essentially ordered causes where our opponent assumes an infinity, the second of the series depends upon the first. This is a consequence of the first difference between essentially and accidentally ordered causes. Now if these causes were infinite so

infinitae ita quod non solum quaelibet posterior sed
quaelibet alia dependet a sua causa proxima prior, ergo
universitas causatorum est ab aliqua causa priori. Non
ab aliqua causa quae est aliquid totius universitatis,
quia tunc esset causa sui. Tota enim universitas dependet et a nullo illius universitatis et hoc voco primum
efficiens. Si igitur sunt infinitae, adhuc dependent ab
aliqua quae non est illius universitatis.

Tum quia si causae infinitae ordinatae essentialiter
concurrant ad productionem alicujus effectus ; et ex
tertia differentia omnes causae essentialiter ordinatae
sunt simul, sequitur quod infinita sunt simul ad causandum hunc effectum, quod nullus philosophus ponit.

Tum tertio, quia prius est principio propinquius,
quinto *Metaphysicae*.* Ergo ubi nullum [*MS* unum]
principium nihil essentialiter prius.

Tum quarto, quia superior causa est perfectior in
causando ex secunda differentia ; ergo in infinitum
superior est in infinitum perfectior ; ergo [*MS* in] infinitae
perfectionis. Et nulla talis est causans de virtute alterius
quia quaelibet talis est imperfecte causans, quia est
dependens incausando ab alia.

Tum quinto, quia effectivum nullam imperfectionem
ponit necessario ; ergo potest esse in aliquo sine imperfectione, quia quod nihil imperfectionis includit potest
poni inter entia sine imperfectione ; sed si nulla causa
est sine dependentia ad prius, in nullo est sine imperfectione ; ergo effectibilitas independens potest inesse
alicui naturae, et illa simpliciter est prima. Ergo
effectibilitas simpliciter prima est possibilis. Hoc

---

* v, cap. xi (1018*b*, 9–11)

that not only would each single cause be posterior to something but every other cause which precedes it would be dependent in turn upon the cause that goes before it, then whole series of effects would be dependent upon some prior cause. Now the latter cannot be a cause that is part of the series, for then it would be its own cause. The series as a whole, then, is dependent on something which does not pertain to the group that is caused, and this I call the first efficient cause. Even if the group of beings caused were infinite, they would still depend upon something outside the group.

Then, too, if an infinite number of essentially ordered causes concurred to produce some effect, it would follow that an infinite number would simultaneously cause this effect, for it follows from the third difference that essentially ordered causes must exist simultaneously. Now no philosopher assumes this.

Then, thirdly, to be prior, a thing must be nearer to the beginning.[11] * Consequently, where there is no beginning, nothing can be essentially prior to anything else.

Then, fourthly, by reason of the second difference, the higher cause is more perfect in its causality, therefore what is infinitely higher is infinitely more perfect, and hence of infinite perfection. Now nothing infinitely perfect can cause something only in virtue of another, because everything of this kind is imperfect in its causality since it depends on another in order to cause its effect.

Then, fifthly, inasmuch as to be able to produce something does not imply any imperfection, it follows that this ability can exist in something without imperfection, because that which implies no imperfection can be asserted of beings without imperfection. But if every cause depends upon some prior cause, then efficiency is never found without imperfection. Hence an independent power to produce something can exist in some nature, and this nature is *simply* first. Therefore, such an efficient power is possible, and this suffices, for later

sufficit, quia inferius ex hoc concluditur quia tale efficiens primum, si est possibile, est in re. Et sic quinque rationibus patet A.

B probatur, scilicet quod infinitas in accidentaliter ordinatis sit impossibilis, nisi ponatur status essentialiter ordinatorum, quia infinitas accidentalis, si ponitur, hoc non est simul, patet, sed successive tantum, ut alterum post alterum, ita quod secundum aliquo modo fluit a priore, non tamen dependet ab ipso in causando. Potest enim causare, illo non existente, sicut illo existente ; sicut filius generat, patre mortuo sicut ipso vivo. Talis infinitas successionis est impossibilis, nisi ab aliqua natura infinite durante, a qua tota successio et quidlibet ejus dependeat ; nulla enim difformitas perpetuatur, nisi in virtute alicujus permanentis quod nihil est illius successionis, quia omnia successiva illius successionis sunt ejusdem rationis, et quia nulla pars successionis potest permanere cum tota successione eo quod tunc non esset pars ejus. Sed est aliquid prius essentialiter, quia quidlibet successionis dependet ab ipso, et hoc in alia ordinatione quam a causa proxima, quia est aliquid illius successionis. Omne igitur quod dependet a causa accidentaliter ordinata, dependet essentialius a causa per se et essentialiter ordinata. Imo negato ordine essentiali negabitur ordo accidentalis quia accidentia non habent ordinem nisi mediante fixo et permanente, nec per consequens habet multitudinem in infinitum. Patet ergo B.

Probatur etiam C, quod scilicet si negetur ordo essentialis, adhuc infinitas est impossibilis. Probo :

we shall prove that if such a first efficient cause is possible, then it exists in reality. And so *A* becomes evident from these five arguments.

Now *B* (namely, that an infinity of accidentally ordered causes is impossible unless we admit that the essentially ordered series has an end) is proved in this way. If we assume an infinity of accidentally ordered causes, it is clear that these causes do not exist simultaneously but only successively, one after the other, so that what follows flows in some way from what precedes. Still the succeeding cause does not depend upon the preceding for the exercise of its causality, for it is equally effective whether the preceding cause exists or not. A son in turn may beget a child just as well whether his father be dead or alive. But an infinite succession of such causes is impossible unless it exists in virtue of some nature of infinite duration from which the whole succession and every part thereof depends. For no change of form is perpetuated save in virtue of something permanent which is not a part of the succession. And the reason for this is that everything of this succession which is in flux, is of the same nature and no part thereof can be coexistent with the entire series for the simple reason that it would no longer be a part of the latter. Something essentially prior to the series then exists, for everything that is part of the succession depends upon it, and this dependence is of a different order from that by which it depends upon the immediately preceding cause where the latter is a part of the succession. Therefore, whatever depends upon an accidentally ordered cause depends more essentially upon an essentially ordered cause. Indeed, to deny the essential order is to deny the accidental order also, since accidents do not have any order save in virtue of what is fixed and permanent. Consequently, neither will an infinite multitude exist. *B*, then, is evident.

Proposition *C* (namely that if an essential order is denied, an infinity is still impossible), also is proved.

quia cum ex prima ratione hic adducta, scilicet quod a
nullo nihil potest esse, sequatur quod aliqua natura sit
effectiva. Si negatur ordo essentialis activorum, ergo illa
in nullius alterius virtute causat, et licet ipsa in aliquo
singulari ponatur causata, tamen in aliquo est non
causata, quod est propositum de natura vel si in quolibet
ponatur causata, statim implicatur contradictio negando
ordinem essentialem, quia nulla natura potest poni in
quolibet causata, ita quod sit ordo accidentalis sub ipsa
sine ordine essentiali ad aliam naturam [sicut patet ex B].

Ad secundam instantiam supra positam, quae dicit
quod ratio procedit ex contingentibus et ita non est
demonstratio, cum dico aliqua natura vere est effecta,
ergo aliquid est efficiens, respondeo quod posset sic argui :
aliqua natura est effecta quod aliquod subjectum mutatur, et ita terminus mutationis incipit esse in subjecto, et
ita ille terminus vel compositum producitur sive efficitur ;
ergo est aliquod efficiens, per naturam correlativorum ;
et tunc potest esse secundum veritatem prima contingens,
sed manifesta. Potest tamen sic argui probando primam
conclusionem sic. Haec est vera : aliqua natura est
effectibilis ; ergo aliqua est effectiva. Antecedens probatur : quia aliquod subjectum est mutabile, quia aliquod
entium est possibile, definiendo possibile contra necessarium ; et sic procedendo ex necessariis. Et tunc
probatio primae conclusionis est de esse quidditative sive,

Proof : From the first reason adduced here, viz. that nothing can come from nothing, it follows that some nature is capable of causing effectively. Now, if an essential order of agents be denied, then this nature capable of causing does not cause in virtue of some other cause, and even if we assume that in one individual it is caused, nevertheless in some other it will not be caused, and this is what we propose to prove to be true of this nature. For if we assume that in every individual this nature is caused, then a contradiction follows immediately if we deny the existence of an essential order, since no nature that is caused can be assumed to exist in each individual in such a way that it is included in an accidental order of causes without being at the same time essentially ordered to some other nature. This follows from proposition *B*.

Then we come to the second objection cited above,[12] namely that when I argue : "Some nature is capable of producing an effect, therefore something is an efficient cause", the argument is not a demonstration, since it proceeds from contingent propositions. I reply that I could indeed argue that some nature is produced because some subject undergoes a change and therefore the term of the change comes into existence in the subject, and consequently this term or the composite [i.e. the subject and term] are produced or effected. Hence by the nature of the correlatives, some efficient cause exists. Formulated in this fashion, this first argument would be based upon a contingent but manifest proposition. However, to prove our conclusion the argument can be reformulated in such a way that it proceeds from necessary premises. Thus it is true that some nature is able to be produced, therefore something is able to produce an effect. The antecedent is proved from the fact that something can be changed, for something is possible ("possible" being defined as contrary to "necessary"). In this case, the proof for the first conclusion proceeds

de esse possibili, non autem de existentia actuali. Sed
de quo nunc ostenditur possibilitas ultra in conclusione
tertia ostendetur actualis existentia.

Secunda conclusio de primo effectivo est illa quod
simpliciter primum effectivum est incausabile. Hoc
probatur, quia est ineffectibile independens effectivum.
Hoc patet prius, quia si sit virtute alterius causativum,
vel ab alio effectibile, ergo vel processus in infinitum,
vel circulus, vel status in aliquo [in]effectibili indepen-
dente effective ; illud dico primum, et aliud patet quod
non est primum ex datis tuis. Ergo ulterius concluditur,
si illud primum est ineffectibile, ergo incausabile, quia
non est finibile, nec materiabile, nec formabile. Probatur
consequentia prima, scilicet quod si est ineffectibile, ergo
est infinibile quia causa finalis non causat nisi quia
causa movet metaphorice ipsum efficiens ad efficiendum ;
nam alio modo non dependet entitas finiti ab ipso ut a
priori. Nihil autem est causa per se nisi ut ab ipso
tamquam a priore essentialiter dependet causatum.
Duae autem aliae consequentiae, scilicet quod si est
ineffectibile, ergo est immateriabile et informabile,
probantur simul ; quia cujus non est causa extrinseca,
nec intrinseca ; quia causalitas causae extrinsecae dicit
perfectionem sine imperfectione. Causalitas vero causae
intrinsecae necessario dicit imperfectionem annexam,
quia causa intrinseca est pars causati. Igitur ratio causae

from what the thing is or from its possible existence, but not from its actual existence. The actual existence of this being which up to now we have shown to be merely possible, however, will be established in the third conclusion.

The *second conclusion* about the first possible efficient cause is this. *Among those things which can produce an effect that which is simply first is itself incapable of being caused.* Proof : Such a being cannot be produced and is independently able to produce an effect. This was proved above, for if such a being could cause only in virtue of something else or if it could be produced, then either a process *ad infinitum* or a circle in causes would result, or else the series would terminate in some being which cannot be produced and yet independently is able to produce an effect. This being I call "first", and from what you grant, it is clear that anything other than this is not first. Therefore, the further conclusion follows that if such a being cannot be produced, it has no causes whatsoever, for it cannot be the result of a final, material or formal cause. Proof of the first consequence, viz. that if such a being cannot be produced, neither can it have any final cause. A final cause does not cause at all unless in a metaphorical sense it moves the efficient cause to produce the effect. Only in this way does the entity of what exists for the sake of an end depend on the end as prior. Nothing, however, is a *per se* cause unless the thing caused depends upon it essentially as upon something prior. Now the other two consequences are proved simultaneously. If something cannot be produced, then it can be the result neither of a material nor of a formal cause. The reason is this. If something has no extrinsic cause, neither does it have an intrinsic cause, for while to be an extrinsic cause does not imply imperfection but perfection, to be an intrinsic cause necessarily includes some imperfection since the intrinsic cause is a part of the thing it causes. For this reason, the very notion of

extrinsecae est naturaliter prior ratione causae intrinsecae ; negato igitur priori, et negatur et posterius.

Probantur etiam eaedem consequentiae, quia causae intrinsecae sunt causatae ab extrinsecis vel secundum esse earum vel in quantum causant compositum vel utroque modo, quia causae intrinsecae non seipsis sine agente constituunt compositum. Ex istis dictis satis patet conclusio secunda.

Tertia conclusio de primo effectivo est ista : primum effectivum est in actu existens, et aliqua natura vere existens actualiter sic est effectiva. Probatio istius : Cujus rationi repugnat esse ab alio, illud si potest esse, potest esse a se ; sed rationi primi effectivi simpliciter repugnat esse ab alio, sicut patet ex secunda conclusione. Similiter etiam ipsum potest esse, sicut patet ex prima ubi posita est quinta probatio ad A, quae minus videtur concludere et tamen hoc concludit. Aliae autem probationes ipsius A possunt tractari de existentia quam proponit haec tertia conclusio, et sunt de contingentibus, tamen manifestis : vel accipitur A de natura et quidditate et possibilitate, et sunt ex necessariis. Ergo effectivum simpliciter primum potest esse ex se ; quod non est a se, non potest esse a se quia tunc non ens produceret aliquid ad esse, quod est impossibile, et adhuc tunc illud causaret se, et ita non esset incausabile omnino.

Illud ultimum, scilicet de existentia primi effectivi

an extrinsic cause has a natural priority over that of intrinsic cause ; to deny what is prior is to deny also what is posterior.

Another way of proving these same consequences is this. Intrinsic causes are caused by extrinsic causes either in their very being or in so far as they cause the composite, or in both of these ways, for the intrinsic causes of themselves and without the intervention of some agent cannot constitute the composite. This suffices to make the second conclusion evident.

The *third conclusion* about this being capable of exercising efficient causality is this. *Such a being actually exists and some nature actually existing is capable of such causality.* Proof: Anything to whose nature it is repugnant to receive existence from something else, can exist of itself if it is able to exist at all. To receive existence from something else, however, is repugnant to the very notion of a being which is first in the order of efficiency, as is clear from the second conclusion. That it can exist, is also clear from the first conclusion [namely *A*], where the fifth argument, which seems to be less conclusive than the others, establishes this much at least.[13] However, the other proofs of proposition *A* can also be used to establish the existence of this being as proposed by this third conclusion, but in this case they are based on contingent though manifest propositions. If *A*, however, is understood of the nature, the quiddity and the possibility, then the conclusions proceed from necessary premises. From all this it follows that an efficient cause which is first in the unqualified sense of the term can exist of itself. Consequently, it does exist of itself, for what does not actually exist of itself, is incapable of existing of itself. Otherwise a non-existent being would cause something to exist; but this is impossible, even apart from the fact that in such a case the thing would be its own cause and hence could not be entirely uncaused.

Another way to establish this last conclusion, viz. the

aliter declaratur, quia inconveniens est universo deesse supremum gradum possibilem in essendo.

Juxta tres conclusiones ostensas de effectivo primo, nota corollarium quoddam quod quasi continet tres conclusiones probatas, quod, scilicet primum effectivum non tantum est prius aliis, sed eo prius aliud esse includit contradictionem. Sic in quantum primum, existit, probatur ut praecedens ; nam in ratione talis primi maxime includitur incausabile, probatur ex secunda ; ergo si potest esse, quia non contradicit entitati, ut probatur ex prima, sequitur quod potest esse a se, et ita est a se.

[*b. De Primitate Finalitatis*]. Juxta tres conclusiones primas de causa effectiva, propono tres conclusiones similes de causa finali. Aliquod finitivum est simpliciter primum, hoc est nec ad aliud ordinabile nec in virtute alterius natum finire alia. Et probatur quinque probationibus similibus illis quae ponebantur ad primum conclusionem de primo effectivo.

Secunda est quod primum finitivum est incausabile. Probatur, quia infinibile, alias non primum, et ultra, ergo ineffectibile. Haec consequentia probatur, quia omne per se agens agit propter finem, ex secundo *Physicorum*,* ubi etiam hoc vult Philosophus de natura, de qua minus videtur quam de agente a proposito. Sed cujus non est aliquod per se efficiens, illud non est effectibile, quia in nullo genere potest per accidens esse primum, sicut patet in proposito specialiter de causis

---

* II, cap. v (196^b, 17–22).

existence of this first efficient cause, would be to argue from the impropriety of a universe that would lack the highest possible degree of being.

A kind of corollary contained, as it were, in these three conclusions concerning the first being able to exercise efficient causality, is the following. Not only is such a cause prior to all the others, but it would be contradictory to say that another is prior to it. And, in so far as such a cause is first, it exists. This is proved in the same way as the preceding. The very notion of such a being implies its inability to be caused (which is proved from the second conclusion). Therefore, if it can exist, owing to the fact that to be is not contradictory to it (as the first conclusion proves), then it follows that it can exist of itself, and consequently that it does exist of itself.

[*b. The Primacy of Finality*]. Concerning the final cause, I propose three conclusions similar to the first three conclusions about the being which is able to produce something. The *first conclusion* is that *some end is simply ultimate*, that is, it can neither be ordained to something else nor exercise its finality in virtue of something else. This is proved by five arguments similar to those advanced for the first conclusion concerning the possibility of a first efficient cause.

The *second conclusion* is that *the ultimate end cannot be caused in any way*. This is proved from the fact that it cannot be ordained for another end ; otherwise it would not be ultimate. It follows in addition that it cannot be caused by an efficient cause. This latter consequence is proved from the fact that every agent *per se* acts for the sake of an end as is said in *Physics*, BK. II,* where the Philosopher understands this proposition to hold also of "nature" where it seems to apply less than in the case of an agent who acts according to purpose.[14] Now a thing cannot be produced if no *per se* efficient cause of it exists, for the first of any given kind of cause is never an incidental cause (*causa per accidens*). This is clear from

agentibus per accidens, quae sunt casus et fortuna quae secundum Aristotelem, secundo *Physicorum*,* reducuntur necessario ad causas per se agentes ut priores, scilicet ad naturam et intellectum ut propositum ; cujus igitur non est aliquid per se agens ejus nullum erit agens, sed cujus non est finis, ejus non est aliquod per se agens ; ergo ipsum erit ineffectibile ; nam finibile excellitur a fine in bonitate et per consequens in perfectione. Et ultra, ut supra ostensum est de causa effectiva prima.

Tertia conclusio est, quod primum finitivum est actu existens, et alicui naturae actu existenti convenit illa primitas. Probatur ut prima via de efficientia.

Sequitur quod primum est ita primum, quod impossibile est aliud prius esse. Et probatur ut corollarium in via priori.

[*c. De Primitate Eminentiae*]. Conclusionibus tribus de utroque ordine causalitatis extrinsecae jam positis, propono tres similes de ordine eminentiae. Aliqua natura eminens est simpliciter prima secundum perfectionem. Hoc patet quia inter essentias ordo essentialis, quia secundum Aristotelem, formae se habent sicut numeri, octavo *Metaphysicae*.† In hoc ordine statur. Quod probatur illis quinque rationibus quae de statu in effectivis sunt superius.

Secunda conclusio est quod suprema natura est incausabilis. Probatur, quia est infinibilis, ex praecedentibus [nam finibile excellitur a fine in bonitate et per consequens in perfectione]. Ergo ineffectibilis. Et ultra,

---

* II, cap. vi (198^a, 5–13).   † VIII, cap. iii (1043^b, 33).

what is said in particular of incidental causes, which are chance and fortune. These, according to Aristotle in *Physics*, BK. II,* must be reduced respectively to the prior causes of "nature" and "intellect" as purpose, neither of which are incidental causes. Hence, whatever has no *per se* efficient cause has no efficient cause whatsoever. But whatever has no end, also has no *per se* efficient cause. Therefore, it will not be something that could be produced, for whatever could be the result of a final cause will be surpassed in goodness, and consequently in perfection, by the end. Further, as has been shown above of the first potential efficient cause [such a being will have no material or formal cause either].

The *third conclusion* is that *the being which can be an ultimate end actually exists and that this primacy pertains to some actually existing nature.* The proof for this is like that used in the first way from efficiency.[15]

It follows that such a being is first in the sense that it is impossible that anything should be prior to it. This is proved in the same fashion as the preceding corollary about the efficient cause.

[*c.* *The Primacy of Pre-eminence*]. Having already established three conclusions of each of the two orders of extrinsic causality, I submit three similar conclusions concerning the order of pre-eminence. The *first conclusion* is that *some eminent nature is simply first in perfection.* This is evident because an essential order exists among essences, for as Aristotle puts it,† forms are like numbers. And in such an order an ultimate nature is to be found. This is proved by the five reasons given above for a first being in the order of efficient causality.

The *second conclusion* is that *the supreme nature cannot be caused.* This is proved from the fact that it cannot be ordained to an end, for whatever is ordained to an end is surpassed in goodness, and therefore also in perfection, by the end. But if it is not ordained to an end, then, it cannot be caused by an efficient cause, and consequently

ergo incausabilis. Illae duae consequentiae sunt probatae ex secunda conclusione de effectivis.

Item, quod suprema natura sit ineffectibilis probatur. Nam omne effectibile habet aliquam causam essentialiter ordinatam, sicut patet ex probatione ipsius B in conclusione prima de primo effectivo. Causa autem essentialiter ordinata excellit effectum. [Igitur, si esset effectibilis, non esset suprema.]

Tertia conclusio est quod suprema natura est aliquod actu existens et probatur ex praecedentibus. Corollarium : aliquam esse naturam eminentiorem vel superiorem ipsa includit contradictionem. Probatur ut corollarium de efficiente et fine.

[*Pars Secunda. De primitatibus ad invicem comparatis*]. Quantum ad secundum articulum dico quod primum efficiens est ultimus finis. Probatio, quia omne efficiens per se agit propter finem et prius efficiens propter finem priorem. Ergo primum efficiens propter ultimum finem. Sed propter nihil aliud a se principaliter et ultimate agit. Ergo, propter se sicut propter finem. Ergo primum efficiens est primus finis. Si enim ageret per se propter finem alium a se, tunc aliquod esset nobilius primo efficiente, quia finis qui est aliquid remotum ab agente intendente finem nobilius eo.

Similiter, primum efficiens est primum eminens. Probatur, quia primum efficiens non est univocum respectu aliarum naturarum effectivarum, sed aequivocum. Ergo eminentius et nobilius eis. Ergo primum efficiens est eminentissimum.

[*Pars Tertia. De divinae naturae unitate*]. Quantum ad tertium articulum dico quod cum sit idem cui inest

it cannot be caused in any way. These last two consequences are proved from the second conclusion about the efficient cause.

Another consideration proves that this supreme nature cannot be an effect. Everything which can be produced has some essentially ordered cause, as is evident from the proof of the proposition *B* in support of the first conclusion about the possibility of a first efficient cause. Now an essentially ordered cause excels its effect ; therefore, if it could be produced, it would not be supreme.

The *third conclusion* is that *the supreme nature actually exists*, and this is proved from what we have said above.[16] Corollary : It is contradictory that any nature should be more excellent or higher than this nature. This is proved in the same way as were the corollaries about the efficient and final cause.[17]

[*Part II. Interrelation of the Three Primacies*]. Regarding the second part, I say that *the first cause is the ultimate end*. Proof : Every *per se* efficient cause acts for the sake of an end, and a prior cause acts for a prior end ; therefore, the first cause acts for the sake of the ultimate end. Now the first efficient cause does not act primarily or ultimately for the sake of anything distinct from itself ; hence, it must act for itself as an end ; therefore, the first efficient cause is the ultimate end. If it were to act *per se* for the sake of any end other than itself, then something would be more noble than the first efficient cause, for if the end were anything apart from the agent intending the end, it would be more noble than the agent.

Now *the first efficient cause is also the supreme nature*. Proof : The first efficient cause is not a univocal cause with reference to the other efficient causes but rather an equivocal cause. Such a cause, therefore, is more excellent and noble than they. Consequently, the first efficient cause is the most excellent.[18]

[*Part III. Unity of the Divine Nature*]. Regarding the third part, I say that since this triple primacy is

triplex primitas, quia cui inest una, insunt et aliae ; et
etiam est ibi triplex identitas, ita quod primum efficiens
est tantum unum secundum quidditatem et naturam.
Ad quod ostendendum ostendo primo quamdam conclusionem praeambulam et secundo principalem conclusionem. Praeambula autem est quod efficiens quod
est primum hac triplici primitate, est necesse esse ex se.
Probatio, quia est penitus incausabile ; nam contradictionem includit aliquod esse prius eo in genere causae
efficientis vel finis, et per consequens in genere cujuscumque causae ; ergo est omnino incausabile. Ex hoc
arguo : nihil potest non esse, nisi cui aliquid incompossibile positive vel privative potest esse. Ei autem
quod est a se et penitus incausabile, non potest aliquid
esse quod ei sit incompossibile positive vel privative ;
ergo etc. Major patet quia nullum ens potest destrui,
nisi per incompossibile sibi vel positive vel privative.
Minor probatur, quia illud incompossibile aut potest
esse a se aut ab alio. Si a se et erit a se. Erit igitur duo
incompossibilia simul, vel neutrum est, quia utrumque
destruit esse alterius. Si ab alio, contra : nulla causa
potest destruere aliquod ens propter repugnantiam sui
effectus ad illud, nisi suo effectui perfectius et intensius
esse det quam sit esse illius alterius destructibilis :
nullius entis ab alio est nobilius esse a causa sua quam
sit esse necessarium a se, quia omne causatum habet esse
dependens, sed quod est ex se habet esse independens.

Ex hoc ultra ad propositum, probatur unitas [*MS*
veritas] naturae primae, quae est principale intentum in
hoc tertio articulo, quod ostenditur tribus rationibus.

Primo sic : quia si duae naturae sunt necesse esse,
aliquibus rationibus propriis realibus distinguuntur ; et
dicantur A et B. Illae rationes aut sunt formaliter neces-

found together (for where one is, there also are the others), it follows further that this triple identity is such that *there is but one first efficient cause according to essence and nature.*[19]

To show this, I will first establish a preliminary conclusion and only afterwards the principal conclusion. Now the preliminary conclusion is this. *The efficient cause which is first by this triple primacy is of itself necessarily existent.* Proof : It is completely incapable of being caused, for it is contradictory that it should have anything prior to it in the order of efficiency or finality, and consequently in any causal order. Hence, it is wholly incapable of being caused. From this I argue, nothing can be non-existent unless something either positively or privatively incompatible with it can exist. Now nothing can be positively or privatively incompatible with a being which exists of itself and is totally uncaused ; therefore, etc. The major is clear, inasmuch as no being can be destroyed except by something positively or privatively incompatible with it. The minor is proved as follows. What is incompatible could exist either of itself or in virtue of some other being. If it can exist of itself, then it will exist of itself. Consequently, two incompatible entities will coexist or rather neither will exist because each will destroy the other. But can this incompatible entity exist in virtue of another being? No, for no cause is able to destroy something by reason of an effect incompatible with the thing to be destroyed unless it is able to give a more perfect and intense existence to its effect than that which the thing to be destroyed possesses. Now the existence which a cause imparts to a being is never as perfect as that of a self-existent being, for the existence of what is caused is dependent whereas that of the self-existent being is independent.

Now to proceed to what we primarily intended to prove in this third part, the unity of this first nature.

Three reasons are adduced by way of proof, the first of which is this. If two necessary natures existed, some reality proper to each would distinguish one from the

sariae, aut non. Si sic, igitur utrumque duabus rationibus formalibus erit necesse esse, quod est impossibile,
quia cum neutra illarum rationum per se includat aliam,
utraque istarum circumscripta, esset necesse esse [MS om.
per alteram, et ita esset aliquid necesse esse per illud,
quo circumscripto, non minus esset necesse esse]. Si
vero per illas rationes quibus distinguuntur neutrum
sit formaliter necesse esse, igitur illae rationes non sunt
rationes necessario essendi, et ita neutrum includitur in
necesse esse, quia quaecumque entitas non est necesse
esse est de se possíbilis ; sed nihil possibile includitur in
necesse esse.

Secundo probatur, quia duae naturae eminentissimae
non possunt esse in universo ; ergo nec duo prima
effectiva. Probatio antecedentis, quia species se habent
sicut numeri, ex octavo *Metaphysicae*,* et per consequens
duae non possunt esse in eodem ordine. Ergo multo
minus nec duae primae vel duae eminentissimae.

Hoc etiam patet tertio per rationem de ratione finis,
quia duo fines ultimi si essent haberent duas coordina-
tiones entium ad se, ita quod ista entia ad illa nullum
ordinem haberent, quia nec ad finem illorum ; nam quae
ordinantur ad unum finem ultimum non possunt ordinari
ad alium, quia ejusdem causati duas esse causas totales
et perfectas in eodem ordine est impossibile ; tunc enim
aliquid esset in aliquo ordine per se causa, quo non
posito, nihilominus causatum illud [aeque perfecte esset].

---

* viii, cap. iii (1043*b*, 33).

other. Let us call these real differences A and B. Now either A and B are formally necessary or they are not. If we assume them to be necessary, then each necessarily existing nature will possess two formal reasons for its necessary existence, for in addition to A or B, each is formally necessary by reason of that part of its nature in which it is like the other. Now this is impossible, for since neither of the two reasons of itself includes the other, if either be excluded, the being would still exist necessarily in virtue of the other. In such a case the being would exist necessarily in virtue of something which, if eliminated, would still leave the nature existing as necessarily as before. On the other hand, if neither nature is formally necessary in virtue of these real differences, then the latter are not of the essence of necessary existence and consequently neither is included in a necessary being. For any entity which is not of itself necessary being is only possible being.[20] Nothing merely possible, however, is included in what exists necessarily.

Second proof : Two pre-eminent natures cannot exist in one universe ; therefore neither can two beings first in the order of efficient causality. Proof of the antecedent : Species are like numbers (*Metaphysics*, BK. VIII)* and hence no two occur in the same order. Still less could two be first or pre-eminent.

This is also evident in the third place from the fact that this Being has the character of an end. Now if there were two ultimate ends, then we should have two separate series of co-ordinated beings where the members of one group would have no relation to the other inasmuch as they are not ordered to the same end. For what is ordered to one ultimate end cannot be ordered to another, as it is impossible to have two total and perfect causes of the same order causing one and the same thing. In such a case, something could be a *per se* cause in a given order, although its effect would exist no less perfectly even should this cause never have existed. Therefore, things

Ordinata ergo ad unum finem nullo modo ordinantur ad alium, nec per consequens ad illa quae ordinantur ad alium, et ita ex eis non fieret universum.

Hoc etiam confirmatur in communi, quia nulla duo possunt esse terminantia totaliter dependentiam alicujus ejusdem, quia tunc illud terminaret dependentiam, quo subtracto, non minus terminaretur illa dependentia, et ita non esset dependentia ad illud; sed ad efficiens et eminens et ad finem dependent aliqua [*MS* alia] essentialiter. Ergo nullae duae naturae possunt esse primo terminantia aliqua [*MS* alia] entia secundum illam triplicem dependentiam. Praecise igitur est aliqua una natura terminans entia secundum illam triplicem dependentiam, et ita habens istam triplicem primitatem.

[*Articulus Secundus. De Proprietatibus Dei Absolutis*]

Ostenso esse de proprietatibus relativis primi entis, ulterius ad ostendendum illius primi infinitatem, et per consequens esse de ente infinito, procedo sic : Primo ostendo quod primum efficiens est intelligens et volens, ita quod sua intelligentia est infinitorum distincte, et quod sua essentia est repraesentativa infinitorum, quae quidem essentia est sua intelligentia. Et ex hoc secundo concludetur sua infinitas. Et sic cum triplici primitate ostensa, erit quadruplex medium ad ostendendum ejus infinitatem. . . .

[*Pars Prima. De Intellectu et Voluntate Primi Entis*].
[Conclusio Prima]. Quod autem sit intelligens et volens arguo sic : Aliquod agens est per se primum agens, quia omni causa per accidens prior est aliqua causa per se, secundo *Physicorum*,* ubi hoc vult de natura de qua

---

* II, cap. vi (198^a, 8–9).

THE EXISTENCE OF GOD

ordered to one end cannot be ordered to another. Neither then, can they be ordered to things which in turn are ordered to something else. Consequently, they would not form one universe [with the latter].

This is also confirmed in general because one and the same thing cannot be totally dependent upon two things. For then it would be dependent upon something which, if removed, would still leave the thing in question as dependent as before. Hence, the thing would not really be dependent upon it at all. Now some things depend essentially upon an efficient cause which is also pre-eminent and they depend essentially upon an end. They cannot, then, be dependent upon two natures in this triple way. Consequently, some one nature is the term of this triple dependence, and thus enjoys this triple primacy.

[*Article II.   Absolute Properties of God*]

Having shown the existence of the relative properties of the First Being, we go on to prove that this Being possesses infinity and, consequently, that an Infinite Being exists. I proceed as follows : First I show that the first efficient cause is endowed with will and possesses such intelligence that this cause understands an infinity of distinct things and that its essence, which indeed is its intelligence, represents an infinity of things. Secondly, I go on from this to infer the infinity of this Being. This approach coupled with the triple primacy which we have established provides four ways of showing the infinity of this Being. . . .

[*Part I.   Intellect and Will*]. [First Conclusion]. I argue that *this being is intelligent and endowed with will* as follows :

Some agent is *per se* and first, for according to *Physics*, BK. II,* every incidental cause is preceded by one that is not incidental but *per se*. In this passage the Philosopher applies this to nature where it would seem to hold still

minus videtur. Sed omne agens per se agit propter finem. Et ex hoc arguitur dupliciter : Primo sic : Omne agens naturale, praecise consideratum ex necessitate et aeque ageret si ad nullum finem alium ageret, sed sit independenter agens ; ergo si non agit nisi propter finem, hoc est quia dependet ab agente amante finem ; tale est primum efficiens ; ergo etc.

Item, si primum agens agit propter finem, aut ergo finis ille movet primum efficiens ut amatus actu voluntatis, aut ut tantum naturaliter amatus. Si ut amatus actu voluntatis, habetur propositum. Si tantum amatus naturaliter, hoc est falsum, quia non naturaliter amat alium finem a se, ut grave centrum, et materia formam. Tunc enim esset aliquo modo ad finem, quia inclinatus ad illum. Si autem tantum naturaliter amat finem qui est ipse, hoc nihil est nisi ipsum esse ipsum. Hoc enim non est salvare duplicem rationem in ipso.

Item arguitur quasi confirmando [*MS* conferendo] rationem jam factam sic. Ipsum primum efficiens dirigit effectum suum ad finem ; ergo vel naturaliter dirigit, vel cognoscendo et amando illum finem. Non naturaliter, quia non cognoscens nihil dirigit nisi in virtute cognoscentis : sapientis enim est prima ordinatio, primo *Metaphysicae*.* Sed primum efficiens nullius alterius virtute dirigit, sicut nec causat ; tunc enim non esset primum ; ergo, etc.

Item, aliquid causatur contingenter ; ergo prima causa contingenter causat ; ergo volens causat. Probatio

---

* I, cap. ii (982^a, 17–18).

less [than of a deliberate cause]. Now every *per se* agent acts for the sake of an end. From this I draw a double argument : First, that every natural agent, considered precisely as natural, acts of necessity [21] and would act just as it does now even if it had no other end but was an independent agent. Therefore, if it acts only because of an end, this is so only because it depends upon an agent which loves the end. But the first efficient cause is such an agent, therefore, etc.

[Secondly,] if the first agent acts for the sake of an end, then this end moves the first efficient cause inasmuch as it is loved either naturally or by an act of the will. If the latter be the case, you grant what I seek to prove. If you assume that the end is loved naturally, the assumption is false, for the first agent loves naturally no end other than itself, as matter, for instance, naturally loves form or the heavy object the centre [of the earth]. If it did, the first agent would be oriented to it as an end, since it is inclined to it by its very nature. But if this end which it loves naturally is nothing other than itself, then we assert nothing more than that the thing is itself.[22] In such a case, however, the twofold [causal] aspect would not be saved.

In confirmation of the argument just given we could argue that the first efficient cause directs its effect to some end. Now, it directs it either naturally or by consciously loving this end. The first alternative is untenable, inasmuch as whatever lacks knowledge can direct its effect to some end only in virtue of something which does possess knowledge, for "to order ultimately" pertains to wisdom according to *Metaphysics*, BK. I.* Now just as the first efficient cause does not cause in virtue of something else, neither does this cause direct its effect to an end by reason of something other than itself, for otherwise it would not be first ; therefore, etc.

Another proof is this. Something causes contingently. Therefore, the first cause causes contingently ;

primae consequentiae : quaelibet causa secunda causat in quantum movetur a prima ; ergo si prima necessario movet, quaelibet alia necessario movetur et quidlibet necessario causatur. Igitur, si aliqua causa secunda contingenter movet, et prima contingenter movebit, quia non causat causa secunda nisi in virtute primae causae, in quantum movetur ab ipsa. Probatio secundae consequentiae : nullum est principium contingenter operandi nisi voluntas, vel aliquid concomitans voluntatem, quia quodlibet aliud agit ex necessitate naturae, ita et non contingenter ; ergo etc.

Contra istam rationem instatur, et primo contra primam consequentiam arguitur sic : quia nostrum velle posset adhuc aliquid contingenter causare, et ita non requiritur quod prima causa illud contingenter causet. Item, Philosophus antecedens concessit, scilicet quod aliquid contingenter causatur, et negavit consequens, intelligendo de velle scilicet quod prima causa contingenter causet ; ponendo contingentiam in inferioribus, non propter contingenter Deum velle, sed ex motu qui necessario causatur in quantum uniformis, sed difformitas sequitur ex partibus ejus, et ita contingentia.

Contra secundam consequentiam : si causat contingenter, ergo volens, non videtur tenere, quia aliqua naturaliter mota possunt impediri, et ita oppositum contingenter et violenter potest evenire.

Ad primum dicendum, quod si Deus est primum movens vel efficiens respectu voluntatis nostrae, idem sequitur de ipsa quod de aliis, quia sive immediate necessario movet eam, sive aliud immediate, et illud necessario motum necessario moveat eam, quia movet

consequently, it causes voluntarily. Proof of the first consequence : Every secondary cause causes in so far as it is moved by the first cause. If the first cause moves necessarily, then, every other cause will be moved necessarily and everything will be caused necessarily. Consequently, if any secondary cause moves contingently, the first cause also moves contingently, since the secondary cause can cause only in so far as it is moved by the first. Proof of the second consequence : The only source of contingent action is either the will or something accompanied by the will. Everything else acts with a natural necessity and, consequently, not contingently ; therefore, etc.

One objection to this argument is directed against the first consequence, namely that our volition would still be able to cause something contingently and therefore it is unnecessary that the first cause should cause contingently. Furthermore, the Philosopher [23] concedes the antecedent (that something is caused contingently), yet denies the consequent (that the first cause causes contingently). He places contingency in the lower beings and not in the fact that God wills things contingently. Contingency arises from motion, which, though it is caused necessarily in so far as it is uniform, gives rise to difformity owing to its parts.

The other objection is to the second consequence. Just because something causes contingently, it does not seem to follow that therefore this cause is endowed with a will, for even what is moved naturally can be impeded. Hence, the opposite can happen either contingently or violently.

To the first objection we must reply that if God is the first mover or efficient cause with regard to our will, then the same holds of our will as of other things. Whether God moves our will immediately with necessity or whether He first moves something else necessarily and this latter in turn moves our will with necessity,

non nisi ex hoc quod movetur, sequitur tandem quod proximum voluntati necessario moveat voluntatem, etiam si proximum voluntati sit ipsamet voluntas, et ita necessario volet, et erit volens necessario. Et sequitur ulterius impossibile, quod necessario causat quodlibet causatum [, et non est aliquid contingens].

Ad secundum dico, quod non voco hic contingens quodcumque non necessarium, vel non sempiternum, sed cujus oppositum posset fieri quando illud fit. Ideo dixi : aliquod contingenter causatum, et non aliquod est contingens. Nunc dico, quod Philosophus non potest consequens negare salvando antecedens per motum ; quia si ille totus motus necessario est a causa sua, quaelibet pars ejus necessario causatur quando causatur, id est, inevitabiliter, ita quod oppositum non potest tunc causari. Et ulterius, quod causatur per quamcumque partem motus, necessario causatur et inevitabiliter. Vel igitur nihil fit contingenter, id est, evitabiliter, vel primum sic causat immediate, quod posset etiam non causare.

Ad tertium dico, quod si aliqua causa potest impedire istam, hoc non est nisi in virtute superioris causae, et sic usque ad primam causam quae si immediatam causam sibi necessario movet, usque ad ultimam erit necessitas ; ergo necessario impediet, et per consequens, non potest alia causa naturaliter causare.

Sic ergo videtur triplici via ostensum quod primum agens est intelligens et volens. Quarum prima est quod natura agit propter finem, et non nisi quia dependens

in any case the will would be necessarily moved by whatever is proximate to it. This would be true even if this proximate cause were itself will. The will, therefore, would will necessarily and would be a necessary voluntary agent. And there is still another absurdity that would follow, viz. that it would cause necessarily anything that is caused, and there would be nothing contingent.

As to the second objection, let me say that by "contingent" I do not mean something that is not necessary or which was not always in existence, but something whose opposite could have occurred at the time that this actually did. That is why I do not say that something is contingent, but that something is *caused contingently.* Now I maintain that the Philosopher cannot deny the consequent and still save the antecedent through the expedient of motion, because if the motion as a whole proceeds from its cause in a necessary manner, every single part of it is caused necessarily at the time it occurs. In other words, it is inevitable, so that the opposite effect could not possibly be caused at just this moment. Furthermore, whatever is caused by any part of this motion is caused necessarily and inevitably. Therefore, either nothing ever happens unavoidably or contingently, or the first cause immediately causes what it was also able not to cause.

To the third objection, I say that if any cause can impede a natural cause, it can do so only in virtue of a higher cause, and so we are forced back again to the first cause. If this first cause necessarily moves the cause immediately below it, this necessity will continue down to the last cause, which will consequently be necessarily impeded in its action. As a result, this last cause could not cause anything naturally.

There appears to be three ways, then, of proving that the first agent is intelligent and endowed with will. The first of these is that nature acts on account of an end,

et directa a cognoscente finem ; secunda est quod ipsum primum agens agit propter finem ; et tertia quod aliquis effectus contingenter fit quando causatur.

[Conclusio Secunda]. Ulterius quoad quaestionem praeambulam ad infinitatem, probo secundo quod ejus intellectio et volitio est idem quod ejus essentia. Et primo de volitione sui ipsius ut objecti, ita quod primam causam amare est idem essentialter cum natura causae et omnis actus voluntatis ejus. Probatio : causalitas et causatio causae finalis est simpliciter prima, secundum Avicennam sexto *Metaphysicae* [cap. v], dicentem quod si de qualibet causa esset scientia, illa quae esset de causa finali esset nobilissima ; ipsa enim quantum ad causalitatem praecedit causam efficientem, quia movet eum ad agendum, et ideo causalitas primi finis et ejus causatio est penitus incausabilis secundum quamcumque causationem in quolibet genere causae. Causalitas autem finis primi est efficiens primum movere sicut amatum. Idem autem est primum finem movere primum efficiens ut amatum ab ipso et primum efficiens amare propter finem, quia nihil aliud est objectum amari a voluntate quam voluntatem amare objectum ; ergo primum efficiens amare primum finem est penitus incausabile, et ita per se necesse esse, et ita erit idem naturae primae. Et quasi convertitur ratio ex opposito conclusionis ; quia si primum amare est aliud a natura prima, ergo est causabile, et per consequens effectibile. Igitur ab aliquo per se efficiente amante finem ; igitur primum amare se esset causatum ex aliquo amore finis priore isto causato ; quod est impossibile.

Hoc ostendit Aristoteles, duodecimo *Metaphysicae*,* de intelligere quia aliter primum non erit optima

---

* xii, cap. ix (1074^b, 28–29).

and it does this, only because it is dependent upon and directed by someone who knows the end. The second is that this first agent acts for the sake of an end. The third is that some effects are caused contingently. But let us proceed with the preliminaries to the proof for infinity.

[Second Conclusion]. The *second conclusion* I establish is this : *the knowledge and volition of this First Being is the same as its essence.* This is true, first, of its volition of itself as object, so that to love the first cause is something essentially identified with the nature of this cause, and the same holds for every act of its will. Proof : The causality and causation of the final cause is simply first according to Avicenna's *Metaphysics*, BK.VI, where he says : "If we had scientific knowledge of any cause, that of the final cause would be the most excellent". The reason is this. The final cause from the standpoint of causality precedes the efficient cause inasmuch as it moves it to act. Therefore, the causality of the ultimate end and its causation is completely incapable of being caused in any way. Now the causality of the ultimate end consists in this. By being loved it moves the first efficient cause. But it is one and the same thing whether the ultimate end moves the first efficient cause by being loved by this cause or whether the first efficient cause loves for the sake of an end. For an object being loved by the will means the same as a will loving an object. Hence, the love by which the first efficient cause loves the ultimate end is completely incapable of being caused. Therefore, it exists necessarily and consequently is the same as the first nature. Or to use the argument in reverse, if this first love is directed towards anything other than the first nature itself, it can be caused and therefore produced, and this by some *per se* efficient cause which in turn loves some end. Consequently, this first love of itself would be caused by some prior love of an end, which is impossible.

Aristotle in his *Metaphysics*, BK. XII,* proves that the knowledge which the First Being possesses is the same as

substantia, quia per intelligere est honorabile ; secundo quia alias laboriosa erit ejus continuatio. Item si non sit illud, erit in potentia contradictionis ad illud. Ad illam naturam sequitur labor, secundum ipsum.

Istae rationes possunt ratione declarari. Prima sic : cum omnis entis in actu primo perfectio ejus ultima sit in actu secundo quo conjungitur optimo, maxime si sit activum et non tantum factivum. Omne autem intelligibile est activum, et prima natura est intelligibilis ex praemissa, sequitur ergo quod ultima ejus perfectio erit in actu secundo. Igitur si ille non sit ejus substantia, substantia ejus non est optima, quia aliud est suum optimum.

Secunda ratio potest declarari sic : potentia solummodo receptiva est potentia contradictionis ; ergo cum hoc non sit hujusmodi ; ergo etc. Sed quia secundum Aristotelem, nec ista est ratio demonstrativa, sed tantum probabilis, aliter propositum ostendatur ex identitate potentiae et objecti in se ; ergo actus erit eis idem. Sed consequentia non valet. Patet instantia : quia angelus intelligit se et amat se, et tamen actus angeli amandi et intelligendi non sunt idem substantiae ejus.

Haec conclusio, videlicet, quod essentia divina sit eadem quod volitio sui ipsius, foecunda [*MS* vera] est ex corollariis. Nam sequitur primo quod voluntas est idem primae naturae ; quia velle non est nisi voluntatis ; ergo illa voluntas cujus velle est incausabile, est

its essence, first, because it would not be the best substance, were such not the case, since this is the most excellent of substances precisely because of the knowledge it possesses. And secondly, because otherwise the First Being would grow weary if it continued to think, for if its thought were not its substance, the latter would be in potency of contradiction [24] to thinking, and this would produce weariness according to Aristotle.

These arguments from authority can be established by reason. As to the first, every being which is in first act finds its ultimate perfection in its second act, through which it is united to that which is best for it.[25] This is true especially if this being is capable of acting in the proper sense of the term and not merely in the sense of producing or fashioning some external object.[26] Now whatever is intelligible is active in the proper sense of the term, and the first nature is intelligible from what we said above. Therefore, it follows that the ultimate perfection of this Being will be in its second act. But if this act is not the substance itself, the latter will not be the best inasmuch as its ultimate perfection is something other than itself.

[Aristotle's] second reason can be put in this way. Only a receptive potency is in potency of contradiction. But this Being has no receptive potencies ; therefore, etc. Since Aristotle, however, did not consider his proof demonstrative but merely probable, some [27] would prove the thesis in another way, viz. since the faculty and the object are identical, therefore the act is identified with them. This inference, however, is invalid as is clear from the case of an angel, which knows and loves itself and nevertheless, its acts of loving and knowing are not identical with its substance.

This conclusion, viz. that the divine essence is identical with its volition, is fruitful because of its corollaries. First of all, it follows that the will is the same as the first nature, because willing is a function only of the will ; wherefore, if the volition itself is uncausable, the same is true of the

etiam incausabilis ; ergo, etc. Et similiter velle intelligitur quasi posterius voluntate ; tamen velle est idem illi naturae ; ergo magis voluntas.

Item, secundo sequitur quod intelligere se est idem illi naturae, quia nihil amatur nisi cognitum ; sicut si amare se ex se est necesse esse, sequitur quod intelligere se est necesse esse ex se.

Et si est intelligere propinquior illi naturae quam velle, ideo sequitur ulterius quod intellectus sit idem illi naturae, sicut prius de voluntate ex velle argutum est.

Sequitur quarto etiam quod ratio intelligendi se sit idem sibi quia necesse esse est ex se, si intelligere sit ex se necesse esse, et ratio intelligendi se quasi praeintelligitur ipsi intellectui.

[Conclusio Tertia]. Ostenso de intelligere se et velle se quod sint idem essentiae primi, ostendo propositum ex aliis, scilicet de omni intelligere et velle ; et sit conclusio tertia ista : nullum intelligere potest esse accidens primae naturae. Probatio, quia de illa natura prima ostensum est esse in se primum effectivum. Ergo ex se habet unde posset quodcumque causabile causare circumscripto alio quocumque, saltem ut prima causa illius causabilis ; sed circumscripta cognitione ejus, non habet unde possit illud causabile causare ; ergo cognitio cujuscumque alterius non est aliud a natura sua. Probatio assumpti, quia nihil potest causare nisi ex amore finis volendo illud, quia non potest aliter esse per se agens, quia nec agere propter finem ; nunc autem ipsi

will to which it belongs ; consequently [the will is identified with the nature]. Furthermore, since the act of the will is conceived as though it were posterior to the will, if the former is identical with that nature, then the latter will be all the more so.

Secondly, it follows that this self-knowledge is identical with that nature, for nothing is loved unless it is known. Hence it follows that just as this self-love exists necessarily in virtue of itself, so also this self-knowledge.

Then too, knowledge, as it were, is more closely connected with that nature than is volition. Therefore, it follows in the third place that the intellect is the same thing as that nature. We prove this in the same way as we previously established the identity of the will from the act of willing.

Fourthly, it follows that whatever is required for this nature to know itself is also identical with the nature,[28] for if the knowledge exists in virtue of itself, then the same is true of the reason for knowing, because the latter, as it were, must first be known to the intellect.

[Third Conclusion]. Having proved that this self-knowledge and self-love of the first being are the same as its essence, I go on to show the same to be true of other acts, namely of all its knowledge and all its acts of volition. Let the *third conclusion* be that *no knowledge can be an accident of the first nature*. Proof : The first nature has been shown to be first in the order of efficiency, and therefore has of itself and apart from anything else, the ability to produce whatever can be produced, at least in so far as it is the first cause of that which can be produced. But without a knowledge of the latter, the first nature would be unable to produce what can be produced. Hence, the knowledge of any of these other beings is not something distinct from its own nature. Proof of the last assumption : Nothing can cause an effect except by willing it for the sake of an end. Otherwise it would not be a *per se* agent, since it would not

velle alicujus propter finem praeintelligitur intelligere ipsum. Ante igitur primum signum, in quo intelligitur causans sive volens A, necessario praeintelligitur intelligens A, ita sine hoc non potest per se efficere, et ita de aliis.

Item probatur idem : quia omnes intellectiones ejusdem intellectus habent similem habitudinem ad intellectum secundum identitatem essentialem vel accidentalem, sicut patet de omni intellectu creato et ejus intellectionibus, quia videntur perfectiones ejusdem generis. Ergo si aliquae habent receptivum, et omnes ; et si aliqua est accidens, et quaelibet, Sed aliqua non potest esse accidens in primo, ex praecedenti quaestione, quia non intellectio sui ipsius ; ergo nulla erit ibi accidens.

Item, intelligere si quod potest esse accidens recipietur in intellectu ut in subjecto ; ergo et in illo intelligere quod est idem intellectui, et ita perfectius intelligere erit in potentia receptiva respectu imperfectioris [quod est absurdum].

Item, idem intelligere potest esse plurium objectorum ordinandorum ; ergo quanto perfectius tanto plurium ; ergo perfectissimum, quo incompossibile est perfectius intelligi, erit idem omnium intelligibilium. Intelligere primi sic est perfectissimum ; ergo idem est omnium intelligibilium, et illud quod est sui est idem sibi, ex proxima praecedente ; ergo intelligere omnium est idem. Et eandem conclusionem volo intelligi de velle.

be acting for an end. But before anything can be willed for the sake of an end, it must be known. Hence, before we can even conceive of the First Being as willing or causing *A*, we must conceive it as knowing *A*, for without such knowledge the first cause would not be properly a cause. And the same holds true of everything else it could produce.

Another proof of the same is that all the acts of knowledge of any given intellect are related in the same way to that intellect, so that either all are accidents or all are of the essence of that intellect. This is clear in regard to all created intellects and their respective acts of knowledge, all of which seem to be of the same kind of perfection. Therefore, if some of the acts are received by the intellect, all the acts are, and if one of them is an accident, the remainder are likewise. But from the preceding conclusion, the self-knowledge of the first being cannot be an accident ; therefore none of its knowledge will be accidental to it.

Furthermore, if some act of knowledge can be an accident, it will be received by the intellect as by its subject. In such a case, however, the act of knowledge which is identical with the intellect and is the more perfect of the two acts of knowledge, would itself be the recipient of the less perfect, which is absurd.[29]

Furthermore, the same act of knowledge can embrace several interrelated objects, and the more perfect this act is, the greater can be the number of objects. Consequently, an act that is so completely perfect that it would be impossible to have anything more perfect, will embrace all that can be known. Now the understanding of the First Being is of such perfection ; therefore there is but one act for all that can be known. Now, from the preceding conclusion, self-knowledge is identical with its very being ; consequently, all knowledge is identical with its being. This same conclusion I wish to be understood of the act of volition.

Item, iste intellectus non est nisi quoddam intelligere ;
sed iste intellectus est idem omnium et ita quod non
potest esse alicujus alterius objecti ; ergo nec intelligere
aliud ; ergo idem intelligere est omnium. Fallacia est
accidentis ex identitate aliquorum inter se concludere
identitatem respectu tertii, respectu cujus extraneantur,
et patet in simili : intelligere est idem quod velle ; si
ergo intelligere ipsum est alicujus, ergo et velle est
ejusdem ; non sequitur, sed tantummodo sequitur quia
est velle, quod quidem velle est aliquid ejusdem, quia
intelligere est ejusdem ; ita quod divisim inferri potest,
non conjunctim propter accidens.

Item, intellectus primi habet actum unum adaequatum sibi et coaeternum, quia intelligere se est idem sibi.
Ergo non potest aliquem habere alium. Consequentia
non valet. Exemplum de beato, qui simul videt Deum
et aliud etiamsi videat Deum secundum ultimum
capacitatis suae, ut de anima Christi ponitur, et adhuc
potest videre aliud.

Item arguitur : intellectus iste habet in se per identitatem perfectionem maximam intelligendi ; ergo et
omnem aliam. Respondeo : non sequitur, quia alia
quae minor est, potest esse causabilis, et ideo differre ab
incausabili ; maxima autem non potest.

[Conclusio Quarta]. Quarta conclusio principalis de
intellectu et voluntate Dei est ista : intellectus primi
intelligit semper et distincto et actu et necessario quod-

It is also said that this intellect is nothing more than a certain kind of knowing ; but this intellect is the same for all things so that it cannot differ for different objects. Therefore, neither is the act of understanding different. Hence, one act of understanding suffices for all objects. However, to argue in all cases from the identity of two things among themselves to their identity with relation to a third object distinct from both, as this argument does, is to commit the fallacy of accident. For instance, just because an act of understanding is identified with the act of willing, it does not follow that whatever is known by the act of knowledge is also loved by the will. All that follows is that an act of volition exists and that this act of will is something which is related to object known [not indeed by a relation of love] but in so far as it is also an act of knowledge. The inference can be made only in disjunction, not in conjunction, for only an incidental relation exists between the two.

Another argument advanced is that inasmuch as the First Being's act of self-knowledge is identical with itself, its intellect has one coeternal and completely adequate act, and therefore can have no other. The inference is invalid. Take the example of one who is beatified. He has an intellectual vision of God and of other things as well. Even though he sees God to the utmost of his ability, as we assume to be the case with the soul of Christ, he can still see something else.

Still another argument employed is this. Since this intellect is identified with the most perfect knowledge possible [viz. knowledge of the supreme nature itself], it also possesses all other knowledge. I reply that this does not follow, for this other lesser knowledge could be caused, and therefore it could be different from the most perfect self-knowledge, which is uncaused.

[Fourth Conclusion]. The *fourth principal conclusion* which concerns the intellect and will of God is this : *the intellect of the First Being knows everything else that can be*

cumque intelligibile, prius naturaliter quam illud sit in se.

Prima pars probatur, quia potest cognoscere quodcumque intelligibile, sic : hoc enim est perfectionis in intellectu, posse distincte et actu cognoscere quodcumque intelligibile. Imo hoc ponere est necessarium ad rationem intellectus, quia omnis intellectus est totius entis sumpti communissime, ut determinabitur distinctione tertia.* Nullam autem intellectionem potest habere intellectus primi nisi eamdem sibi, ex proxima ; igitur cujuslibet intelligibilis habet intelligere actuale et distinctum, et hoc idem sibi, et ita semper et necessario.

Secunda pars, de prioritate, probatur sic : quia quidquid est idem sibi, a se est necesse esse, sicut patuit prius. Sed esse aliorum non a se est non necesse esse ; ergo necesse esse ex se est prius natura omnium non necessario. Aliter probatur, quia esse cujuslibet alterius dependet ab ipso ut a causa, et ut causa est alicujus causabilis, necessario includitur cognitio ejus ex parte causae ; ergo illa cognitio erit prior naturaliter ipso esse cogniti. Secunda pars etiam conclusionis probatur aliter, quia artifex perfectus distincte cognoscit omne agendum antequam fiat ; alias non perfecte operaretur, quia cognitio est mensura juxta quam operatur ; ergo Deus est omnium producibilium a se habens notitiam distinctam et actualem, vel saltem habitualem, priorem eis. Contra istam instatur de arte, quia ars universalis sufficit ad universalia ; ergo, etc. Responsionem quaere.

---

* *Opus oxoniense*, ɪ, dist. ɪɪɪ, q. iii.

known with a knowledge that is eternal, is distinct, is actual, is necessary and is prior by nature to the existence of these things in themselves.

Proof of the first part. To be able to know actually and distinctly each and every other thing that can be known is something that pertains to the perfection of knowledge. Indeed, the very notion of an intellect makes it necessary to assume the possibility of such knowledge, for every intellect (as will be determined in distinction three) has to do with all being in general. But the intellect of the First Being can have no knowledge that is not one with itself (from the preceding conclusion). Therefore, it knows everything intelligible actually and distinctly. Since this knowledge is identified with the First Being, it is eternal and necessary.

The second part about the priority of this knowledge is proved as follows. As we have made clear above, whatever is identical with this Being, exists necessarily. But the existence of other things which are not self-existent is not necessary. Necessary being, however, is prior by nature to everything that does not necessarily exist.— Another proof is this. Every being other than the first depends upon the latter as upon a cause. Now to be a cause of something, it must necessarily possess a knowledge of what it can cause. Consequently, this knowledge will be naturally prior to the existence of the thing known. —Still another proof for the second part of this conclusion is the following. The perfect artisan has a distinct knowledge of everything to be done before he does it. Otherwise he would not act perfectly, for knowledge is the norm which regulates his work. God, therefore, has some previous distinct knowledge, either actual or at least habitual, of everything that he can make.—Against this last argument, the objection is raised that the possession of some universal art suffices for the production of both the universal and the singular. For the solution to this objection, see what I have said elsewhere.[30]

[*Pars Secunda. De Infinitate Primi Entis*]. His ostensis praeambulis, arguo infinitatem quatuor viis : primo per viam efficientiae ubi ostendetur propositum dupliciter : primo quia ipsum est primum efficiens omnium ; secundo, quia efficiens, puta distincte cognoscens omnia factibilia : tertio ostendetur infinitas per viam finis : et quarto per viam eminentiae.

[Via Prima]. Primam viam ex parte causae tangit Philosophus, octavo *Physicorum* * et duodecimo *Metaphysicae*,† quia movet motu infinito ; ergo habet potentiam infinitam.

Haec ratio roboratur quantum ad antecedens sic : aeque concluditur propositum si possit movere per infinitum, sicut si moveret per infinitum, quia aeque oportet eum esse in actu ; sicut illud posse patet de primo quantum est ex se ; licet igitur non moveat motu infinito sicut intelligit Aristoteles, tamen si accipiatur antecedens istud quod quantum est ex parte sua potest movere, habetur antecedens verum et aeque sufficiens ad inferendum propositum.

Consequentia probatur sic : quia si ex se non virtute alterius movet motu infinito, ergo non ab alio accipit sic movere, sed in virtute sua activa habet totum effectum suum simul, quia independenter ; sed quod simul habet in virtute infinitum effectum est infinitum ; ergo, etc.

Aliter roboratur prima consequentia sic : primum movens simul habet in virtute sua omnes effectus

---

* viii, cap. x (266ᵃ, 10–24).   † xii, cap. vii (1073ᵃ, 3–13).

[*Part II. The Infinity of the First Being*]. Now that these preliminary conclusions have been established, I argue in four ways for the infinity [of the First Being]. The notion of efficiency really provides two of the arguments, the first of which is drawn from the fact that this Being is the first efficient cause of all other things ; the second, that as efficient cause, this Being has a distinct knowledge of all that can be made. The third way is that of finality ; the fourth, that of eminence.

[*a*. First Proof]. The Philosopher treats of the first way from efficient causality in *Physics*, BK. VIII,* and his *Metaphysics*, BK. XII,† where he argues that the First Being has infinite power, because it moves with an endless movement.

The antecedent can be reinforced inasmuch as the desired conclusion follows equally well from the fact that the First Being *can* cause such motion as it would if it actually did so ; for in either case, the actual existence of such a being would be necessarily required. Now it is clear that, so far as the First Being exists in virtue of itself, it has this ability to produce endless movement. Therefore, even though such a being may not actually cause an endless movement as Aristotle thought, still the proposed conclusion can be inferred with equal validity if the antecedent be understood of the ability of the first cause to produce such movement.

The proof of the consequence is this. If the First Being, by itself and not in virtue of another, moves with an infinite movement, then it has not received such power of movement from another. Hence it has in its power at one and the same time the totality of its effect, because it has this power independently. But, whatever has an infinite effect in its power at one and the same moment is infinite ; therefore, etc.

Another way to reinforce the first consequence is this. At one and the same moment, the First Mover has in its power all the possible effects to be produced by motion.

possibiles produci per motum ; sed illi sunt infiniti, si motus infinitus ; ergo, etc.

Contra istas declarationes Aristotelis : quidquid sit de antecedente, tamen consequentia prima non videtur bene probari. Non primo modo, quia duratio major nihil perfectionis addit ; nam albedo quae uno anno manet non est perfectior quam si tantum uno die maneret ; ergo motus quantaecumque durationis non est perfectior effectus quam motus unius diei. Ergo ex hoc, quod agens habet in virtute sua activa simul movere motu infinito, non concluditur major perfectio hic quam ibi, nisi quod agens diutius movet et ex se ; et ita esset ostendendum quod aeternitas agentis concluderet ejus infinitatem ; alias ex infinitate motus non posset concludi.

Tunc ad formam, ultima propositio illius roborationis negatur, nisi de infinitate durationis. Secunda roboratio etiam consequentiae improbatur quia non major perfectio intensiva concluditur ex hoc quod agens quodcumque ejusdem speciei potest producere successive quotcumque quamdiu manet, quia quod potest in tempore uno in unum tale, potest eadem virtute in mille talia, si mille temporibus maneat. Et non est possibilis apud philosophos infinitas nisi numeralis effectuum producibilium, per motum scilicet generabilium et corruptibilium, quia in speciebus finitatem ponebant ; ergo non magis sequitur infinitas intensiva in agente ex hoc quod potest in infinita numero successive, quam si posset

If the motion is without end, however, these effects are infinite ; therefore, etc.

Against these statements of Aristotle : Whatever is to be said of the antecedent, the first consequence still does not seem to be validly established. Certainly not in the first way for a perfection does not increase simply because it endures for a greater length of time. Whiteness which exists for a year does not become any more perfect than if it existed just for a day. Therefore, movement which continues for howsoever long a time, is not a more perfect effect than the movement which lasts for a day. Consequently, just because at one and the same moment an agent virtually possesses infinite movement, we cannot conclude to any greater perfection in this case than in any other—except that here the agent moves by itself and for a longer time. And so we would have to prove that the eternity of the agent implied its infinity ; otherwise, the latter could not be inferred merely from the endlessness of the movement.

As to the form of the argument, the last proposition of the reinforced argument [viz. that whatever has an endless effect virtually is infinite] may be denied if used to prove anything more than an infinity of duration. Also the second reinforcement of the consequence breaks down, inasmuch as we cannot conclude to greater intensive perfection merely from this that an agent, if it remains in existence long enough, can produce successively any number whatsoever of the same species. For what an agent can do in one moment to one thing, by the very same power it can do to a thousand in a thousand such moments, if it exists for such a length of time. However, according to the philosophers, who assumed only a finite number of species, the only infinity possible is the numerical infinity of effects that come into existence and go out of existence through motion. Hence, there is no more reason for concluding that the agent is intensively infinite [31] just because it can do an infinite number of

in duo tantum, tantum enim est possibilis infinitas numeralis secundum philosophos. Si quis autem probet infinitatem specierum possibilem, probando aliquos motus coelestes esse incommensurabiles, et ita numquam posse redire ad uniformitatem, etiam si per infinitum durarent, et 'infinitae conjunctiones specie causarent infinita generabilia specie, de hoc, quidquid sit in se, nihil tamen ad intentionem Philosophi, qui infinitatem specierum negaret.

Ultima probabilitas quae occurrit pro consequentia Philosophi declaranda est ista : quidquid potest in aliqua multa simul quorum quodlibet requirit aliquam perfectionem sibi propriam, illud concluditur esse perfectius ex pluralitate talium, ita videtur de primo agente esse concedendum, quod si posset causare simul infinita, quod esset ejus virtus infinita, et per consequens si primum agens simul habet virtutem causandi infinita, quantum est ex se simul posset ea producere, licet natura effectus non permittat, adhuc sequitur infinitas virtutis ejus. Haec consequentia ultima probatur : quia potens causare albedinem et nigredinem, non est minus perfectum quia non sunt simul causabilia. Haec enim non simultas est ex repugnantia eorum et non est ex defectu agentis.

Et ex isto probo infinitatem sic : si primum haberet omnem causalitatem formaliter simul, licet non possent causabilia simul poni in esse, esset infinitum, quia simul, quantum est ex se, posset infinita producere, et posse

things successively (for only a numerical infinity is possible according to the philosophers) than there would be if it could do but two. But suppose someone should prove that an infinity of species is possible by proving that some heavenly movements are incommensurable and so the same arrangement would never recur even though the movement should continue *ad infinitum*. The infinite variety of [planetary] conjunctions, then, would cause an infinite variety in the effects that can be produced. Whatever is to be said of this view, however, it is definitely not the position of Aristotle, who denies the infinity of the species.[32]

The final probable interpretation advanced to reinforce the Philosopher's reasoning may be put in this way. If an agent can do many things at once, where each of the things in question needs some perfection proper to itself, then the greater the number of such things, the greater the perfection of the agent. And so it seems that we must concede that if the power of the First Agent could produce an infinity of effects at one and the same time, it must be infinite. This conclusion would follow even where the nature of the effect was such as to make its simultaneous existence in an infinite number impossible, provided that, so far as the causal power of the agent was concerned, it could produce simultaneously an infinite multitude.—This last inference is proved as follows. An agent that can cause both whiteness and blackness is not less perfect because it cannot cause the two simultaneously, for this inability to exist simultaneously arises from the repugnance of the effects to each other, and not from any defect in the agent.

From this I prove infinity in this way : If the First Being at one and the same time *formally* possessed all causal power, even though the things which it could cause could not be given simultaneous existence, it would be infinite, because—as far as it is concerned—it has power enough to produce an infinite number all

plura simul concludit majorem potentiam intensive ;
ergo si habet perfectius quam si haberet omnem causalitatem formaliter, magis sequitur infinitas intensiva. Sed
habet omnem causalitatem cujuslibet rei secundum totum
quod est in re ipsa eminentius quam si esset formaliter.

Licet ergo omnipotentiam proprie dictam secundum
intentionem theologorum tantum creditam esse et non
naturali ratione credam posse probari, sicut dicetur
distinctione xlii et *Quodl.* q. vii,* tamen probatur naturaliter infinita potentia, quae simul, quantum est ex se, habet
omnem causalitatem, quae simul posset in infinita, si
essent simul factibilia.

Si objicis, primum non potest ex se simul in infinita,
quia non est probatum quod sit totalis causa infinitorum,
hoc nihil obstat, quia si haberet simul unde esset totalis
causa, nihil perfectius esset quam nunc sit, quando habet
unde sit prima causa : tum quia illae secundae causae
non requiruntur propter perfectionem in causando, quia
tunc remotius a prima esset perfectius, quia perfectiorem
requireret causam, sed si requiruntur causae secundae
cum prima, secundum philosophos, hoc est propter imperfectionem effectus, ut primum cum alia causa imperfecta posset causare imperfectum, quod secundum ipsos,
non posset immediate causare : tum quia perfectiones
totae secundum Aristotelem eminentius sunt in primo
quam si ipsae formalitates earum sibi inessent, si possent
inesse. Quod probatur, quia causa secunda proxima

---

* *Opus oxoniense*, i, dist. xlii, q. unica ; *Quodlibet*, q. vii.

at once, and the more one can produce simultaneously, the greater the power in intensity. But if the First Being possessed such power in an even more perfect way than if it had it formally [as Avicenna, for instance, assumes], its intensive infinity follows *a fortiori*. But the full causal power that each thing may have in itself, the First Being possesses even more perfectly than if it were formally present.

Therefore, although I believe that the omnipotence in the proper sense of the word as the theologians understand it,[33] cannot be proven by natural reason, but is only believed (as will be shown in dist. XLII and *Quodlibet* q. vii),* nevertheless we can establish naturally the existence of an infinite power which on its part possesses simultaneously the fulness of causality and could produce an infinite number of things at once, if only they were capable of existing simultaneously.

It is objected that the First Cause on its part cannot cause an infinite number of effects at one time, so long as it is not proved that it is the total cause of these effects. This objection, however, presents no obstacle, since the requirements to be a total cause would not make it any more perfect than it would have to be if it were the First Cause. This is clear, first of all, because secondary causes are not required simply to supply some additional perfection to the causality, for if that were the case, the more remote effect would be the more perfect inasmuch as it would require a more perfect cause. But if secondary causes are needed in addition to the First Cause, the reason, according to the philosophers,[34] lies in the fact that the effect is imperfect. That is to say, the First Cause, which immediately would be unable to cause anything imperfect, could do so in conjunction with another imperfect cause. Also, the First Being, according to Aristotle, contains all the perfections in a more perfect manner than if they were formally present, were this latter possible. The proof of this lies in the fact that

primae totam perfectionem suam causativam habet a sola prima ; ergo totam perfectionem illam eminentius habet causa prima quam secunda causa habens ipsam formaliter. Consequentia patet, quia prima respectu illius causae secundae est causa totalis et aequivoca. Consimiliter quaeratur de tertia causa respectu secundae vel respectu primae. Si respectu primae, habetur propositum. Si respectu secundae, sequitur secundam eminenter continere perfectionem totalem quae est formaliter in tertia. Sed secunda habet a prima quod sic continet perfectionem tertiae, ex praeostensa ; ergo prima eminentius habet continere perfectionem tertiae quam secunda ; et sic de omnibus aliis usque ad ultimam ; quare [concluditur] primam causam habere eminenter totalem perfectionem causativam omnium et perfectius quam si haberet causalitatem omnium formaliter, și esset possibile. Videtur judicio meo posse concludere ratio Aristotelis de substantia infinita, quae accipitur ex octavo *Physicorum* * et duodecimo *Metaphysicae* † superius posita.

Juxta istam viam efficientiae arguitur quod habeat potentiam infinitam, nam virtus quae potest super extrema distantia in infinitum, est infinita. Sed virtus divina est hujusmodi in creatione. Inter enim extrema creationis est infinita distantia, sicut inter aliquid et nihil. Sed hoc antecedens ponitur tantum creditum, et verum est de creatione in ordine reali, ita scilicet quod non-esse quasi durative praecederet esse reale existentiae creaturae. Non tamen est minor credita de creatione qua ordine naturae esse sequitur non-esse, quo modo loquitur Avicenna de creatione quinto [*read* sexto] *Metaphysicae* ‡ ; sed est sufficienter demonstrata quia saltem prima natura

---

* viii, cap. x (266ª, 10–24).   † xii, cap. vii (1073ª, 3-13).
‡ *Metaphysica*, vi, cap. ii.

the secondary cause closest to the first receives all of its causal perfection exclusively from the first. Consequently, the First Cause has the whole of this perfection in a more eminent way than the second cause, which possesses it formally. The consequence is evident, since the first is the total equivocal cause of the second. We can argue the same way regarding the relation of the third cause to the second or first cause. If we take it in relation to the first, we have the proposed conclusion. If we take it in relation to the second, then it follows that the second cause contains the total perfection found formally in the third. But as we have shown, the second cause owes this all to the First Cause ; therefore, the First Cause must contain the perfection of the third in an even more perfect way than does the second. And the same is true with all the other causes down to the very last. Therefore, we conclude that the First Cause contains eminently the total causal perfection of all the other causes, and this in a way that is even more perfect than if it contained this causality formally, were that possible. To my mind, it seems that Aristotle's argument for an infinite substance in *Physics*, BK. VIII,* and *Metaphysics*, BK. XII,† can be made to hold.

Using this way of efficiency, some [35] argue that the First Cause has infinite power, because any power which can bridge the distance between infinite extremes is itself infinite. The divine power in creation, however, is of such a nature, for between the extremes of creation (i.e. between nothing and something) an infinite distance intervenes. If existence be understood as true of the real order where non-existence precedes existence by a priority of duration, then the antecedent is an assumption based on faith alone ; whereas if we take creation as Avicenna does in *Metaphysics*, BK. VI,‡ in the sense that non-existence precedes existence merely by a priority of nature, then the antecedent is no longer an assumption of faith.[36] For it is sufficiently demonstrated that the first

post Deum est ab ipso et non a se, nec accipit esse aliquo praesupposito. Ergo illud creatur. Nam si est primum effectivum, quodlibet aliud ab eo totum esse suum capit ab eo, quia aliter secundum aliquid ejus non dependet ab eo, nec illud esset tunc primum effectivum. Sed quod sic capit totum esse suum ab aliquo, ita quod per naturam suam habet esse post non-esse, creatur ; ergo, etc. Sed sic accipiendo prius natura tam esse quam non-esse, non sunt extrema mutationis [*MS* univocationis] quam causet ista virtus, nec illud effici requirit mutari.

Sed quidquid sit de antecedente, consequentia non probatur ; quia quando inter extrema nulla est distantia media, sicut est in continuo cujus extrema sunt duo puncta, ista dicuntur praecise distare ratione extremorum inter se ; tanta ergo est distantia quantum est majus extremum. Exemplum : Deus distat in infinitum a creatura etiam suprema possibili, non quidem propter aliquam distantiam mediam inter extrema, sed propter infinitatem unius extremi ; sic ergo contradictoria non distant per aliqua media, quia contradictoria sunt immediata, ita quod quantumcumque parum recedit aliquid ab uno extremo, statim est sub altero ; sed distant [*MS* differunt] propter extrema in se. Tanta ergo est distantia ista quantum est illud extremum quod est perfectius : illud est finitum ; ergo, etc. Confirmatur, quia posse totaliter super terminum positivum hujus distantiae est posse super distantiam sive super transitum ab extremo in extremum ; ergo ex posse super istum transitum non sequitur infinitas, nisi sequatur ex

nature after God does not exist of itself but is dependent upon Him ; neither is anything [viz. matter] presupposed in order to give it existence. Consequently, it is created. For if a first efficient cause exists, everything else receives its total being from it. Otherwise, these other beings would not be dependent upon it, nor could it really be the first efficient cause. But anything that receives its total being from another so that by its nature it has existence after non-existence, is created ; therefore, etc. If we understand nature as being prior to both existence and non-existence in this [viz. ontological] sense, then existence and non-existence are not termini of a change ; neither does "to be produced in this way" necessarily imply "to be changed".

Whatever is to be said of the antecedent of this argument, the consequence remains unproved. When there is no interval between the extremes as is the case in a continuum, whose extremes are two points, it is how one extreme compares with the other that determines how "distant" it is said to be. Consequently, it will be as distant from, as it is greater than, the other. God, for example, is infinitely distant from even the greatest creature possible, not indeed because of any interval between the two, but because of the infinity of the one extreme. And so I argue that contradictories are distant from one another in virtue of the extremes themselves, and not by reason of some interval between them, for contradictories are immediate. No matter how little something departs from one extreme, it immediately comes under the other. In the present instance, then, there will be as much "distance" as there is [entity] in the more perfect extreme. But the latter is finite ; therefore, etc. This is confirmed, inasmuch as to possess complete power over the positive term of this "distance" is to have power over the distance or the passage from one extreme to the other. Infinity, therefore, cannot be inferred from the power of the agent to effect this transi-

posse totaliter super terminum ejus positivum. Terminus
ille est finitus ; ergo posse super transitum ad istum terminum non concludit virtutem activam infinitam
demonstrative.

Quod autem dicitur communiter, contradictoria distare in infinitum, potest sic intelligi, id est, indeterminate ;
quia sicut nulla est ita parva distantia quae non sufficiat
ad contradictoria, sic nulla est ita magna, etiam si
esset major maxima possibili, quin ad illa contradictoria
se extendere. Est igitur eorum distantia infinita, id est,
indeterminata ad quamcumque scilicet magnam vel par-
vam. Et ideo ex tali infinitate distantiae, id est, indeterminata, non sequitur consequens de infinita potentia
intensive, sicut nec sequitur ad minimam distantiam, in
qua salvatur sic infinita distantia, id est, indeterminata ;
et quod non sequitur ad antecedens, nec ad consequens.
Contradictoria ergo maxima distantia est et oppositio,
sed privative et indeterminate ; contrarietas vero est
maxima positive, sicut patet decimo *Metaphysicae.**

[Via Secunda]. Ostenso proposito per viam primae
efficientiae, quia illa prima efficientia infert infinitatem,
sequitur secunda via ex hoc quod est intelligens distincte
omnia factibilia, ubi arguo sic : Intelligibilia sunt
infinita, et hoc actu in intellectu omnia intelligente.
Ergo intellectus ista simul actu intelligens est infinitus.
Talis est intellectus primi.

Hujus enthymematis probo antecedens et consequentiam. Quaecunque sunt infinita in potentia, ita
quod in accipiendo alterum post alterum nullum possunt
habere finem, illa omnia, si simul actu sunt, sunt actu
infinita. Intelligibilia sunt hujusmodi respectu intel-

---

* x, cap. iv (1055^a, 9).

THE EXISTENCE OF GOD   68

tion, unless it is already implied by its power to produce the positive extreme. But the latter, in the present case, is finite ; consequently, it is not demonstratively established that infinite power is required to effect such a transition.

Still, the common saying that "contradictories are infinitely distant" can be understood in the sense of "indeterminately". For just as no "distance" is too small to produce a contradiction, so likewise, none is too great, even if it were greater than the greatest possible. Therefore this "distance" is infinite in the sense that it is not determined to any definite interval, howsoever great or small. Such an infinity or indeterminateness, then, does not imply the consequent about a power that is intensively infinite, just as the minimum distance characterised by such an infinity does not imply it. For what does not follow from the antecedent, does not follow from the consequent. Contradictories, therefore, are at the greatest "distance" and in the greatest opposition to each other, but privatively and indeterminately. Positively, however, the greatest "distance" is between contraries, as is clear from *Metaphysics*, BK. X.*

[*b.* Second Proof]. Having established the proposed conclusion by the first way of efficiency inasmuch as the first efficient cause implies infinity, we proceed to the second, where, from the fact that the First Being knows distinctly everything that can be made, we argue as follows : The things that can be known are infinite in number. But they are all actually known by an intellect which knows all things. Therefore, that intellect is infinite which, at one and the same moment, has actual knowledge of all these things. Now such is the intellect of the First Being.

I prove the antecedent and consequence of this enthymeme. Things potentially infinite or endless in number, if taken one at a time, are actually infinite if they actually exist simultaneously. Now what can be known is of such

lectus creati. Satis patet. Et in intellectu divino sunt simul omnia actu intellecta quae ab intellectu creato successive sunt intellecta. Ergo ibi sunt infinita actu intellecta. Hujus syllogismi probo majorem, licet satis evidens videatur, quia omnia talia acceptibilia quando sunt simul existentia, aut sunt actu finita aut sunt actu infinita. Si actu finita, ergo accipiendo alterum post alterum, tandem omnia possunt esse actu accepta. Ergo si non possunt esse omnia actu accepta, si talia actu simul sunt, sunt actu infinita.

Consequentiam primi enthymematis sic probo : quia ubi pluralitas requirit vel concludit majorem perfectionem quam paucitas, ibi infinitas numeralis concludit infinitam perfectionem. Exemplum : posse ferre decem majorem perfectionem requirit virtutis motivae quam posse ferre quinque : ideo posse ferre infinita concludit infinitam virtutem motivam. Ergo in proposito, cum intelligere A sit aliqua perfectio, et intelligere B sit similiter alia perfectio, numquam intelligere idem est ipsius A et B et aeque distincte, ut duo intelligere essent, nisi perfectiones [*MS* perfectiores] duorum intelligere includuntur in illo uno eminenter, et sic de tribus, et ultra de infinitis.

Consimiliter etiam quia de ipsa ratione intelligendi argueretur sicut de intellectu et actu argutum est : quia major perfectio concluditur in actu intelligendi ex pluralitate illorum quorum ratio intelligendi distincte, quia oportet quod includant eminenter perfectiones omnium propriarum operationum intelligendi, quarum quaelibet secundum propriam rationem aliquam perfectionem ponit ; ergo infinitae concludunt infinitam.

Secundo, juxta istam viam de intelligere primi propositum sic ostendo ; causa prima, cui secundum

a nature so far as a created intellect is concerned, as is sufficiently clear. Now all that the created intellect knows successively, the divine intellect knows actually at one and the same time. Therefore, the divine intellect knows the actually infinite. I prove the major of this syllogism, although it seems evident enough. Consider these potentially infinite things as a whole. If they exist all at once, they are either actually infinite or actually finite. If finite, then if we take one after the other, eventually we shall actually know them all. But if we cannot actually know them all in this way, they will be actually infinite if known simultaneously.

The consequence of this first enthymeme, I prove as follows. Whenever a greater number implies or requires greater perfection than does a smaller number, numerical infinity implies infinite perfection. For example, greater motive power is required to carry ten things than to carry five. Therefore, an infinite motive power is needed to carry an infinity of such things. Now in the point at issue, since to know *A* is one perfection and to know *B* also is another perfection, it follows that *A* and *B* as two equally distinct objects will never be known by one and the same act of knowledge unless the latter includes in a more eminent way these two perfections. The same holds for three objects, and so *ad infinitum*.

A similar argument to that based on the intellect and the act of knowing could be constructed in regard to the reason for knowing (*ratio intelligendi*).[37] For the greater the number of things known distinctly through this medium of knowledge, the more perfect is the act of knowing since the act by which all things are known must include in a more eminent way the perfections of each proper act of knowledge, where each of these includes some perfection proper to itself. Where the latter are infinite, therefore, infinite perfection is required.

A second proof from the knowledge of the First Being in support of our thesis is this. Suppose a secondary

ultimum suae causalitatis causa secunda aliquid perfectionis addit in causando, non videtur sola posse ita
perfectum effectum causare, sicut ipsa cum secunda, quia
causalitas sola primae diminuta est respectu causalitatis
ambarum ; ergo si illud quod natum est esse a causa
secunda et prima simul sit multo perfectius a sola prima,
secunda nihil perfectionis addit primae ; sed omne
finitum omni finito addit aliquam perfectionem ; ergo
talis causa prima est infinita. Ad propositum, notitia
cujuscumque nata est gigni ab ipso sicut a causa proxima,
et maxime illa quae est visio sive intuitiva intellectio ;
ergo si illa alicui intellectui inest sine actione quacumque
talis objecti, tantummodo ex virtute alterius objecti
prioris, quod natum est esse causa superior respectu talis
cognitionis, sequitur quod illud objectum superius est
infinitum in cognoscibilitate, quia inferius nihil sibi addit
in cognoscibilitate : tale objectum superius est natura
prima, quia ex sola praesentia ejus apud intellectum
primi, nullo alio objecto concomitante, est notitia
cujuscumque objecti in intellectu ejus ; ergo nullum
aliud intelligibile aliquid sibi addit in cognoscibilitate ;
ergo est infinitum in cognoscibilitate sic, ergo est in
entitate, quia unumquodque sicut se habet ad esse, sic
ad cognoscibilitatem, ex secundo *Metaphysicae.**

[Via Tertia]. Item, tertia via, scilicet ex parte finis
arguitur sic : voluntas nostra omni finito aliquid aliud
majus potest appetere et amare, sicut intellectus intelligere ; et videtur quod plus est inclinatio naturalis ad
summe amandum bonum infinitum ; nam inde arguitur
inclinatio naturalis ad aliquid in voluntate, quia ex se,

---

* II, cap. i (993^b, 30–31).

cause can add some perfection to the causality of the First Cause, even when the latter acts to the utmost of its power. In such a case, if the First Cause were to act alone, its effectiveness would seem to be less perfect than that of the two causes together. Therefore, if something which a secondary cause can produce together with the First Cause, can be done much more perfectly by the First Cause alone, the secondary cause adds no perfection to the first. But a finite thing always adds some perfection to what is finite. Hence, a first cause whose causality cannot be perfected is infinite. To apply this to the question at issue. Knowledge of any object is by its very nature apt to be engendered by that object as its proximate cause, and this is especially true of intuitive knowledge or vision. Therefore, if some intellect possesses such knowledge without any action on the part of the object known, but solely in virtue of some prior object which by nature is a higher cause of such knowledge, it follows that the higher object is infinitely intelligible, because the lower object adds nothing to it in the way of cognoscibility. Now, the supreme nature is such a superior object, since in the absence of all other objects by the mere fact that it is present to the intellect of the First Being, it gives to that intellect a knowledge of every object without exception. Therefore, nothing else that can be known adds anything to this nature in the way of cognoscibility. Consequently, it is infinitely intelligible ; therefore, its entity is also infinite, for a thing can only be known to the extent that it has entity, according to *Metaphysics*, BK. II.*

[c. Third Proof]. The fact that the First Being is also the ultimate end provides a third way of arguing to infinity. Our will can always love and seek something greater than any finite being, even as our intellect is always able to know more. And, what is more, there seems to be a natural inclination to love an infinite good to the greatest degree possible, because the free will of

sine habitu, prompte et delectabiliter vult illud voluntas libera : ita videtur quod experimur actu amandi bonum infinitum : imo non videtur voluntas in alio perfecte quietari. Et quomodo non illud naturaliter odiret, si esset objectum sui objecti, sicut naturaliter odit non esse, secundum Augustinum, *De libero arbitrio*, libri [tertii] capitulo [octavo] * Videtur etiam si infinitum repugnaret bono, quod nullo modo quietaretur in bono sub ratione infiniti, nec in illud faciliter tenderet, sicut nec in repugnans suo objecto. Confirmabitur illa ratio in sequenti via de intellectu.

[Via Quarta]. Item quarto propositum ostenditur per viam eminentiae et arguo sic : eminentissimo incompossibile est aliquid esse perfectius, sicut prius patet. Finito autem non est incompossibile esse aliquid perfectius ; quare, etc. Minor probatur quia infinitum non repugnat enti ; sed omni finito magis est infinitum.

Ad istud aliter arguitur, et est idem : cui non repugnat infinitum esse intensive, illud non est summe perfectum nisi sit infinitum, quia si est finitum potest excedi vel excelli, quia infinitum esse sibi non repugnat : enti non repugnat infinitas ; ergo perfectissimum ens est infinitum. Minor hujus quae in praecedenti argumento accipitur, non videtur a priori ostendi ; quia sicut contradictoria ex rationibus propriis contradicunt, nec potest per aliquid manifestius hoc probari, ita non repugnantia ex rationibus propriis non repugnant, nec videtur posse ostendi, nisi explicando rationes ipsorum :

* III, cap. vi, viii (Migne, P.L., XXXII, 1280, 1282).

itself and without the aid of any habit promptly and delightfully loves this good, so that we seem to experience an act of love for an infinite good. Indeed it seems that the will is not perfectly satisfied with anything else. And if such an infinite good were really opposed to the natural object of the will, why is it that the will does not naturally hate an infinite good, just as it naturally hates non-existence, according to Augustine in *De libero arbitrio*, III, viii ?* For it seems that if "infinite" and "good" were incompatible, then there would be no way in which the will could be satisfied in such a good, nor could it readily tend towards such a good just as it cannot readily tend towards anything which is opposed to its proper object. This argument will be confirmed in the following by a similar argument from the intellect.

[*d*. Fourth Proof]. The thesis is shown also by the way of eminence, and here I argue that it is incompatible with the idea of a most perfect being that anything should excel it in perfection, as has been previously explained. Now there is nothing incompatible about a finite thing being excelled in perfection ; therefore, etc. The minor is proved from this, that to be infinite is not incompatible with being ; but the infinite is greater than any finite being.

Another formulation given to the same argument is this. That to which intensive infinity is not repugnant is not all perfect unless it be infinite, for to be infinite is compatible with it. And if it is finite, it can be exceeded or excelled. Now infinity is not repugnant to being, therefore the most perfect being is infinite. The minor of this proof, which was used in the preceding argument, cannot, it seems, be proven *a priori*. For, just as contradictories by their very nature contradict each other and their opposition cannot be made manifest by anything more evident, so also these terms [viz. "being" and "infinite"] by their very nature are not repugnant to each other. Neither does there seem to be any way of

ens per nullius notius explicatur ; infinitum intelligimus per finitum, hoc vulgariter sic expono : infinitum est quod aliquod finitum datum secundum nullam habitudinem finitam praecise excedit, sed ultra omnem talem habitudinem assignabilem adhuc excedit.

Sic tamen propositum suadetur : sicut quidlibet ponendum est possibile, cujus non apparet impossibilitas, ita et compossibile cujus non apparet incompossibilitas. Hic incompossibilitas nulla apparet quia de ratione entis non est finitas, nec apparet ex ratione entis quod sit passio convertibilis cum ente ; alterum istorum requiritur ad repugnantiam praedictam : passiones enim primae entis et convertibiles satis videntur notae sibi inesse.

Item sic suadetur : infinitum suo modo non repugnat quantitati, id est, in accipiendo partem post partem ; ergo nec infinitum suo modo repugnat entitati, id est in perfectione simul essendo.

Item, si quantitas virtutis est simpliciter perfectior quam quantitas molis, quare erit infinitum possibile in mole et non in virtute ? Quod si est possibilis, est in actu, sicut ex tertia conclusione patet supra de primitate effectiva et etiam inferius probabitur.

Item, quare [MS quia] intellectus, cujus objectum est ens, nullam invenit repugnantiam intelligendo aliquod infinitum ; imo videtur perfectissimum intelligibile ? Mirum est autem, si nulli intellectui talis contradictio patens fiat circa primum ejus objectum, cum discordia in sono faciliter offendat auditum ; si enim disconveniens

proving this except by explaining the meaning of the notions themselves. "Being" cannot be explained by anything better known than itself. "Infinite" we understand by means of finite. I explain "infinite" in a popular definition as follows : The infinite is that which exceeds the finite, not exactly by reason of any finite measure, but in excess of any measure that could be assigned.

The following persuasive argument can be given for what we intend to prove. Just as everything is assumed to be possible, if its impossibility is not apparent, so also all things are assumed to be compatible, if their incompatibility is not manifest. Now there is no incompatibility apparent here, for it is not of the nature of being to be finite ; nor does finite appear to be an attribute coextensive with being. But if they were mutually repugnant, it would be for one of these reasons. The coextensive attributes which being possesses, seem to be sufficiently evident.

Another persuasive argument adduced is this. Infinity, in its own way, is not opposed to quantity (that is, where parts are taken successively) ; therefore, neither is infinity, in its own way, opposed to entity (that is, where perfection exists simultaneously).

Again, if the quantity characteristic of power is simply more perfect than that characteristic of mass, why is it possible to have an infinity [of small parts] in an [extended] mass and not an infinite power ? And if an infinite power is possible, then it actually exists, as is evident from the third conclusion about the first efficient cause, and will also be proved again later.[38]

Again, why is it that the intellect, whose object is being, does not find the notion of something infinite repugnant? Instead of this, the infinite seems to be the most perfect thing we can know. Now, if tonal discord so readily displeases the ear, it would be strange if some intellect did not clearly perceive the contradiction between infinite and its first object [viz. being] if such existed.

statim ut percipitur offendit, cur nullus intellectus ab
intelligibili infinito naturaliter refugit sicut a non conveniente, suum ita primum objectum destruentem ?

Per illud potest colorari illa ratio Anselmi de summo
bono cogitabili, *Proslogion*,* et intelligenda est ejus
descriptio sic. Deus est quo cognito sine contradictione
majus cogitari non potest sine contradictione. Et quod
addendum sit contradictione, patet : nam in cujus
cognitione vel cogitatione includitur contradictio, illud
dicitur non cogitabile, quia sunt tunc duo cogitabilia
opposita nullo modo faciendo unum cogitabile, quia
neutrum determinat alterum, ut quod homo sit irra-
tionalis est incogitabile. Unde sicut in rebus nihil est
nisi sit simplex vel compositum ex potentia et actu, ita
in conceptibus. Contradictoria autem nihil faciunt unum
nec simplex, nec compositum.

Summum cogitabile praedictum, sine contradictione
potest esse in re. Hoc probatur primo de esse quiddita-
tibo : quia in tali cogitabili summo quiescit intellectus ;
ergo in ipso est ratio primi objecti intellectus scilicet
entis, et hoc in summo.

Et tunc arguitur ultra, quod illud sit loquendo de
esse existentiae. Summe cogitabile non est tantum in
intellectu cogitante, quia tunc posset esse, quia cogitabile
possibile, et non posset esse, quia repugnat rationi ejus
esse ab aliqua causa, sicut patet prius in secunda conclusione de via efficientiae. Majus ergo cogitabile est

---

* Cap. iii (Migne, P.L., CLVIII, 228).

For if the disagreeable becomes offensive as soon as it is perceived, why is it that no intellect naturally shrinks from the infinitely intelligible as it would from something out of harmony with, and even destructive of, its first object ?

In this same way Anselm's argument in the *Proslogion* * about the highest conceivable good can be touched up. His description must be understood in this way. God is a being conceived without contradiction, who is so great that it would be a contradiction if a greater being could be conceived. That the phrase "without contradiction" must be added is clear, for anything, the very knowledge or thought of which includes a contradiction, is called "inconceivable", for it includes two conceivable notions so opposed to each other that they cannot in any way be fused into a single conceivable object, since neither determines the other. Thus "man is irrational" cannot be conceived. Hence, just as in the world of reality nothing exists that is not either simple or at least composed of act [the determining element] and potency [the determinable element], so also with concepts. Contradictories, however, do not form a unity, be it simple or composed.

It follows then, that the greatest object conceivable without contradiction can actually exist in reality. This is proved first of its essential being, for in such an object the intellect is fully satisfied ; therefore, in it the primary object of the intellect, viz. "being", is verified and this in the highest degree.

It is further argued, then, that this being actually exists because the highest conceivable object is not one which is merely in the intellect of the thinker, for then it both could exist, because as something possible it is conceivable, and yet could not exist, because the idea of existing in virtue of some cause is repugnant to its very nature. This latter was shown above in the second conclusion of the proof from efficiency.[39] Therefore, what

quod est in re quam quod est tantum in intellectu. Non est autem hoc sic intelligendum, quod idem si cogitetur per hoc sit majus cogitabile si existat, sed omni quod est in intellectu tantum est majus aliquod quod existit.

Vel aliter coloratur sic : majus cogitabile est quod existit, id est perfectius cognoscibile, quia visibile sive intelligibile intellectione intuitiva. Cum [*read* Quod autem] non existit, nec in se, nec in nobiliori, cui nihil addit, non est visibile. Visibile autem est perfectius cognoscibile non visibili, sed tantum modo intelligibili abstractive ; ergo perfectissimum cognoscibile existit. De differentia intellectionis intuitivae et abstractivae et quomodo intuitiva est perfectior, tangetur distinctione tertia * et alias quando locum habebit.

[Via Inefficax]. Ultimo ostenditur propositum ex negatione causae extrinsecae [*read* intrinsecae] ; quia materia finitur per formam, sicut potentia per actum et perfectionem et esse formae ejus. Et e converso forma finitur per materiam sicut actus per potentiam. Forma ergo quae non est nata esse in materia est infinita ; cujusmodi est Deus.

Haec ratio non valet, quia secundum ipsos angelus est immaterialis ; ergo in natura est infinitus. Non possunt dicere, quod esse angeli finiret essentiam ejus, quia secundum eos est accidens essentiae et posterius naturaliter ; et sic in primo signo naturae essentia secundum se ut prior esse, videtur infinita intensive, et per consequens in secundo signo naturae non erit finitabilis per esse.

---

* *Opus oxoniense*, I, dist. III, q. iii.

exists in reality is conceivably greater than what exists only in the intellect. This is not to be understood, however, in the sense that something conceived if it actually exists, is, by the fact of existing, conceivable to any greater extent. The meaning is that whatever exists is greater than whatever is solely in the intellect.

Or the argument could be retouched in this way. Whatever exists is conceivable to a greater extent [than what does not] ; that is to say, it can be known more perfectly, because it is intuitively intelligible or visible. What does not exist either in itself or in something more noble to which it adds nothing, is not capable of being intuited. Now what can be seen is able to be known more perfectly than what can not be intuited, but known only abstractively. Therefore, the most perfect thing that can be known exists. The difference between intuitive and abstractive knowledge, and the superiority of the former over the latter, will be treated in distinction three and elsewhere as occasion offers.[40]

[e. An Ineffective Proof]. Finally, some [41] argue to the proposed conclusion from the absence of any intrinsic cause, for matter is determined by form as the potential is determined by act, perfection, and the existence of its form. Conversely, the form is limited by matter as act is limited by potency. Any form incapable of being in matter, therefore, is infinite. God is of such kind.

This reason does not hold, for according to these men,[42] the angel is immaterial ; therefore, its nature is infinite. They cannot avoid this conclusion by saying that the existence of the angel limits its essence, for they maintain that existence is accidental to the essence and naturally posterior to it. And so in the first instance of nature,[43] the essence, considered in its own right and as prior to existence, seems to be intensively infinite. Consequently, it cannot be limited by existence in the second instance of nature.

Breviter respondeo ad argumentum : nam quaelibet entitas habet intrinsecum sibi gradum suae perfectionis, in quo est finitum, si est finitum, et in quo infinitum, si potest esse infinitum, et non per aliquid accidens sibi.

Arguitur etiam : si forma finitur ad materiam, ergo si non ad illam, non finitur. Fallacia consequentis : sicut corpus finitur ad corpus ; igitur si non ad corpus, erit infinitum ; ultimum ergo coelum erit actu infinitum; sophisma est istud tertio *Physicorum*,* quia sicut prius corpus in se prius finitur propriis terminis antequam ad aliquid aliud finiatur, ut de coelo, ergo ita forma finita prius est in se finita quam finiatur ad materiam, quia est talis natura in entibus quod finitur, id est antequam uniatur materiae ; nam secunda finitas praesupponit primam et non causat eam ; ergo in aliquo signo naturae erit essentia [angeli] finita ; ergo non finitur per esse ; ergo in secundo signo non finitur per esse. Breviter dico unam propositionem, quod quaecumque essentia absoluta finita in se, est finita ut praeintelligitur omni comparatione sui ad aliam essentiam.

[Solutio Quaestionis]

Ex dictis patet solutio quaestionis : nam ex primo articulo habetur quod aliquod ens existens est simpliciter primum triplici primitate, videlicet efficientiae, finis et eminentiae, et ita simpliciter quod incompossibile est aliquid esse prius ; et in hoc probatum est esse de Deo quantum ad proprietates respectivas Dei ad creaturam, vel in quantum determinat dependentiam respectus creaturarum ad ipsum. Ex secundo articulo habetur

---

* III, cap. iv (203^b, 20–22).

Briefly, then, I reply to the argument. If an entity is finite or infinite, it is so not by reason of something incidental to itself, but because it has its own intrinsic degree of finite or infinite perfection respectively.

It is also argued that,[44] if form is limited with reference to matter, where there is no matter, there the form is infinite. This is the fallacy of asserting the consequent, just as is the following : a body is limited with reference to a body ; therefore, if a body is not limited with reference to another body, it will be infinite ; hence, the outermost heaven will be actually infinite. This is the fallacy of *Physics*, BK. III.* For, just as a body is first limited in itself by its own proper boundaries before it is limited with respect to anything else (as is the case with the heavens), so the finite form is first limited in itself before it is limited with respect to matter. That is to say, it is of such a nature that it is limited, and this, prior to any union with matter ; for the second limitation presupposes, and does not cause, the first. The finite character of the angelic essence, then, is something that is prior by nature to its existence. Consequently, it is not its subsequent existence that makes such an essence limited. To put the argument briefly in one sentence, I say that every finite essence is such absolutely and prior to any reference it may have to another essence.

[*Solution of the Question*] [45]

The solution to the question, then, is clear from the foregoing, for the first article establishes the existence of some being that is simply first by the triple primacy of efficiency, finality and eminence, and is first in such an unqualified sense that it would be impossible for anything to be prior to it. This is to establish the existence of God so far as the divine properties that have reference to creatures are concerned, or in so far as creatures are dependent upon him. The second article shows in four

quadruplex via quod illud primum est infinitum : primo videlicet, quia primum efficiens ; secundo, quia primum agens omnia factibilia, secunda via continet quatuor conclusiones de intelligere primi ; tertio, quia finis ultimus ; quarto, quia eminens.

Juxta primam exclusa est quaedam via inutilis de creatione. Juxta secundam tangitur alia via de perfectione primi objecti et intellectualitate. Juxta quartam exponitur ratio Anselmi, *Proslogion*, Deus est quo majus cogitari non potest. Ultimo excluditur via inutilis ex immaterialitate inferens infinitatem.

Ex praemissis conclusionibus probatis et ostensis, arguitur sic ad quaestionem : aliquod ens tripliciter primum in entibus existit in actu et illud tripliciter primum est infinitum ; ergo aliquod infinitum ens existit in actu, et istud est perfectissimum conceptibile et conceptus perfectissimus absolutus quem possumus habere de Deo naturaliter quod sit infinitus, sicut dicitur distinctione tertia.* Et sic probatum est Deum esse quantum ad conceptum vel esse ejus perfectissimum conceptibilem vel possibilem haberi a nobis de Deo.

[Ad Argumenta Principalia]

Ad argumenta hujus quaestionis : ad primum dico quod causa infinita activa ex necessitate naturae non compatitur aliquid sibi contrarium, sive sit ei contrarium aliquid formaliter [*MS om.* id est, secundum aliquod quod convenit sibi essentialiter] sive virtualiter, id est, secundum rationem effectus sui quem virtualiter includit ; utroque enim modo impediret quodlibet incompossibile suo effectui, sicut argutum est prius.

Contra : numquid philosophi ponentes Deum agere ex necessitate naturae non ponebant esse aliquid malum

---

* *Opus oxoniense*, I, dist. III, q. i.

ways that this First Being is infinite, first, because it is the first efficient cause ; secondly, because as first agent it knows all that can be made (this second way contains four conclusions regarding the knowledge of the first being) ; thirdly, because it is the last end ; and fourthly, because it is most excellent.

In our treatise on the first way, we rejected as useless a certain argument regarding creation. With the second, we considered another way based on the perfection of the first object and its intelligibility. In connection with the fourth, we expounded the argument of Anselm in the *Proslogion*, cap. ii, namely that God is that, greater than which nothing can be thought. Finally, we rejected as useless the argument that would infer infinity from immateriality.

Having proved these conclusions, one can answer the question as follows. *In the realm of beings there actually exists a being which has a triple primacy, and this being is infinite. Therefore, some infinite being actually exists.* This notion of God as an infinite being is the most perfect absolute concept we can have of him, as we point out in dist. III.[46] Consequently, we prove that God, conceived under the most perfect aspect possible to us, actually exists.

[Reply to the Arguments at the Beginning]

To the first [47] of the arguments at the beginning of the question, I say that an infinite cause that acts by a necessity of nature would not suffer anything contrary to itself, whether such a thing be formally contrary (i.e. opposed to some essential perfection of the First Cause) or only virtually contrary (i.e. opposed to some effect which it includes virtually). For in either case, an infinite cause would impede anything incompatible with its effect, as the argument states above.

To the contrary : Did not the philosophers who assumed that God acted out of a necessity imposed by

in universo ? Respondeo, sicut patuit probando Deum esse agens per cognitionem, non potuerunt salvare aliquod malum fieri posse contingenter in universo, sed tantum unus ordo causarum produceret aliquid quod esset receptivum alicujus perfectionis ; alius autem ordo de necessitate produceret oppositum illius perfectionis, ita quod ista perfectio non posset tunc induci concurrentibus omnibus causis, licet absolute productum ab aliquibus [*MS* aliis quibus], consideretur secundum rationem suae speciei, esset receptivum illius perfectionis, cujus oppositum necessario evenit ; ergo secundum eos sicut causae efficientes in una coordinatione necessario agunt, ita causae efficientes impedientes in alia coordinatione necessario agunt impediendo. Unde aequali necessitate qua sol agit ad dissolvendum, agit Saturnus ad condensandum. Cum ergo omnis defectus materiae reducatur ad causas efficientes quae sunt defectuosae in virtute, si quaelibet causa efficiens agit necessario, tunc nihil defectus vel monstruositatis vel malitiae erit in universo quin necessario accidat. Quid autem possunt philosophi dicere de libero arbitrio nostro et malitia moris, dicendum est alias.

Ad secundum dico, quod consequentia non valet. Ad probationem ostendo quod non est consimilis incompossibilitas dimensionum in replendo locum et essentiarum in simul essendo ; non enim una entitas ita replet totam naturam entis quin cum ea posset stare alia entitas. Hoc autem non debet intelligi de repletione locali, sed quasi commensuratione essentiali ; sed una dimensio replet eumdem locum secundum ultimum capacitatis suae, itaque una entitas simul potest esse cum cum alia,

his nature, also admit the existence of evil in the universe? As I have already made clear in proving that God acts with knowledge,[48] I reply that they could not consistently explain the contingent character of the evil in the universe. All they could maintain would be that one order of causes could produce something capable of receiving a given perfection, whereas another order of necessity would produce the opposite of this perfection. In other words, if we considered all the causes actually concurring at that time, this perfection could not be induced at this particular moment. Absolutely speaking, however, if we consider not this particular event, but one similar in kind, then a thing produced by some of these causes could also be the recipient of a perfection which *de facto* was necessarily absent at this particular time. According to them, therefore, just as the efficient causes in one group act necessarily, so the impeding efficient causes of the other group act necessarily. The sun dissolves something, then, with the same necessity with which Saturn condenses it. Therefore, since every defect of matter is due to a deficiency in the strength of the efficient causes, if each efficient cause acts necessarily, then every defect, monstrosity, or evil in the universe occurs necessarily. What the philosophers can say of our free will and moral evil, however, will have to be treated elsewhere.

To the second argument,[49] I say that the consequence is invalid. As to the proof adduced in its favour, I show that there is no parity between the impossibility of several extended things filling the same place and several essences existing simultaneously. For no entity so fills the whole nature of being as to render impossible the coexistence of another. "Coexistence" in this latter case, however, should not be understood in the sense of filling a place, but rather as a kind of essential commensuration.[50] The extension of one thing, however, fills any place to the utmost of its capacity. More than one entity, therefore,

12

sicut posset respectu loci cum corpore replente locum esse aliud corpus non replens locum. Similiter alia consequentia non valet, quia corpus infinitum si esset cum alio, fieret totum majus utroque ratione dimensionum, quia dimensiones alterius corporis essent aliae a dimensionibus corporis infiniti et ejusdem rationis cum eis, et ideo totum esset majus propter dimensionum diversitatem, et totum non majus, quia dimensio infinita non potest excedi. Hic autem tota quantitas infinitae perfectionis nullam additionem recipit in ratione talis quantitatis ex coexistenti alicujus finiti secundum talem qualitatem.

Ad tertium dico, quod consequentia non valet, nisi illud quod demonstratur in antecedente, a quo alia separantur, sit finitum. Exemplum : si esset aliquod ubi infinitum per impossibile, et corpus infinitum replet illud ubi, non sequeretur : hoc corpus est hic, ita quod non alibi ; ergo est finitum secundum ubi, quia ly hic non demonstrat nisi infinitum. Item, secundum Philosophum, si motus esset infinitus et tempus infinitum, non sequitur : iste motus est in hoc tempore et non in alio ; ergo est finitum secundum tempus. Ita ad propositum, oporteret probare illud quod demonstratur per ly hoc esse finitum. Quod si assumatur, petitur conclusio in praemissa.

Ad ultimum dico, quod Philosophus infert moveri in non-tempore ex hoc antecedente, quod potentia infinita est in magnitudine, et intelligit in consequente moveri proprie, ut distinguitur contra mutationem, et hoc modo consequens includit contradictionem, et etiam antecedens, secundum eum. Qualiter autem teneat illa consequentia, sic declaro : si potentia est infinita et agit ex

can exist at once, even though one body cannot fill a place already occupied by another. The other consequence is also invalid, for if an infinite body were to coexist with another body, the reason the combination of the two would be greater than either taken singly lies in the nature of extension, for the dimensions of this other body would be different from those of the infinite body and still they would be qualitatively the same. Therefore, the union of two extended bodies implies an increase in extension because of the distinct dimensions and yet the sum total could not represent an increase, because an infinite extension cannot be exceeded. In our case, however, the total amount of infinite perfection is not increased quantitatively by the coexistence of some qualitatively similar finite entity.

To the third [51] *argument,* I say that the consequence does not hold unless, in the antecedent, the thing singled out from all the others is something finite. For example, to assume the impossible, if an infinite place were occupied by an infinite body, it still would not follow that this body is "here" in such a way that it is nowhere else, because the word "here", in this case, only designates what is infinite. Then too, according to the Philosopher,[52] if motion and time were infinite, from the proposition "this motion is at this time and not at another", it does not follow that motion is finite in duration. Consequently, if the desired conclusion is to be established, it would be necessary to prove that whatever is designated by the word "this" is finite. To assume it simply begs the question.

To the last [53] *argument,* I say that the Philosopher argues that if the antecedent be true (viz. that some power is of infinite magnitude), it would move instantaneously, where he understands "moves" in the proper sense as different from mutation. In this sense, according to him, the consequent as well as the antecedent is self-contradictory. I will show, however, how this consequence could be made

necessitate naturae, ergo agit in non-tempore. Quia si agat in tempore, sit illud A, et accipiatur alia virtus finita quae in tempore finito agit, sit illud B ; et augmentetur virtus finita quae est B secundum proportionem illam quae est B ad A. Puta, si A [*MS* B] est centuplum vel milletuplum ad B [*MS* A], accipiatur virtus centupla ad illam virtutem finitam datam, vel milletupla. Igitur illa virtus sic augmentata movebit in A tempore, et ita virtus illa et infinita in aequali tempore movebunt, quod est impossibile, si virtus infinita movet secundum ultimum potentiae suae et necessario. Ex hoc ergo quod virtus est infinita sequitur quod si agat ex necessitate, agit non in tempore. Ex hoc autem quod ponitur in antecedente, quod est in magnitudine sequitur si agit circa corpus quod proprie moveat illud corpus, quod loquitur de virtute extensa per accidens. Talis autem virtus si ageret circa corpus, haberet partes hujus corporis diversimode distantes respectu ejus : puta unam partem corporis propinquiorem et aliam remotiorem ; habet etiam resistentiam aliquam in corpore, circa quod agit, quae duae causae, scilicet resistentia et diversa approximatio partium mobilis ad ipsum movens, faciunt successionem esse in motu et corpus proprie moveri. Ergo ex hoc quod in antecedente illo ponitur virtus in magnitudine sequitur quod proprie movebit, et ita jungendo illa duo simul, scilicet quod est infinitum et quod est in magnitudine, sequitur quod [*MS om.* proprie] in non-tempore movebit, quod est contradictio. Sed istud non sequitur de virtute infinita quae non est in magnitudine, ipsa enim licet in non-tempore agat, si in non-tempore agit, quia hoc sequitur infinitatem, tamen non proprie

to hold. If a power is infinite and acts by necessity of
nature, then it acts instantaneously. If it were to act in
time, let us call this time *A*. Now take another finite
power, which acts in the finite time *B*. Then let the
finite power, which acts in *B* time, be increased by the
amount that *A* exceeds *B*, e.g. if *A* is one hundred or one
thousand times as great as *B*, let the finite power be
increased a hundred—or a thousand fold. Now, this
increased power would act in *A* time. Consequently,
this finite power would act in the same time as the infinite, which is impossible if the infinite power moves
necessarily and to the utmost of its ability. Therefore,
if an infinite power acts necessarily, it follows that it
acts instantaneously. On the other hand, however, if
we assume, as the antecedent does, that this power has
magnitude, i.e. is extended accidentally, then it follows
that if it acts on a body, it moves this body in the proper
sense of moving. But if such a power acted upon a
body, it would be at unequal distance from the different
parts of this body, that is, one part of the body would
be closer, whereas another would be farther away.
Then, too, this power would meet with some resistance
in the body on which it acts. Now these two causes
(viz. resistance and the difference in distance between
the mover and the various parts of the thing moved)
give rise to succession in motion and, therefore, cause
the body to be moved in the proper sense of that term.
From the fact, then, that we assume in the antecedent
a power with magnitude, it follows that it moves in the
proper sense, and thus by combining these two notions
simultaneously, namely that it is infinite and that it has
magnitude,[54] it follows that it moves in the strict sense
of the term and, nevertheless, does so instantaneously,
which is a contradiction. This contradiction, however,
does not follow from the notion of an infinite power which
has no magnitude. For although it would act instantaneously, were it infinite and necessarily acting, still it

movebit, quia non habebit in passo illas duas rationes successionis. Non igitur vult Philosophus quod infinita potentia proprie moveat in non-tempore, sicut argumentum procedit, sed quod infinita potentia in magnitudine proprie moveat et non in tempore, quae sunt contradictoria. Et ex hoc sequitur quod talis antecedens includit contradictoria, scil. quod virtus infinita sit in magnitudine.

Sed tunc est dubitatio : cum potentiam motivam ponat infinitam et naturaliter agentem, videtur sequi quod necessario ageret in non-tempore ; licet non moveat in non-tempore ; imo tunc nihil movebit aliud proprie loquendo. Et quod hoc sequatur patet : quia illud probatum fuit prius per rationem potentiae infinitae necessario agentis.

Respondet Averroes duodecimo *Metaphysicae*,* quod praeter primum movens, quod est infinitae potentiae, requiritur movens conjunctum potentiae finitae, ita quod ex primo movente sit infinitas motus et ex secundo sit successio, quia aliter non posset esse successio nisi concurreret illud finitum, quia si solum infinitum ageret, ageret in non-tempore. Illud improbatur distinctione octava quaestione ultima,† ubi in hoc arguitur contra philosophos, qui ponunt primum agere ex necessitate quidlibet quod immediate agit.

Sed Christianis non est argumentum difficile, qui dicunt Deum contingenter agere. Ipsi enim possunt faciliter respondere, quia licet virtus infinita necessario agens agat secundum ultimum sui, et ita in non-tempore, quidquid immediate agit, non tamen virtus infinita contingenter et libere agens ; sicut enim est in potestate ejus agere vel non agere, ita est in potestate ejus in

---

* xii, com. 41.   † *Opus oxoniense*, i, dist. viii, q. v, nn. 3, 8 ff.

would not move, properly speaking, since the two reasons for succession would be absent in that on which it acts. The Philosopher, therefore, does not mean that an infinite power would move instantaneously as the argument assumes, but that a power infinite in magnitude, though it is not in time, nevertheless moves in the proper sense, which is a contradiction. From this it follows that such an antecedent includes contradictory notions, namely a power infinite in magnitude.

But a doubt arises. Since an infinite motive power acting of necessity is assumed, it would seem to follow necessarily that this power acts instantaneously, even though it may not move instantaneously. Consequently, it follows further, that no agent will move another properly speaking. That this would follow is clear from what was just proved above regarding an infinite necessarily acting power.

Averroes in *Metaphysics*, BK. XII,* replies that it is not enough simply to have an infinitely powerful First Mover. What is further required is that this First Mover and some additional finite power co-operate in such a way that the infinity of the motion is due to the First Mover, whereas the succession is due to the other. Without the co-operation of some finite mover, succession would be impossible ; for if only the infinite agent acted, it would act instantaneously. This solution will be disproved in the last question of distinction eight † where the philosophers who assume that whatever the First Cause does immediately, it does with necessity, are attacked.

But for Christians, who say that God acts contingently, the objection presents no difficulty, since they can answer it with ease. For, even if an infinite power which acts necessarily and to the utmost of its power, does instantaneously whatever it does immediately, this is not true of an infinite power which acts freely and contingently. As it is in the power of such an agent either to act or not to act, so it has the power either to act in time or to act

tempore agere vel in non-tempore agere ; et ita facile
est salvare primum movere corpus in tempore, licet sit
infinitae potentiae, quia non necessario agit nec secundum ultimum potentiae quantum scilicet posset agere,
neque in tam brevi tempore in quam brevi posset agere.

instantaneously. Consequently, it is easy to defend the position that the First Cause moves a body in time even if it be of infinite power, for it does not act necessarily neither to the full extent of its power nor in as short a time as it could.

IV

THE UNICITY OF GOD

Summary of the Argument

QUESTION : Is there but one God ?

PRO ET CONTRA

BODY OF THE QUESTION

First opinion : The unicity of God is known only by faith

Scotus's opinion : Natural reason can prove the unicity of God

First proof :	From the infinite intellect
Second proof :	From the infinite will
Third proof :	From the infinite goodness
Fourth proof :	From the infinite power
Fifth proof :	From absolute infinity
Sixth proof :	From necessity of existence
Seventh proof :	From the omnipotence

Reply to the arguments for the first opinion

REPLY TO THE ARGUMENTS AT THE BEGINNING

[IV. DE UNITATE DEI] *

Quaero utrum sit tantum unus Deus?

[Pro et Contra]

Et quod non arguitur :

Quorum dicuntur multi domini et dii multi.†

Item, si Deus est, ergo dii sunt. Probatur consequentia, quia singulare et plurale idem significant, licet differant in modo significandi ; ergo idem includit praedicatio proportionaliter accepta ; ergo sicut singulare includit singulare, ita plurale includit plurale. Probatur secundo [*MS* tertio], quia sicut Deus est quo majus cogitari non potest, ita dii sunt quibus majores cogitari non possunt. Illa autem quibus majora cogitari non possunt sunt in effectu. Quod videtur, quia si non essent in effectu, possent cogitari majora eis ; ergo, etc.

Praeterea, omne ens per participationem reducitur ad aliquid tale per essentiam. Individua in quacumque specie creata sunt entia per participationem, alioquin non essent multa ; ergo reducuntur ad aliquid tale per essentiam. Ergo est aliquis homo, aliquis bos per essentiam, etc. Quidquid autem est per essentiam, non per participationem, est Deus ; ergo, etc.

Item, plura bona sunt paucioribus meliora. Sed quaecumque meliora sunt ponenda in universo ; ergo, etc.

Item, quidquid si est, est necesse esse, est simpliciter

* *Opus oxoniense*, I, dist. II, q. iii (Assisi 137, f. 18r^b-19r^b; cf. Vatican ed., VOL. II, 222-243).

[IV. THE UNICITY OF GOD]

I ask whether there is but one God?

[Pro et Contra]

Some argue there is not merely one God [1] :

[Arg. i]. "For indeed there are many gods and many lords".

[Arg. ii]. Also, if God exists, then gods exist. Proof of the consequence : (1) Singular and plural signify the same, although they differ in the way in which they do so. Therefore, the predication proportionately implies the same. As the singular mode then implies a singular thing, so the plural implies several things.[2] (2) Just as God is that greater than which nothing can be conceived, so gods are those greater than which nothing can be thought. Things that could not be conceivably greater, however, actually exist. This is clear from the fact that if they did not actually exist, we could think of something greater than they. Therefore, etc.

[Arg. iii]. Furthermore, everything which is a being by participation can be traced back to something which is such by its very essence.[3] Now the individuals in any created species are beings by participation ; otherwise more than one individual per species would not exist. Therefore, they can be traced back to something which is such by its very essence. Consequently, there is some man who is by his essence, some ox which is by its essence, and so on. Now whatever is by its essence and not by participation is God. Therefore, etc.

[Arg. iv]. Likewise, a greater number of good things is better than a lesser number.[4] But we should assume the best to exist in the universe. Therefore, etc.

[An additional argument].[5] Also, whatever is a

necesse esse ; sed alius Deus si est, est necesse esse ; ergo, etc. Major probatur : da oppositum praedicati "non est necesse esse simpliciter", et sequitur oppositum subjecti quod scilicet si est, est possibile esse et non necesse esse. Respondeo : Debet inferri oppositum subjecti sic, " non est necesse esse, si est", ubi negetur habitudo inter antecedens et consequens.

Contra :

Deuter. 6.* Audi Israel : Dominus Deus tuus Deus unus est ; et Is.† : Extra me non est Deus.

[Corpus Quaestionis]

In illa quaestione conclusio est certa ; sed dicunt aliqui quod haec conclusio non est demonstrabilis, sed tantum accepta per fidem. Et ad hoc sequitur auctoritas Rabbi Moysi, xxiii cap.,‡ quod unitas Dei accepta est a Lege. Hoc etiam arguitur per rationem, quia si per naturalem rationem posset cognosci Deum esse unicum, ergo posset cognosci Deum esse singularem naturaliter ; ergo posset cognosci singularitas Dei et essentia ut singularis, quod falsum est et supra [*read* contra] prius dictum est in quaestione de subjecto theologiae.

[*Opinio Scoti*]

Videtur tamen quod illa unitas posset naturali ratione ostendi ; et hoc sumendo viam primo ex infinito

---

* Deut. vi. 4. † Isaias, xlv. 5.
‡ *Doctor perplexorum*, i, cap. lxxv.

necessary being, if it exist, is necessary being without qualification. But if another God exists, He is a necessary being. Therefore, etc. Proof of the major : If you grant the opposite of the predicate (viz. "[it] is not necessary being without qualification"), the opposite of the subject follows (viz. "It is not necessary but only possible being, if it exists").—Reply : The opposite of the subject which is to be inferred is this. "It is not a necessary being, if it exists." Here, then, the relation between antecedent and consequent may be denied.

To the contrary :

In *Deuteronomy* * we read : "Hear O Israel, the Lord our God is one Lord", and in *Isaias*† : "There is no God besides me".

[Body of the Question]

In this question, the conclusion is certain.

[*First Opinion*]

Some say,[6] however, that the unicity of God cannot be demonstrated but is accepted only on faith. And in this they follow the authority of Rabbi Moses [Maimonides] ‡ who says that it is known from the Law that God is one. Reason supports this view, for if the mind by its natural powers could know that God is one, then it could also know naturally that God is singular. In this case, natural reason could know the singularity of God and could also know the essence of God as singular, which is false and contradicts what was said in the question about the subject of theology.[7]

[*Scotus's Opinion*]

Nevertheless, it seems that natural reason could establish the unicity of God by arguing from (1) the infinite

intellectu ; secundo ex infinita voluntate ; tertio ex infinita bonitate ; quarto ex ratione infinitae potentiae ; quinto ex ratione infiniti absolute ; sexto ex ratione necesse esse ; septimo ex ratione omnipotentiae.

[*Prima Via*]. Ex parte intellectus infiniti arguitur sic primo. Intellectus infinitus cognoscit intelligibile quodcumque perfectissime quantum est intelligibile in se ; ergo si sunt dii, sint A et B. A cognoscit B perfectissime, quantum scilicet B est cognoscibile : sed hoc est impossibile. Probatio : quia aut cognoscit B per essentiam B, aut non. Si non, et B est cognoscibile per essentiam, ergo non cognoscit B perfectissime et quantum scilicet est cognoscibile. Nihil enim cognoscibile per essentiam perfectissime cognoscitur, nisi cognoscitur per essentiam suam, vel per aliquid perfectius includens essentiam suam quam ipsa sit in se. Essentia autem B in nullo perfectius includitur quam in B, quia tunc B non esset Deus. Si autem cognoscit B per essentiam ipsius B, ergo actus ipsius A est posterius naturaliter essentia ipsius B, et ita A non erit Deus. Quod autem actus ipsius A sit posterior ipso B probatio, quia omnis actus cognoscendi qui non est idem objecto est posterior objecto ; neque enim prior neque simul natura est actus cum aliquo alio ab actu, quia tunc actus posset intelligi sine objecto, sicut econverso.

Si dicatur quod illa intelligit B per essentiam ipsius A, quae simillima est ipsi B, sic videlicet quod A intelligit B in ratione speciei communis ipsi A et ipsi B. Contra : neutra salvat responsio quod A intelligat B perfectissime, et per consequens non est Deus, quia cognitio alicujus in simili tantum, et in universali non est cognitio perfectissima et intuitiva ipsius rei, et ita A non cognosceret B intuitive nec perfectissime, quod est propositum.

intellect, (2) the infinite will, (3) the infinite goodness, (4) the infinite power, (5) the notion of infinity considered absolutely, (6) the nature of necessary being, and (7) omnipotence.

[*First Proof*]. The first argument, based on the infinite intellect, is this. Such an intellect knows whatever can be known in the most perfect way that it could be known. Suppose then that two gods existed, let us call them *A* and *B*. *A*, therefore, would know *B* as perfectly as *B* could be known. This, however, is impossible. Proof : Either *A* knows *B* through the essence of *B* or not. If not, and *B* can be known through its essence, then *A* knows *B* neither in the most perfect manner nor to the extent that *B* can be known. For nothing that can be known through its essence is perfectly known unless it be known either through its essence or through something which includes the essence in a more perfect way than the latter exists in itself. But the essence of *B* is not included in anything more perfect than *B*, for it it were, *B* would not be God. But if *A* knows *B* through the latter's essence, then *A*'s act of knowledge is posterior to the essence of *B* and therefore *A* would not be God. I prove that in such a case *A*'s act would be posterior to *B* in this fashion. Every act of knowing not identical with its object is posterior to that object. For an act by nature is simultaneous only with itself. Neither is it prior to its object, for then the act could be known without the object and vice versa.

But suppose we say that *A* through its own essence knows *B* because of the great similarity between the two, so that *A* knows *B* through some nature common to *A* and *B*. To the contrary : This answer saves neither of these two points : viz. (1) that *A* knows *B* most perfectly, and therefore, (2) that *A* is God. For any such knowledge that is merely general and in virtue of some likeness is neither perfect nor intuitive. Consequently, *A* would not know *B* intuitively or most perfectly, which is what we set out to prove.

Secundo ex parte intellectus arguitur sic, unica intellectio non potest habere duo objecta adaequata, A est objectum adaequatum suae intellectioni, quia A habet pro objecto adaequato essentiam suam ; ergo non habet essentiam B pro objecto adaequato. Esset autem B objectum adaequatum intellectioni A, si posset simul intelligere perfecte A et B. Major patet, quia aliter actus adaequatur objecto, quo abstracto, non minus quietaretur et adaequaretur, et ita frustra esset tale objectum.

[*Secunda Via*]. Quantum ad secundam viam arguitur sic : Voluntas infinita est recta ; ergo diligit quodlibet diligibile quantum est diligibile, et quanto amore potest si sit infinitum. B autem est diligendus in infinitum cum ponitur esse alius Deus. Et per consequens sit bonum infinitum et infinite a voluntate sic potenter diligere diligendum ; ergo voluntas A diligit B infinite : sed hoc est impossible, quia A naturaliter diligit plus se quam B. Probatio : quilibet enim naturaliter plus [*MS* prius] esse suum quam esse alterius, cujus non est pars vel effectus. A autem nihil est ipsius B nec ut pars nec ut effectus ; ergo plus diligit A se naturaliter quam ipsum B. Sed voluntas libera, quando est recta, conformatur voluntati naturali, alioquin voluntas naturalis non esset semper recta ; ergo A si habet istam voluntatem rectam, actu elicito plus diligit se quam B, ergo non B infinite.

Secundo sic de voluntate : aut A fruitur B aut utitur. Si utitur eo, ergo habet A voluntatem inordinatam. Si fruitur B et fruitur A, ergo A est beatus in duobus objectis, quorum neutrum dependet ab alio, quia sicut A beatus est in se, sic et in B ; sed consequens est impossibile, quia nihil potest esse actu beatum in duobus

A second argument based on the intellect is this. One and the same act of intellection cannot have two adequate objects. Now A is its own adequate object of intellection, for the essence of A is the adequate object of A's intellection. Consequently B's essence is not its adequate object. But if A could know perfectly both itself and B at one and the same time, then B would be an adequate object of A's intellection. The major is evident, for otherwise the intellect could be perfectly satisfied and have all that it is capable of even though its adequate object were non-existent. Such an object, consequently, would be useless.

[*Second Proof*]. A second way is this. Any will that is infinite wills things the way they should be willed. Therefore, it loves whatever is lovable to the extent that it is lovable. If the object is infinitely lovable, then such a will loves it to the utmost of its ability. But since B is assumed to be another God, it must be loved infinitely. Consequently, B inasmuch as it is infinitely good must be loved infinitely by any power capable of infinite love. The will of A, then, loves B infinitely. Now this is impossible since A naturally loves itself more than B.[8] Proof : Everything naturally loves its own being more than any other if it is neither a part nor an effect of this other. But A is neither a part nor the effect of B ; therefore A loves itself naturally more than B. But a free will that loves things as they should be loved conforms itself to this natural will ; otherwise the natural will would not always be as it should be. Therefore, if A wills as it should, then it elicits a greater act of love for itself than for B and hence does not love B infinitely.

A second argument based on the will runs as follows. Either A finds its happiness in B or it simply uses B. If it merely uses B, then A's love is inordinate.[9] If it finds its happiness in B as well as in itself, then A is beatified by two distinct objects, neither of which depends upon the other, for A is made just as happy by B as it is by itself.

objectis beatificantibus totalibus. Probatio :   quia
utroque destructo, nihilominus esset beatus ; ergo in
neutro est beatus.

[*Tertia Via*]. De tertia via, scilicet de ratione infiniti
[boni], arguitur sic : voluntas ordinate potest appetere
majus bonum et magis amare majus bonum. Sed plura
bona infinita, si sint possibilia, plus includunt bonitatis
quam unum infinitum ; ergo voluntas ordinate plus
posset amare plura infinita quam unum, et per consequens in nullo uno objecto infinito quietaretur. Sed
hoc est contra rationem boni quod sit infinitum et non
quietativum cujuscumque voluntatis.

[*Quarta Via*]. Quantum ad quartam viam de potentia
infinita arguo sic : non possunt esse duae causae totales
ejusdem effectus in eodem ordine causae ; sed infinita
potentia est causa totalis respectu cujuscumque effectus
in ratione primae causae ; ergo nulla alia potest esse in
ratione causae primae respectu alicujus effectus, et ita
nulla alia causa infinita in potentia. Primam propositionem probo : quia tunc posset aliquid esse causa
alicujus a quo illud non dependeret. Probatio : a nullo
aliquid   dependet   essentialiter,   quo   non   existente,
nihilominus esset ; sed si C habet duas causas totales
A et B, et in eodem ordine, utroque eorum non existente,
nihilominus esset ipsum C ab altero eorum, quia non
existente A, nihil minus est ipsum C ab ipso B et non
existente B, nihil minus est C ab A.

Juxta illud arguitur de unitate cujuscumque primi
in quacumque primitate praedicta. Nihil enim est
excessum a duobus primo excedentibus ; vel finitum
essentialiter ordinatur [*MS* ordinantur] ad duos primos
fines. Esset [*MS* essent] enim aliquid ad finem, quo non

But the consequent is impossible, for nothing finds its complete happiness in each of two objects.[10] Proof : Either object could be destroyed and nevertheless the being would still be happy. Therefore in neither object is it completely happy.

[*Third Proof*]. The third way, based on the notion of the infinite good, is this. It is proper for a will to seek the greater good and love it more ardently. But if more than one thing could be infinitely good, then together they would contain more goodness than a single infinite good. An orderly will, consequently, could not be perfectly satisfied with but one infinite good. Yet to be unable to satisfy perfectly any will whatsoever contradicts the very notion of an infinite good.

[*Fourth Proof*]. My fourth argument, from infinite power, is this. Two causes of the same order cannot each be the total cause of the same effect. But an infinite power is the total primary cause of every single effect that exists. Therefore, no other power can be the total primary cause of any effect. Consequently, no other cause is infinite in power. My proof of the first proposition : If this proposition did not hold, then a thing could be the cause of something which does not depend upon it. Proof : Nothing depends essentially on anything if it could exist even when this other is non-existent. But if *C* has two total causes, *A* and *B*, each of which is in the same order, then either could be non-existent and still *C* would continue to exist in virtue of the other. For if *A* were non-existent, *C* would still exist by reason of *B* and if *B* were non-existent, *C* would exist by reason of *A*.

This argument can be used to establish the unicity of any of the primacies mentioned above [viz. efficiency, finality and eminence].[11] What exists for the sake of an end is never essentially ordered to two ultimate ends, for then, as we argued above, it would exist for the sake of something which, as non-existent, would still be the

existente, nihil minus esset finitum, ut prius argutum
est ; et excessum esset essentialiter ab aliquo, quo non
existente, nihil minus haberet essentiale excedens, quo
mensuraretur essentialiter et a quo acciperet suam
perfectionem essentialiter : quod est impossibile ; ergo
impossibile est aliquorum duorum infinitorum duos esse
fines primos vel duorum excessorum duo prima eminentia.

[*Quinta Via*]. De quinta via dico, quod infinitum non
potest excedi, et arguo sic ; quaecumque perfectio potest
numerari in diversis plus perfectionis habet in pluribus
quam in uno, sicut dicitur VIII *De Trinitate*, c. 1* ;   ergo
infinitum omnino in pluribus numerari non potest.

[*Sexta Via*]. De sexta via primo arguo sic : species
plurificabilis scilicet in individuis non determinatur ex
se ad certum numerum individuorum, sed quantum est
ex se compatitur infinitatem individuorum, sicut patet
in speciebus omnibus corruptibilibus ; ergo si ratio
necesse esse sit plurificabilis in individuis, non determinat se ad certum numerum, sed compatitur infinitatem
quantum est ex se.   Sed si possent esse infinita necesse
esse, sunt infinita necesse esse ; ergo, etc.   Consequens
est falsum ; ergo et antecedens ex quo sequitur.
    Ista ratio in alia forma fiat ex ratione primitatis sic :
Unum unius rationis se habens ad plura unius rationis
non determinatur ad illam pluralitatem sive ad deter-
minationem certam illorum.   Non est instantia in natura
respectu suppositorum nec in causa respectu causatorum,
nisi instes in proposito.   Sed deitas erit unum unius ra-

---

* VIII, cap. i (Migne, P.L., XLII, 947–948).

end for whose sake the other exists. Neither is anything excelled to the ultimate degree by two most perfect beings, for then something could be non-existent and still excel something either as its essential measure of perfection or as that from which it receives its essential perfection. This, however, is impossible. It is not possible, then, that two infinite beings should be ultimate ends, or that of two more perfect beings, both should be the most excellent.

[*Fifth Proof*]. As to the fifth way, I say that what is absolutely infinite, cannot be excelled. And I argue thus. Any perfection that can exist in numerically different things is more perfect if it exist in several than if it exist merely in one, as [Augustine] points out in *De Trinitate*, BK. VIII, c. i.* Therefore, what is absolutely infinite cannot be found in several numerically different things.

[*Sixth Proof*]. The sixth way that I argue is this. A species which can be multiplied in more than one individual, is not of itself determined to any certain number of individuals but is compatible with an infinity of individuals. This is evident in the case of all perishable species. Therefore, if the perfection of necessary existence can be multiplied in more than one individual, it is not of itself restricted to any certain number, but is compatible with infinity. But if an infinity of necessary beings can exist, they do exist. Therefore, etc. The consequence is false ; hence the antecedent is also false.

This argument can be reformulated on the basis of [God's] primacy as follows. One thing of a given kind is not related to others of its kind in such a way that it is limited to just this plurality or to a certain number of such things. There is nothing in the nature itself which requires that there be just so many individuals, nor in a cause that says there must be only so many things caused, unless you insist on what we seek to prove [viz. that the nature is such that it be found in but one individual]. But "deity" is one given kind of thing, and

tionis et per te se habet ad plura unius rationis, ergo ex se non determinatur ad certam pluralitatem singularium nec potest determinari aliunde, quia hoc repugnat primo, ergo deitas est in suppositis infinitis. Ista ratio videtur quod fundatur super hoc quod primitas est de se indeterminata.

Secundo arguo sic et juxta istam viam. Si sint plura necesse esse, aliquibus perfectionibus realibus distinguuntur. Sint illae A et B. Tunc sic : aut illa duo distincta per A et B sunt formaliter necesse esse per A et per B, aut non. Si non, ergo A non est ratio formalis essendi necessario, nec B. Per consequens, nec ergo ea includens est necessarium primo, quia includit aliquam entitatem quae non est formaliter necessitas essendi, nec necessaria ex se. Si autem illa sint formaliter necesse esse per A et B, et praeter haec utrumque est necesse esse per illud in quo convenit unum cum alio, ergo utrumque habet in se duas rationes, quarum utrumque formaliter est necesse esse. Sed hoc est impossibile, quia neutra illarum includit alteram ; utraque ergo illarum circumscripta, esset tale necesse esse per reliquam, et ita aliquid esset formaliter necesse esse per rationem aliquam, qua circumscripta, nihilominus esset necesse esse, quod est impossibile.

[*Septima Via*]. De septima via, scilicet omnipotentia, videtur quod non sit per rationem naturalem demonstrabile, quia omnipotentia, ut alias patebit, non potest concludi ratione naturali, ut catholici intelligunt omnipotentiam, nec concluditur ex ratione infinitae potentiae. Tamen ex omnipotentia credita arguitur sic propositum. Si A est omnipotens, ergo potest facere circa quod-

according to you is found in more than one individual of its kind. Therefore, deity as such is not determined to any certain number of individuals nor can it be so determined by anything other than itself, for this would be repugnant to what is truly first. Therefore, deity exists in an infinite number of individuals. This argument, as we see, is based upon the notion that primacy of itself is indetermined.

The second argument I give, based on this way, runs as follows. If several necessary beings existed, they would be distinguished from one another by some real perfections. Let us call these *A* and *B*. Then I argue, either these two necessary beings which differ by *A* and *B* are necessary formally in virtue of *A* and *B*, or they are not. If not, then *A* is not a formal reason for necessary existence, and the same is true of *B*. Hence, whatever includes *A* or *B* is not primarily a necessary being, because it includes some entity which is neither its necessity of existence nor is it necessary of itself. If, however, these two beings are formally necessary in virtue of *A* and *B*, in addition to being necessary by reason of what they have in common, then each being contains two reasons why it is formally necessary. This, however, is impossible for neither of these two reasons includes the other, and hence if either of the two were absent, the being would still exist necessarily in virtue of what remains. In such an impossible situation, something would owe its formal necessity to what could be removed and still leave the being a necessary being.

[*Seventh Proof*]. As regards the seventh way, from omnipotence, it seems that the thesis cannot be demonstrated by natural reason, for omnipotence—as Catholics understand the term—cannot be demonstrated from natural reason, nor does it follow from the notion of infinite power, as will be shown later. Still, if omnipotence be accepted on faith, then one can argue that if *A* is omnipotent, it can make everything other than itself

cumque aliud ipsum esse vel non esse, et ita posset destruere B, et ita faceret B nullipotentem, et sic sequitur quod B non est Deus.

Ista ratio non valet, sicut quidam respondent ad eam, quia B non est objectum omnipotentiae, quia omnipotentia pro objecto respicit possibile ; B autem ponebatur necessarium sicut A.

Ideo arguitur aliter declarando sic rationem Richardi secundo *De Trinitate*, cap. xvii vel ultimo,* ubi dicit sic : facile efficere poterit quisquis omnipotens fuerit ita quod omne aliud nihil possit, sicut omnipotens per suum velle [*MS add* vel sicut omnipotens suo velle] potest producere quodcumque possibile, ita suo nolle potest impedire vel destruere omne possibile. Sed si A est omnipotens, potest velle omnia alia a se esse et ita suo velle ipsa in esse producere. Non necesse est autem quod B velit omnia illa esse quae vult A, quia voluntas B contingenter se habet ad illa, sicut voluntas A ad illa quae B vult, si est Deus. Si autem B nolit illa esse, ergo nullum illorum est. Ergo si sint duo omnipotentes, uterque illorum faceret alium nullipotentem, non destruendo illum sed prohibendo per suum nolle esse volitorum ab alio.

Quod si dicas quasi sophisticando quod concordent in voluntate sua, quamvis nulla sit necessitas, sed quasi fecerint pactum, adhuc probo quod neuter eorum erit omnipotens ; nam si A est omnipotens, potest producere suo velle quodcumque producibile volitum aliud a se. Ex hoc sequitur quod B nullum poterit producere suo velle, et ita non est omnipotens. Quod autem hoc sequitur, patet ex quarta via, quia impossibile est duas

* I, cap. xxv (Migne, P.L., CXCVI, 902).

come into existence or go out of existence. Consequently, it can destroy B and thus render B impotent. From this it follows that B is not God.

Some [12] object that this reason does not hold since B is not an object of omnipotence, for omnipotence has as its object only what can, yet need not, exist, whereas B is assumed to be just as necessary as A.

Wherefore, we must reformulate the argument of Richard [of St Victor] in his work *De Trinitate** where he says : "Whoever will have been omnipotent, will easily be able to make everything else impotent". Just as an omnipotent being can produce whatever is possible simply by willing that it should be, so also he can impede or destroy everything that is possible by willing that it should not be. But if A is omnipotent, he can will everything other than himself and so, by his will, cause everything to exist. It is not necessary, however, that B will everything which A wills because the will of B is related only contingently to what A wills, even as the will of A is related contingently to what B wills, assuming here that each is God. But if B wills that none of these things should exist, then none will exist. Consequently, if two omnipotent beings exist, each will make the other impotent, not indeed by destroying the other, but because one by his positive will could keep non-existent what the other wills should exist.

And if you say, to argue sophistically, that they voluntarily agree on a common way of acting through some sort of pact, even though there is really no intrinsic necessity that they do so, still I prove that neither will be omnipotent. For if A is omnipotent, by willing he can produce every possible thing that can be produced and thus B can produce nothing by willing and hence will not be omnipotent. That this follows is clear from what was said in the fourth way. For it is impossible that two total causes should produce one and the same effect,

causas esse totales unius effectus, quia ex quo totaliter causatus est ab una, impossibile est quod sit ab alia.

[*Ad Argumenta Pro Prima Opinione*]

Ad argumenta primo enim ad illa quae sunt pro alia opinione respondeo ad auctoritatem Rabbi Moysi et dico quod Deum esse unum creditur in Lege quia enim populus fuit rudis et pronus ad idolatriam. Ideo indiguit instrui per Legem de unitate Dei, licet per naturalem rationem posset demonstrari. Ita etiam acceptum est a Lege quod Deus sit : Exod. III * : Ego sum qui sum, et Apostolus ad Hebraeos,† dicit quod oportet accedentem ad Deum credere quia est, et tamen non negatur Deum esse demonstrabile. Ergo pari ratione nec negandum est posse demonstrari per rationem Deum esse unum, licet accepta sit a Lege. Illa etiam possunt demonstrari utile est communitati tradi etiam per viam auctoritatis et propter negligentiam communitatis in inquirendo veritatem et etiam propter impotentiam intellectus, et propter errores inquirentium per demonstrationem, quia veritatibus suis multa falsa permiscent, ut dicit Augustinus XVIII *De Civitate Dei*,‡ et ideo quia simplices sequentes tales demonstratores possent dubitare, cui esset asserendum vel assentiendum. Ideo tuta est via et stabilis et communis, auctoritas certa [*MS add.* circa] quae non potest fallere nec falli.

Ad secundam rationem de singulari dico quod aliud est singularitatem esse conceptam vel ut objectum vel ut partem objecti, aliud singularitatem esse praecise modum concipiendi sive sub quo concipitur objectum. Exemplum cum dico "universale" [*MS* "velle"], objectum conceptum est pluralitas, sed modus concipiendi, id est modus sub quo concipitur, est singularitas. Ita in

---

* Exodus, III. 14.   † Heb. XI. 6.
‡ XVIII, cap. xli (Migne, P.L., XLI, 601).

for what is caused completely by one cannot be caused by the other.

[Reply to the arguments for the First Opinion] [13]

First I answer the arguments for the other opinion, replying first to the authority of Rabbi Moses. I say that the reason God's unicity was a matter of belief in the Law is to be found in the fact that the people were uneducated and prone to idolatry. Consequently, they needed the Law to tell them that there is but one God even though this truth could be demonstrated by natural reason. The fact that God exists is also known from the Law, for instance, *Exodus*, III* : "I am who am", and the Apostle to the Hebrews † : "For he who comes to God must believe that God exists". Nevertheless, we do not deny that God's existence is demonstrable. On the same grounds, then, we must not deny that reason can demonstrate that there is but one God just because this is accepted from the Law. Indeed it is good that many things demonstrable in themselves be transmitted to the human race by way of authority also because of man's weakness of intellect, his neglect to seek the truth and because of the mistakes he makes when he tries to demonstrate something. As Augustine says in the *City of God*, ‡ much falsity is mixed with truth, and since simple people following such demonstrators could still be in doubt about what they must assent to, the firm, safe and common way is by means of authority so certain it can neither deceive nor be deceived.

As for the second reason about the singular, I say that it is one thing to conceive singularity as an object or part of an object. It is quite another thing to have singularity as a mode of conception or as the aspect under which the object is conceived. For example, when I say "a universal", the object conceived is plurality, but singularity is the mode of conception, that is, it is conceived as a singular thing. So also with logical intentions. When

intentionibus logicis, cum dico "singulare", quod concipitur est singularitas, sed modus sub quo concipitur
est universalitas, quia quod concipitur ut concipitur
habet indifferentiam ad plura. Ita dico in proposito,
quod essentia divina potest concipi ut singularis, ita quod
singularitas sit concepta vel ut objectum vel ut pars
objecti. Non tamen sequitur quod essentia possit cognosci ut est singularis, ita quod singularitas sit modus
concepti. Cognoscere enim sic aliquid ut singulare est
illud cognoscere ut hoc sicut album videtur ut hoc. Et
hoc modo praedictum est quod non cognoscitur essentia
divina sub ratione singularitatis, et ideo in argumento
est fallacia figurae dictionis, commutando rem in modum.

[Ad Argumenta Principalia]

Ad rationes principales, dico quod Apostolus loquitur
de idolis et ideo de diis nuncupative, et subdit ibi * :
Nobis autem unus est Deus, quia omnes dii gentium
daemonia.†

Ad secundam dico quod consequentia non valet, quia
numerus non est talis modus cognoscendi grammaticus
sicut alii modi grammaticales, qui praecise dicunt modum
concipiendi rei absque aliqua realitate correspondente
tali modo concipiendi ; unde [nec] dicunt praecise aliquid in re, a quo moveri possit intellectus ad talem
modum concipiendum, quamvis illud motivum non sit
aliquid in re (masculinitas enim non requirit aliquid
masculinum in re sed aliquid correspondens masculi-
nitati, scilicet potentiam activam vel aliquid hujusmodi).
Sed numerus vere includit rem substratum [*MS* sub-
tractam]. Unde sequitur "Homines currunt, ergo plures
homines currunt". Sed non sic de aliis consignificatis

* 1 Cor. VIII. 6.   † Ps. XCV. 5.

I say "singular", it is singularity that is conceived, but the mode of conception is that of a universal, for what I conceive is indifferent to being more than one. And so my answer to their assumption is this. The divine essence can be conceived as singular in the sense that singularity is conceived either as the object or part of the object. From this, however, it does not follow that the divine essence can be known as singular in such a way that singularity is the mode of conception, for to know something as singular in this way is to know it as "a this" just as a white object is seen as *this* white object. As we said above,[14] the divine essence is not known under the aspect of singularity in this manner. Therefore, the argument involves a fallacy of speech by substituting the mode for the thing.

[Reply to the Arguments at the Beginning]

To the initial arguments,[15] I say that the Apostle is speaking of idols and hence of so-called "gods", for in the same passage he adds : "Yet for us there is only one God", "for all the gods of the Gentiles are devils".

To the *second argument*,[16] I declare the consequence to be invalid inasmuch as number is not like some of the other grammatical modes which express precisely a mode of conception without any reality that corresponds to the conceptual mode, and consequently do not express precisely something in reality by which the intellect could be moved to conceive a thing the way it does, even where that motive be not something in the thing as such. For a noun to be masculine, for instance, it is not necessary that the thing designated by the noun be itself masculine. It suffices if it have something resembling masculinity, namely some active power or some such thing. Number, on the contrary, includes the underlying thing. Consequently, from the proposition "Men are running" it follows that several men are running. Such is not the

nominis vel verbi, quia non [*MS* bene] sequitur : "Deus est, igitur Deus est masculinus", quia ad masculinitatem sufficit aliquid in re a quo ille modus concipiendi possit accipi, puta activitas. Dico ergo quod illud solum "Dii" conceptum sub modo plurali includit contradictionem, quia modus concipiendi repugnat ei quod concipitur sub modo. Cum igitur probatur consequentia, quia idem includit singulare et plurale, dico quod singulare includit illud sub modo concipiendi convenienti ipsi concepto sed plurale includit illud sub modo impossibili illi concepto, et ideo singulare includit rationem quasi in se veram prout includit conceptum et modum concipiendi ; plurale autem prout includit ista duo includit rationem quasi in se falsam ; et ideo non sequitur quod plurale sit verum de plurali, sicut singulare de singulari, quia de eo cujus est ratio in se falsa nihil est verum. Per illud patet ad aliam probationem, quo majus cogitari non potest, quia non sunt dii cogitabiles sine contradictione, quia modus repugnat rei conceptae, et ideo major est glossanda sicut prius est dictum in quaestione praecedenti. Ad sensum autem et veritatem requiritur quod ratio subjecti non includit contradictionem, sicut dictum est in quaestione secunda hujus distinctionis.*

Ad tertiam dico quod illa major propositio non est prima, sed reducitur ad istam, "omne imperfectum reducitur ad perfectum". Et quia omne ens per participationem est imperfectum, et tantum illud ens est perfectum quod est ens per essentiam, ideo sequitur

---

* *Opus oxoniense*, i, dist. ii, q. ii, n. 5.

case, however, with the other co-significates of a noun or verb, for from the proposition "God is" [where the noun God or *Deus* is masculine gender] it does not follow that God Himself is masculine, for it suffices for a noun to be masculine if there is something about the reality that would justify this gender, for instance, activity. I say, therefore, that the subject "gods" conceived in the plural form includes a contradiction since the mode of conception is repugnant to what is conceived under this mode. As for the proof of the consequence, viz. that the singular and plural include the same thing, I reply that the singular includes it in a conceptual mode that is in harmony with the thing conceived whereas the plural includes it in a conceptual mode that is incompatible with the thing conceived. So far as the conceptual mode and the thing conceived are concerned, then, the singular includes a notion that is, as it were, true in itself, whereas the plural includes a notion that is, as it were, false in itself. Consequently, it does not follow that the plural is true of several as the singular is true of one, for nothing is true that is false in itself. And in this way we can answer the other proof for the consequence based on the proposition : "There is something in comparison with which nothing greater can be conceived." For "gods" is not something conceivable without contradiction, since the mode of conception is repugnant to the thing conceived. Consequently, the major must be glossed the way it was in the previous question. For if the proposition is to be true or to make any sense, it is necessary that the notion of the subject includes no inherent contradiction, as has been pointed out in the second question of this distinction.*

To the *third argument* [17] I reply that its major premise is not a primary truth but is reduced to this : "Everything imperfect is traced back to something perfect".[18] Since every being by participation is imperfect and only that being which is such by its essence is perfect, therefore this

14

propositio illa, scilicet quod "omne ens per participationem reducitur ad ens per essentiam quod est perfectum". Ut igitur vere possit sequi conclusio, haec autem major de [im]perfecto sic habet distingui. Aliquid est imperfectum secundum perfectionem simpliciter, quae non necessario habet imperfectionem concomitantem quia non includit in se limitationem, sicut "hoc bonum", "hoc verum", "hoc ens", et hujusmodi imperfectio reducitur ad perfectum ejusdem rationis, scilicet "bonum", "ens", et "verum", quae important perfectiones simpliciter. Aliquid autem est imperfectum secundum perfectionem non simpliciter, quae de ratione sui includit limitationem et ideo necessario habet imperfectionem annexam, ut "hic homo", "hic asinus", et hujusmodi imperfecta non reducuntur ad perfectum per essentiam absolute ejusdem rationis sicut ad rationem specificam quia ipsa adhuc includit imperfectionem, quia limitationem ; sed reducuntur ad perfectum primum quod continet ea supereminenter et aequivoce. Quod ergo imperfectum est primo modo, reducitur ad perfectum simpliciter secundum perfectionem illius rationis, quia aliquid secundum istam rationem potest esse simpliciter perfectum. Quod autem est imperfectum secundo modo non reducitur ad aliquid perfectum secundum perfectionem ejusdem rationis, quia enim illa imperfectionem includit. Ideo illa non potest esse perfectum simpliciter propter illam limitationem. Sed reducitur ad aliquid simpliciter perfectum aequivocum, eminenter includens illam perfectionem. Et ideo bonum imperfectum reducitur ad perfectum bonum, sed lapis, qui est imperfectus, non reducitur ad lapidem perfectum simpliciter, sed ad summum ens et ad summum bonum, quae includunt virtualiter illam perfectionem.

proposition follows : "Every being by participation is traced back to a perfect being that is such by its essence". Hence in order that the conclusion follow, the major premise regarding the "imperfect" must be distinguished as follows. Something is imperfect according to pure perfection. A pure perfection inasmuch as it includes no limitation in itself does not necessarily include some concomitant imperfection. Something imperfect according to pure perfection, for instance, would be "this good", "this true thing", "this being". Such imperfect things are reducible to something perfect of the same character, namely to "the Good", "the True", "Being", all of which imply pure perfection. Other things, however, are imperfect according to mixed perfection. A mixed perfection is one which includes some limitation and therefore necessarily has some added imperfection. "This man", "this donkey", and such like, would be imperfect in this way. Such things are not reduced specifically to something which possesses the same perfection absolutely by its essence, for the latter would still be imperfect because it is limited. They are reduced, however, to a perfect First Being which contains them in a more perfect and equivocal manner. What is imperfect in the first way, then, is reduced to a pure perfection of the same formal character, for something of this kind can be simply perfect. What is imperfect in the second way, however, cannot be reduced to something perfect of the same formal character, for the latter includes imperfection. Such a thing by reason of this limitation, then, cannot be simply perfect, but it is reduced to something which is simply perfect and which is of a different character, but includes the perfection of the imperfect being in a more excellent way. Consequently, an imperfect good is reduced to a perfect good, but an imperfect stone is not reduced to a stone which is simply perfect, but to the Highest Being and the Greatest Good which virtually include this perfection.

Ad ultimum dicitur quod plura bona finita sunt meliora paucioribus bonis finitis, non autem plura bona infinita. Sed hoc non videtur respondere ad argumentum, quia quaecumque si essent meliora essent, videntur ponenda esse in entibus, et maxime in ente supremo quod est necesse esse, quia ibi quidquid posset esse bonum est, et necesse est ibi esse. Sed plura bona infinita si essent essent meliora. Videtur igitur quod plura bona infinita sunt ponenda in natura summi boni.

Ad illud respondeo, quod cum dicitur in majori "illa quae si essent essent meliora, sunt ponenda ibi", dico quod aut per ly "si" implicatur positio possibilis aut positio incompossibilium. Si primo modo dico quod major est vera et minor falsa, quia implicatio illa in minori non possibilis sed incompossibilium. Si autem ly "si" implicet positionem incompossibilium, tunc minor est vera et major falsa, quae enim non essent meliora nisi ex positione incompossibilium, non essent meliora, nec etiam sunt bona, sicut illud quod non est nisi ex positione incompossibilium, omnino non est, sicut nec illud positum a quo dependet.

To the *last*,[19] some say [20] that a greater number of finite goods is better than a lesser number, but that the same is not true of infinite goods. This, however, does not seem to answer the difficulty, for it seems that whatever is better, if it can exist, should be assumed to exist in some being and in particular in that being which is supreme and exists necessarily, for whatever can be a good exists there and it is necessary that it exist there. Now if several infinite goods existed, this would be better. Therefore in a nature of the highest good it seems that more than one infinite good must be assumed to exist.

To this I reply that when the major premise declares that "those things are to be assumed to exist which would be better if they did exist", the term "if" implies the assumption of something possible or something impossible. If the first, then I say the major is true and the minor false, for what the minor implies is not possible but includes incompatible notions. But if the term "if" implies the assumption of the impossible, then the minor is true and the major false. For if some things are better only inasmuch as they assume the coexistence of incompatible notions, then they are not really better, nor for that matter are they really good. It is the same with something that can exist only if we assume the coexistence of incompatible notions. Such a thing is simply non-existent, and the same is true of the impossible basis postulated for it.

V

CONCERNING HUMAN KNOWLEDGE

Summary of the Argument

QUESTION : Can any certain and unadulterated truth be known
naturally by the intellect of a person in this life without the
special illumination of the Uncreated Light ?

PRO ET CONTRA

BODY OF THE QUESTION

[V. DE COGNITIONE HUMANA] *

Ultimo quantum ad materiam istam cognoscibilitatis, quaero *an aliqua veritas certa et sincera possit naturaliter cognosci ab intellectu viatoris absque lucis increatae speciali illustratione.*

[Pro et Contra]

Arguo quod non :

IX *De Trinitate,* cap. ultimo sexto vel decimo quinto † : Intueamur inviolabilem veritatem ex qua definiamus qualis esse mens hominis sempiternis rationibus debeat. Et ibidem, cap. decimo quinto : Aliis supra nos regulis manentibus vel approbare vel improbare convincimur quando aliquid recte vel non recte probamus vel improbamus. Et ibidem, cap. decimo septimo : Artem ineffabiliter pulchram super aciem mentis simplici intelligentia capientes. Et eodem, cap. octavo vel undevigesimo ‡ : In illa veritate ex qua temporalia sunt facta omnia formam conspicimus, atque inde conceptam notitiam tamquam verbum apud nos habemus.

Item, libro duodecimo, cap. secundo ** : Sublimioris rationis est judicare de istis corporalibus secundum rationes sempiternas.

Item, in eodem duodecimo, cap. decimo quarto vel trigesimo secundo †† : Non solum rerum sensibilium in locis positarum stant incommutabiles rationes, etc. Et quod intelligat ibi de rationibus aeternis vere in Deo, probatur per hoc quod ibidem dicit quod paucorum est

* *Opus oxoniense,* I, dist. III, q. iv (Assisi 137, f. 30v^b-33r^b; cf. Vatican ed., VOL. III, 123-172).
† IX, cap. vi (Migne, P.L., XLII, 966).
‡ cap. vii (Migne, P.L., XLII, 967).
** XII, cap. ii (Migne, P.L., XLII, 999).
†† XII, cap. xiv (Migne, P.L., XLII, 1010).

[V. CONCERNING HUMAN KNOWLEDGE]

Finally, on the subject of what we can know, I ask *whether any certain and unadulterated truth can be known naturally by the intellect of a person in this life without the special illumination of the Uncreated Light ?*

[Pro et Contra]

I argue that no such truth can be known [1] :

[Arg. I]. From [St Augustine] : *De Trinitate,* BK. IX †: "But we gaze upon the indestructible truth by reason of which we may define perfectly what the mind of man should be according to the eternal reasons". And again : "When we accept or reject something correctly, our incontestable conviction arises from other immutable rules above our minds". And again : "Grasping by simple intelligence the unspeakably beautiful art that lies beyond the eye of the mind. . .". And in the same work ‡ : "In the eternal truth from which all temporal things are made, we behold the form . . . and we have within us like a Word the knowledge of what we have conceived".

[Arg. II]. Also in BK. XII ** : "But it pertains to higher reason to judge of these corporeal things according to eternal reasons".

[Arg. III. And in the same BK. XII ††: " And not only are there immutable reasons for sensible things posited in place, etc. . .". That Augustine here is speaking of the eternal reasons that are really in God is proved by the fact that he says in the same passage that

ad illas pervenire. Si autem intelligeret de primis principiis, non est paucorum pervenire ad illa sed multorum, quia omnibus sunt communia et nota.

Item, libro decimo quarto, cap. decimo quinto vel trigesimo quarto,* loquens de injusto qui multa recte laudat et vituperat in moribus hominum, ait : Quibus regulis judicat, etc. Et in fine ait : Ubi sunt illae regulae scriptae nisi in libro illo lucis. Liber ille lucis est intellectus divinus. Igitur vult ut in illa luce injustus videt quae sunt juste agenda et quod in aliquo impresso vel per aliquod impressum ab illo videtur, ut ibidem dicit : Unde omnis lex justa in cor hominis non migrando, sed tamquam imprimendo transfertur sicut imago ex annulo, etc. in ceram transit et annulum [*MS.* ceram] non relinquit. Igitur in illa luce videmus, a qua imprimitur in cor hominis justitia ; illa autem est lux increata.

Item, XII *Confessionum* † : Si ambo videmus verum nec tu in me nec ego in te, sed ambo in ea quae supra mentem est incommutabili veritate. Multae autem sunt auctoritates Augustini in multis locis ad probandum hanc conclusionem.

Ad oppositum :

Rom. I ‡ : Invisibilia Dei a creatura mundi per ea quae facta sunt intellecta conspiciuntur. Istae rationes aeternae sunt invisibilia Dei ; ergo cognoscuntur ex creaturis ; igitur ante visionem istarum habetur certa cognitio creaturarum.

---

* XIV, cap. XV (Migne, P.L., XLII, 1052).
† XII, cap. XXV (Migne, P.L., XXXII, 840).   ‡ Rom. I. 20.

it is the privilege of the few to attain them. For he would not say this if he were speaking of first principles, since the latter are not the privilege of the few but the many, inasmuch as first principles are common and known to all.

[Arg. IV]. Also in Book XIV,* speaking of the unjust man who correctly praises and blames many things in the mores of men, he asks : "By what norms do they judge, etc. . .". And at the end, he adds : "Where are these rules written except in that book of light. . .". That "book of light", however, is the divine intellect. Therefore, he wishes to say that it is in this light that the unjust man sees what justice demands must be done. And he sees this in something or by something impressed upon him by this light, for as Augustine says in the same place : ". . . whence every just law is transferred to the heart of man not by passing from one place to another, but by being impressed, as it were, even as the image is transferred from the ring to the wax without leaving the ring". Therefore, we see in that light by which justice is imprinted upon the heart of man. This light, however, is the Uncreated Light.

[Arg. V]. Likewise, in the *Confessions*, BK. XII † : "If both of us see the truth, you do not see it in me, nor do I see it in you, but both of us see it in that immutable truth which is above the mind". Now there are many other places where statements of Augustine could be found to support this conclusion.

To the contrary :

Romans I ‡ : "For since the creation of the world, God's invisible attributes are clearly seen . . . being understood through the things that are made. . .". Now the invisible things of God are these eternal reasons. Consequently, they are known from creatures. Therefore, even before these eternal reasons are seen, we have certain knowledge of creatures.

[Corpus Quaestionis]

[Opinio Henrici]

In ista quaestione est opinio una talis quod intentiones generales habent inter se ordinem naturalem. De duabus quae sunt ad propositum, videlicet de intentione entis et veri [*MS* ubi] loquamur.

Intentio prima est entis, quod probatur per illud *De causis,** propositionis quartae : Prima rerum creaturarum est esse, et in commento primae propositionis : Esse est vehementioris adhaerentiae. Et ratio est quia entitas est absoluta ; veritas decit respectum ad exemplar. Ex hoc sequitur quod ens possit cognosci sub ratione entitatis, licet non sub ratione veritatis, et per consequens ipsum quod est verum potest cognosci antequam cognoscatur ipsa veritas.

Haec etiam conclusio probatur ex parte intellectus, quia ens potest concipi simplici intelligentia et tunc concipitur illud quod verum est ; sed ratio veritatis non concipitur nisi intelligentia componente et dividente ; compositionem et divisionem praecedit simplex intelligentia.

Si autem quaeratur de notitia entis, sive ejus quod verum est, dicitur quod intellectus ex puris naturalibus potest sic intelligere verum. Quod probatur, quia inconveniens est naturam esse expertem propriae operationis secundum Damascenum,† et hoc magis inconveniens est in natura perfectiori secundum Philosophum, ıı *De caelo et mundo,* ‡ de stellis, quia magnum inconveniens esset stellas habere virtutem progressivam et non habere instrumenta ad progrediendum ; igitur cum propria

---

* *Liber de causis,* prop. i, iv.
† *De fide orthodoxa,* ıı, cap. xxiii (Migne, P.G., xcıv, 949).
‡ ıı, cap. viii (290ᵃ, 30).

[Body of the Question]

[The opinion of Henry of Ghent]

One opinion [2] regarding this question maintains that a natural order exists among general notions. Let us discuss two of these which are relevant here, viz. the notion of "being" and the notion of "true".

That "being"is the first of these notions is proved from the fourth proposition of the *Liber de Causis* * : "The first of created things is being" ; and in the commentary on the first proposition : "Being is of stronger adherence". The reason for this is that entity is something absolute, whereas truth implies a relation to an exemplar. From this it follows that a thing can be known as an entity even though its truth value is as yet unknown. Consequently, the thing which is true can be known before its truth is known.

The way the mind functions provides a further proof. A being can be grasped by an act of simple understanding, and in such a case the thing which is true is known. But the truth value itself is known only by an act of judgment. Simple understanding, however, precedes an act of judgment.

Now if we ask about our knowledge of a being or of the thing which is true, they tell us that the intellect by reason of its purely natural powers can know the "true" in this sense. The proof is this. It is hardly fitting that any nature exist without its proper activity, as Damascene says.† The more perfect the nature in question the less fitting that it should lack such operation, as the Philosopher points out in speaking of the stars in *De caelo et mundo*, BK. II.‡ For it would be highly improper for the stars to have the power of progressive movement and still lack the means necessary for locomotion. If the proper

operatio intellectus sit intelligere verum, videtur inconveniens quod natura non concesserit intellectui illa quae
sufficiunt ad hanc operationem.

Sed si loquamur de cognitione veritatis, respondetur
quod sicut est duplex exemplar, creatum et increatum,
secundum Platonem in *Timaeo*,* videlicet exemplar
factum et non factum, sive creatum et non creatum
(exemplar creatum est species universalis causata a re,
exemplar increatum est idea in mente divina), ita duplex
est conformitas ad exemplar et duplex veritas ; una est
conformitas ad exemplar creatum et isto modo posuit
Aristotelis, veritates rerum cognosci per conformitatem
earum ad speciem intelligibilem ; et ita videtur Augustinus ponere viii° *De Trinitate*, cap. vii † ubi vult quod
rerum notitiam generalem et specialem ex sensibus collec-
tam habemus, secundum quam de quocumque occurrent
veritatem judicamus, quod ipsum sit tale vel tale.

Sed quod per tale exemplar acquisitum in nobis
habeatur omnino certa et infallibilis notitia veritatis de
re, hoc videtur omnino impossibile et hoc probatur
triplici ratione secundum istos. Prima sumitur ex parte
rei de qua exemplar est extractum, secunda ex parte
subjecti in quo est, et tertia ex parte exemplaris in se.

Prima ratio est talis : Objectum illud a quo abstrahitur
exemplar est mutabile. Igitur non potest esse causa
alicujus immutabilis, sed certa notitia alicujus de aliquo
sub ratione veritatis in eo habetur per rationem immutabilem ; igitur non habetur per tale exemplar.
Haec dicitur ratio Augustini *Octoginta tres quaestionum*,
quaestio ix, ‡ ubi dicit quod a sensibus non est

---

* *Timaeus*, 28.   † viii, cap. vi (Migne, P.L., xlii, 966).
‡ q. ix (Migne, P.L., xl, 13).

operation of the intellect, however, is to know the thing which is true, it seems hardly fitting that nature should not endow the intellect with what is prerequisite for such an operation.

But as for knowing the truth itself, they tell us that there are two exemplars, one created, the other uncreated. This is in accord with Plato, who mentions in the *Timaeus** one exemplar that is made, i.e. created, and one that is not made, i.e. uncreated. The created exemplar is the species of the universal caused by the thing. The uncreated exemplar is the idea in the divine mind. Consequently, a twofold truth and twofold conformity to an exemplar exists. One is the conformity to the created exemplar, and it was in this sense that Aristotle maintained that the truths of things are known through their conformity to the intelligible species.[3] Augustine, also, seems to hold this view in his work *De Trinitate*, BK. VIII,† where he maintains that the knowledge of things gleaned from the senses is both of a general and of a particular nature. In virtue of such knowledge we judge the truth of any occurrence to be such or such.

But it seems wholly impossible that such an acquired exemplar should give us infallible and completely certain knowledge of a thing. The advocates of this opinion give three reasons for such a conclusion. The first is based upon the thing from which the exemplar is abstracted, the second upon the subject in which the exemplar inheres and the third upon the exemplar itself.

The first reason runs something like this. The object from which the exemplar is abstracted is itself mutable ; therefore it cannot be the cause of something unchangeable. But it is only in virtue of some immutable reason that someone can be certain that something is true. An exemplar such as this, then, provides no such knowledge. They claim this to be Augustine's argument in his *Eighty-three Questions*, q. ix,‡ where he tells us not to look

expectanda veritas, quia sensibilia sine intermissione mutantur.

Secunda ratio talis est : Anima est ex se mutabilis et passiva erroris ; igitur per nihil mutabilius ea potest ratificari sive regulari ne erret. Sed tale exemplar in ea est mutabilius quam ipsa anima sit. Igitur illud exemplar non perfecte regulat animam ne erret. Requiritur ergo specialis influentia superior. Haec dicitur ratio Augustini *De vera religione* * : Lex omnium artium, etc.

Tertio ratio : notitiam veritatis nullus habet certam et infallibilem nisi habeat unde possit verum discernere a verisimili, quia si non possit discernere verum a falso [*MS* secundo] vel a verisimili, potest dubitare se falli. Sed per exemplar praedictum creatum non potest discerni verum a verisimili ; ergo, etc. Probatio minoris : Species talis potest representare se tamquam se vel alio modo se tamquam objectum, sicut est in somniis, si repraesentet se tamquam objectum, falsitas est, si se tamquam se, veritas est. Igitur per talem speciem non habetur sufficiens distinctivum quando repraesentat se ut se vel ut objectum, et ita nec sufficiens distinctivum veri a falso.

Ex istis concluditur quod certam scientiam et infallibilem veritatem si contingat hominem cognoscere, hoc non convenit ei aspiciendo ad exemplar a re per sensus acceptum quantumcumque sit depuratum et universale factum, sed requiritur quod respiciat ad exemplar increatum. Et tunc modus ponendi est iste : Deus non ut cognitum habet rationem exemplaris ad quod aspiciendo cognoscitur sincera veritas. Est enim cognitum

---

* cap. xxx (Migne, P.L., xxxiv, 147).

for truth from the senses, for what the senses perceive constantly undergoes change.

The second reason goes like this. Of itself the soul is changeable and subject to error. Now a thing which is even more changeable than the soul itself cannot correct this condition or prevent the soul from erring. But the exemplar which inheres in the soul is even more mutable than the soul itself. Consequently, such an exemplar does not regulate the soul so perfectly that it makes no mistake. Some special higher influence, then, is required. This, they say, is the argument Augustine uses in his work *De vera religione** : "Since the law of all arts", etc.

The third reason is that no-one possesses certain and infallible knowledge of the truth unless he can distinguish the truth from what has only the appearance of truth, for if he is unable to tell the true from the false or from what appears to be true, he can still be in doubt whether he is being deceived or not. Now truth cannot be distinguished from what merely appears to be true by means of the aforesaid exemplar. Therefore, etc. Proof of the minor : Such a species can either represent itself as species or, as happens in dreams, present itself as an object. In the latter case, we have falsity ; in the former, truth. There is nothing about such a species then that suffices to differentiate the first mode of representation from the second and thus to distinguish the true from the false.

From all this they conclude that if man can know the infallible truth and possess certain knowledge it is not because he looks upon an exemplar derived from the thing by way of the senses, no matter how much such an exemplar may be purified and universalised. It is necessary that he look upon the uncreated exemplar. And the way they assume this to take place is this.[4] God does not function as exemplar in the sense that He is the object known so that unadulterated truth is known by looking at Him. For God is known only under some general

in generali attributo. Sed est ratio cognoscendi ut
nudum exemplar et propria ratio cognoscendi ut nudum
exemplar et propria ratio essentiae creatae.

Qualiter autem possit esse ratio cognoscendi et non
cognitum ponitur exemplum, quia sicut radius solis
quandoquo derivatur quasi obliquato aspectu a suo fonte
quandoque directe. Quod videtur in radio primo modo
derivato, licet sol sit ratio videndi, non tamen ut visus in
se. Ejus autem quod videtur secundo modo in radio, sol
est ita ratio cognoscendi quod etiam est cognitus. Quando
igitur ista lux increata intellectum quasi directo aspectu
illustrat, tunc ut visa est ratio videndi alia in ipsa. Intellectum autem nostrum pro statu viae quasi obliquato
aspectu illustrat, et ideo est intellectui nostro ratio
videndi non visa.

Ponitur autem qualiter habeat triplicem rationem
respectu actus videndi, scilicet lucis actuantis, speciei
immutantis, et caracteris sive exemplaris configurantis.
Et ex hoc concluditur ultra quod requiritur specialis
influentia, quia sicut illa essentia non videtur naturaliter
a nobis in se, ita ut illa essentia est exemplar respectu
alicujus essentiae naturaliter non videtur. Secundum
Augustinum *De videndo Deum*.* In ejus enim potestate est videri ; si vult, videtur ; si non vult, non videtur. Ultimo additur quod perfecta notitia veritatis est
quando duae species exemplares concurrunt in mente,
una inhaerens, scilicet creata, alia illapsa, scilicet non
creata ; et sic contingimus verbum perfecte veritatis.

(Arguo contra istam opinionem in se, secundo contra
rationes fundamentales adductas vel econverso. Primum
includit quartum articulum, qui est quasi ad hominem

---

* cap. vi (Migne, P.L., xxxiii, 603).

attribute. But God is the reason why we know inasmuch as He is the sole exemplar and the proper reason for the created essence.

The following example is used to explain how God can be the reason why we know and yet not be known in Himself. Some sunlight is reflected while other rays come directly from their source. And even though the sun is the reason why we see something by reflected sunlight, the sun itself is not seen. But for an object illumined by direct light, the sun is a reason for knowing that is also known. In similar fashion, then, when the Uncreated Light as it were illumines an intellect by a direct glance, then this Light as seen is the reason for seeing the other things in it. In the present life, however, this Uncreated Light illumines our intellect indirectly as it were. Consequently, though unseen itself, it is the reason why our intellect sees.

Now they claim that the uncreated exemplar is related to the act of vision in three ways, viz. as a stimulating light, as a transforming species, and as the character or exemplar which produces a like form [in the intellect]. From this they conclude further that a special influence is required. For just as naturally we do not see this essence in itself, neither do we see it naturally as the exemplar of any essence. As Augustine puts it in his work *De videndo Deum* * : "It is in His power to be seen. If he wishes it, He is seen ; if He does not wish it, He is not seen". Finally, they add that perfect knowledge of truth results when the two exemplar species concur in the mind, viz. the created exemplar which inheres in the soul and the uncreated exemplar which enters from without. And it is in this way that we have the word of truth perfectly.

(First [5] I argue against the opinion in itself ; secondly I refute the reasons adduced in its favour or turn them to my advantage. Under the first heading falls the fourth article. It is an *argumentum ad hominem*, as it were, whereas

et tertium qui est ad rem, secundum includit primum articulum hic et tertium et sextum. Quintus ergo articulus est solutio quaestionis.)

Contra istam opinionem, primo ostendo quod istae rationes non sunt rationes fundamentales alicujus opinionis verae, nec secundum intentionem Augustini, sed sunt pro opinione Academicorum. Secundo ostendo quomodo illa opinio Academicorum, quae videtur concludi per istas rationes, falsa sit. Et tertio respondeo ad rationes istas quatenus minus concludunt. Quarto arguo contra conclusionem istius opinionis. Quinto solvo quaestionem. Sexto ostendo quomodo rationes istae quatenus sunt Augustini concludunt illam intentionem Augustini, non illam ad quam hic inducuntur.

[*Articulus Primus. Rationes Henrici sunt pro Opinione Academicorum*]. Primo, istae rationes videntur concludere impossibilitatem certae cognitionis naturalis. Prima, quia si objectum continue mutatur nec potest haberi aliqua certitudo de ipso sub ratione immutabilis. Immo nec in quocumque lumine posset certitudo haberi, quia non est certitudo quando objectum alio modo cognoscitur quam se habet. Igitur nec est certitudo cognoscendo mutabile ut immutabile. Patet etiam quod antecedens hujus rationis, videlicet quod sensibilia continue mutantur, falsum est. Haec enim est opinio quae imponitur Heraclito IV *Metaphysicae*.*

Similiter, si propter mutabilitatem exemplaris, quod est in anima nostra, non posset esse certitudo, cum quidquid ponitur in anima subjective sit mutabile, etiam ipse actus intelligendi, sequitur quod per nihil in anima rectificatur anima ne erret. [Non Duns] [8] (Sequitur etiam quod ipse actus intelligendi cum sit mutabilior quam ipsa anima in qua est, numquam erit verus nec veritatem continebit.)

* IV, cap. v (1010^a, 6).

the third article is *ad rem*. The second heading includes the material in the third and sixth articles. The fifth article, therefore, is the solution to the question.)

Against this opinion, in the first [article] I show that these arguments are not a basis for any true opinion. Neither are they in accord with the mind of Augustine. Instead they lead to the view of the Academicians.[6] In the second [article], I show how the view of the Academicians, which seems to follow from these reasons, is false. In the third, I answer these arguments in so far as they are inconclusive. In the fourth, I argue against the conclusion of this opinion [of Henry]. In the fifth, I solve the question. In the sixth, I show how these reasons, in so far as they are Augustine's, prove what Augustine intended to prove rather than what they are here used to prove.

[*Article I. Henry's Arguments lead to Scepticism*]. First, these reasons seem to imply the impossibility of any certain natural knowledge. Consider the first.[7] If an object is continually changing we can have no certitude about it by any kind of light, for there can be no certitude when an object is known in some way other than the way in which it is. Neither is there any certitude in knowing a changeable thing as unchangeable. It is also clear that the antecedent of this argument is false, viz. that what the senses can perceive is continually changing. This is the opinion attributed to Heraclitus in *Metaphysics*, BK. IV.*

Likewise, if the mutability of the exemplar in our soul makes certitude impossible, then it follows that nothing in the soul could prevent it from erring, for everything inhering in such a subject is also mutable—even the act of understanding itself.[8] (It follows further that, inasmuch as the act of understanding is even more mutable than the soul in which it resides, it will never be true nor contain truth.)

Similiter, secundum istam opinionem species creata inhaerens concurrit cum specie illabente, sed quando aliquid concurrit quod repugnat certitudini, non potest certitudo haberi, sicut enim ex altera de necessario et altera de contingenti non sequitur conclusio nisi de contingenti, ita ex certo et incerto concurrentibus ad aliquam cognitionem, non sequitur cognitio certa.

Idem patet etiam de tertia ratione, quia si species ipsa abstracta a re concurrat ad omnem cognitionem et non potest judicari quando illa repraesentat se tanquam se et quando se tamquam objectum ; ergo quodcumque aliud concurrat, non potest haberi certitudo per quam discernatur verum a verisimili. Istae igitur rationes videntur concludere omnem incertitudinem et opinionem Academicorum.

Quod autem ista conclusio non sit secundum intentionem Augustini probo. Augustinus II *Soliloquiorum* * : Spectabilia disciplinarum quisque verissima esse nulla dubitatione concedit. Et Boethius *De hebdomadibus* † : Communis animi conceptio est quam quisque probat auditam. Et Philosophus II *Metaphysicae* ‡ : Prima principia sunt omnibus nota. Ex his tribus auctoritatibus, arguitur sic quod convenit omnibus alicujus speciei, sequitur naturam specificam. Igitur cum quisque habet certitudinem infallibilem de primis principiis et ultra cuilibet est naturaliter evidens forma syllogismi perfecti I *Priorum*,** scientia autem conclusionum non dependet nisi ex evidentia principii et ex evidentia illationis syllogisticae, igitur cuilibet naturaliter scita potest esse quaecumque conclusio demonstrabilis ex principiis per se notis.

* II, cap. xi (Migne, P.L., xxxII, 893–894).
† (Migne, P.L., LXIV, 1311).
‡ II, cap. i (993^b, 4).
** *Analytica priora*, I, cap. ii (24^b, 22–26).

Likewise, according to this opinion, the created species which inheres in the soul concurs with the species that enters from without. But no certitude is possible where something incompatible with certitude concurs. For just as we can infer only a contingent proposition from a necessary and a contingent proposition combined, so also a concurrence of what is certain and what is uncertain does not produce certain knowledge.

The same reasoning clearly applies to the third argument. For if the species abstracted from the thing is a concurrent factor in all knowledge, and if we cannot judge when such a species represents itself as such and when it represents itself as object, then it makes no difference what concurs with such a species. We shall never have a certain norm for distinguishing the true from what merely appears to be true. These arguments then seem to lead to the conclusion that all is uncertain, the opinion of the Academicians.

That such a conclusion is not what Augustine intended I prove from the second book of his *Soliloquies* * : "Everyone concedes without hesitation that the proofs of the sciences are most true". And Boethius says in *De hebdomadibus* † : "A common conception of the mind is that which is conclusive for anyone who hears it". And the Philosopher in *Metaphysics*, BK. II, ‡ says : "First principles are known to all. . .". On the basis of these three testimonies, the following argument is constructed. Whatever pertains to all the members of a given species, springs from the specific nature itself. Now since the knowledge of conclusions depends solely upon the evidence of first principles and of the syllogistic inference, then if everyone has infallible certitude about first principles and further, if the form of the perfect syllogism as defined in *Prior Analytics*, BK. I,** is naturally evident to everyone, then anyone can know naturally any conclusion demonstrable from self-evident principles.

Secundo apparet quod Augustinus concedit certitudinem eorum quae cognoscuntur per experientiam
sensuum. Unde dicit xv *De Trinitate*, cap. xiii vel xxxii * :
Absit ut ea quae didicimus per sensus corporis vera esse
dubitemus per ea quippe didicimus caelum et terram et
mare et omnia quae in eis sunt. Si non dubitamus de
veritate eorum et non fallimur, ut patet ; ergo certi
sumus de cognitis per viam sensus. Nam certitudo habetur quando excluditur dubitatio et deceptio.

Patet etiam tertio quod Augustinus concedit certitudinem de actibus nostris, ibidem xv, cap. xii vel xxxi †
sive dormiat sive vigilet vivit, quia et dormire et in
somniis videre viventis est. Quod si dicas : vivere non
esse actum secundum sed primum, sequitur ibidem : Si
aliquis dicat, scio me scire, me vivere, falli non potest,
etiam quotiescumque reflectendo super primum scitum ;
et ibidem : Si quis dicat, volo esse beatus, quomodo non
impudenter respondetur, forte falleris, et ibi reflectendo
in infinitum scio me velle etc. Ibidem : Si quispiam
dicat errare nolo, nonne eum errare nolle verum est.
Et alia, inquit, reperiuntur quae contra Academicos
valent qui nihil sciri ab homine posse concedunt.
Sequitur ibidem *De tribus contra Academicos libris* ‡
quos qui intellexerit, nihil eum contra perceptionem
veritatis argumenta eorum multum movebunt. Item
eodem xv, cap. viii vel xxxviii ** : Illa quae sciuntur ut
numquam excidere possint et ad naturam ipsius animae
pertinent cujusmodi est illud quod nos vivere scimus.

(Notandum quod quattuor sunt cognitiones in quibus
est nobis necessaria certitudo, scilicet de scibilibus

---

* xv, cap. xii (Migne, P.L., XLII, 1075).
† loc. cit. (1074).
‡ *Libri tres contra Academicos* (Migne, P.L., XXXII, 905–958).
** xv, cap. xv (Migne, P.L., XLII, 1078).

Secondly, it is clear that Augustine concedes the certitude of those things known through sense experience. Hence he says in *De Trinitate*, BK. XV * : "Far be it that we should doubt about those things which we learn to be true through our bodily senses, for through these we learn the heavens, the earth, the sea and all that are in them". If then we are not deceived nor in doubt about the truth of these things, as is clearly the case, we are certain of things known through the senses, for where doubt and deception are excluded, we have certitude.

Thirdly, it is clear that in the same work Augustine also concedes that we have certitude regarding our actions.† " He is alive whether he be asleep or awake, for it is a part of living also to sleep and to see in dreams". And if it be objected that to live is not a second act but a first act,[9] he adds in the same place : "If anyone should say, 'I know that I know or that I live', he cannot be deceived, no matter how often he reflect on this first knowledge". And in the same place : "And if one says, 'I am happy', how can one say without being impudent, 'Perhaps you are deceived'? And if I reflect *ad infinitum*, I know that I will, and so on". And in the same place : "If anyone says I do not wish to err, will it not be true that he does not wish to err. . .". "And other arguments", he says, "can be found which hold against the Academicians, who maintain that nothing can be known by man". And in the same work : "If anyone has read our *Contra Academicos*,‡ the arguments against the perception of truth given by the Academicians will not move him". Likewise, in the same book ** : "Those things which are known in such a way that they can never slip from the mind but pertain to the nature of the soul itself, of such kind is the knowledge that we live. . .".

(Note [10] that there are four kinds of knowledge of which we are necessarily certain, viz. (1) things knowable

simpliciter ; de scibilibus per experientiam ; de actibus nostris ; et de cognitis a nobis ut nunc per sensus ; exemplum triangulus habet tres, etc. ; luna eclipsatur ; vigilo ; illud est album. Primum et tertium tantum egent sensu ut occasione, quia simpliciter est certitudo si omnes sensus errarent, secundum et quartum tenent per illud, scilicet quod frequenter evenit a non libero habet illud pro per se causa naturali, ex hoc sequitur propositum tam in secundo quam in quarto aliquando additur propositio necessaria. Itaque auctoritates Augustini dimittas usque ad articulum secundum, qui est ad rem vel qui est solutio). (Primum est manifestum, tertium conceditur esse per se notum, alias non judicaretur quid esset per se notum. Secundum et quartum habent infinitas per se notas quibus jungunt alias ex pluribus sensibus).

Sic patet primum quomadmodum rationes illius non concludunt et quod hoc falsum sit et contra Augustinum.

[*Articulus Secundus. Reprobatio Scepticismi*]. Quantum ad secundum articulum ut in nullis cognoscibilibus locum habeat error Academicorum, videndum est qualiter de tribus cognoscibilibus praedictis dicendum est, videlicet de principiis per se notis et de conclusionibus, et secundo de cognitis per experientiam, et tertio de actibus nostris, utrum possit naturaliter haberi certitudo infallibilis.

[*a. De Notitia Principiorum*]. Quantum ergo ad certitudinem de principiis dico sic. Termini principiorum per se notorum talem habent identitatem ut alter evidenter necessario alterum includat, et ideo intellectus componens illos terminos, ex quo apprehendit

in an unqualified sense, (2) things knowable through experience, (3) our actions, (4) things known at the present time through the senses. An example [of each] : (1) A triangle has three [angles equal to two right angles], (2) The moon is eclipsed, (3) I am awake, (4) That is white. The first and third require the senses merely as an occasion, because even if all the senses erred, there would still be certitude purely and simply. The second and fourth hold in virtue of this proposition : "Whatever happens frequently through something that is not free, has this something as its natural *per se* cause". From this principle certitude follows in the second and fourth cases when the other proposition is necessary. Therefore you can let the arguments from the authority of Augustine go until the second article, which is *ad rem*, or to the [fifth article] which is the solution.) (The [11] first is manifest, the third is conceded to be self-evident ; otherwise we could not judge what is self-evident. The second and fourth have an infinity of self-evident truths to which others are added which are based on the testimony of several senses.)

And so the first article is clear, viz. that the reasons [of Henry] are inconclusive, that his opinion is false and not in accord with the mind of Augustine.

[*Article II. The Rejection of Scepticism*]. As regards the second article, lest the error of the Academicians be repeated in regard to any of those things which can be known, we must see what is to be said of the three types of knowledge mentioned above, viz. whether it is possible to have infallible certitude naturally : (1) of self-evident principles and conclusions, (2) of things known by experience, and (3) of our actions.

[*a. Certitude of First Principles*]. As to the certitude of principles, I have this to say. The terms of self-evident principles are so identical that it is evident that one necessarily includes the other. Consequently, the intellect uniting these terms in a proposition, from the

eos, habet apud se necessariam causam conformitatis illius actus componendi ad ipsos terminos quorum est compositio, et etiam causam evidentem talis conformitatis, et ideo necessario patet sibi illa conformitas cujus causam evidentem apprehendit in terminis. Igitur non potest in intellectu apprehensio esse terminorum et compositio eorum, quin stet conformitas illius compositionis ad terminos, sicut stare non potest album et album, quin stet similitudo. Haec autem conformitas compositionis ad terminos est veritas compositionis. Ergo non potest stare compositio talium terminorum quin sit vera. Et ita non potest stare perceptio illius compositionis et perceptio terminorum, quin stet perceptio conformitatis compositionis ad terminos, et ita perceptio veritatis quia prima percepta evidenter includunt perceptionem istius veritatis.

Confirmatur ratio ista per simile per Philosophum IV *Metaphysicae* * ubi vult quod oppositum principii non potest in intellectu alicujus venire, scilicet hujusmodi impossibile idem esse et non esse, quia tunc essent opiniones contrariae simul in mente ; quod utique verum est de opinionibus contrariis, id est repugnantibus formaliter, quia opinio opinans esse de aliquo et opinio opinans non esse de eodom, sunt formaliter repugnantes. Ita arguam in proposito, repugnantiam aliquam intellectionum in mente, licet non formalem ; si enim stat in intellectu notitia totius et partis, et compositio eorum, cum ista includant sicut causa necessaria conformitatem compositionis ad terminos, si stet in intellectu haec opinio, quod ipsa compositio sit falsa, stabunt notitiae repugnantes ; non formaliter, sed notitia una stabit cum

---

* IV, cap. iii (1005^b, 23–24).

very fact that it grasps these terms, has present to itself the necessary cause, and what is more—the evident cause, of the conformity of this proposition with the terms that compose it. This conformity, then, the evident cause of which the intellect perceives in the terms, cannot help but be evident to the intellect. That is why the intellect could not apprehend these terms and unite them in a proposition without having this relationship of conformity arise between the proposition and the terms, any more than two white objects could exist without a relationship of similarity arising between them. Now it is precisely this conformity of the proposition to the terms that constitutes the truth of a judgment. Such terms then cannot be combined in a judgment without being true, and so it is that one cannot perceive this proposition and its terms without also perceiving the conformity of the proposition to the terms, and therefore, perceiving the truth. For what is first perceived evidently includes the perception of the truth of the proposition.

In *Metaphysics*, BK. IV,* the Philosopher confirms this reasoning by a simile. There he points out that the opposite of a first principle such as "It is impossible that the same thing be and not be", cannot enter the mind of anyone because then the mind would possess contrary opinions simultaneously. This is indeed true of contrary opinions, that is, propositions formally opposed to each other. For the opinions attributing existence and non-existence to one and the same thing are formally opposed. And so in the question at hand, I argue that there is some kind of repugnance existing between intellections in the mind, even though it is not exactly a formal opposition. For if the intellect possesses the knowledge of "whole" and of "part" and combines them in a proposition, since they include the necessary reason for the conformity of the proposition to the terms, if the intellect were to think this proposition false, two mutually repugnant acts of knowledge would coexist, even though the

alia, et tamen erit causa necessaria oppositae notitiae
ad illam, quod est impossibile. Sicut enim impossibile
est album et nigrum simul stare, quia sunt contraria
formaliter, ita impossibile est simul stare album et illud
quod est praecise causa nigri, ita necessario quod non
potest esse sine eo absque contradictione.

Habita certitudine de principiis primis patet quomodo
habebitur de conclusionibus illatis ex eis propter evidentiam syllogismi perfecti, cum certitudo conclusionis
tantumodo dependeat ex certitudine principiorum et ex
evidentia illationis.

Sed numquid in ista notitia principiorum et conclusionum non errabit intellectus si sensus omnes deci-
piantur circa terminos ? Respondeo quantum ad istam
notitiam, quod intellectus non habet sensus pro causa,
sed tantum pro occasione, quia intellectus non potest
habere notitiam simplicium nisi acceptam a sensibus.
Illa tamen accepta virtute sua potest simul componere
simplicia, et si ex ratione talium simplicium sit complexio
evidenter vera, intellectus virtute propria et terminorum
assentiet illi complexioni non virtute sensus a quo
accipit terminos exterius. Exemplum : si ratio totius
et ratio majoritatis accipiatur a sensu et intellectus
componat istam : Omne totum est majus sua parte, intellectus virtute sui et istorum terminorum assentiet
indubitanter isti complexioni et non tantum quia vidit

opposition is not precisely formal. The one act of knowledge would be co-present with the other even though the first is the necessary cause of the very opposite of the second, which is impossible. For just as it is impossible for white to be at the same time black because the two are formally contraries, so it is also impossible to have the white where you have the precise cause of blackness. The necessity in this case is of such a kind that it would be a contradiction to have the one [viz. the knowledge of the terms and the proposition] without the other [viz. the knowledge of the conformity between the two].

Once we have certitude of first principles, it is clear how one can be certain of the conclusions drawn from such principles, since the perfect syllogism is evident,[12] and the certitude of the conclusion depends solely upon the certitude of the principles and the evidence of the inference.

But will the intellect not err in its knowledge of principles and conclusions, if all the senses are deceived about the terms? I reply that so far as this kind of knowledge goes, the senses are not a cause but merely an occasion of the intellect's knowledge, for the intellect cannot have any knowledge of the terms of a proposition unless it has taken them from the senses. But once it has them, the intellect by its own power can form propositions with these terms. And if a proposition be evidently true by reason of the terms involved, the intellect by its own power will assent to this proposition in virtue of the terms and not by reason of the senses from which it externally received the terms. To give an example : If the notion of "whole" and the notion of "greater than" be taken from the senses and the intellect form the proposition "Every whole is greater than its part", the intellect by its own power and in virtue of the terms will assent to this proposition without the shadow of doubt. And it does not assent to this because it sees these terms verified in some thing, as it does when it

terminos conjunctos in re, sicut assentit isti : Sortes
est albus, quia videt terminos in re uniri.

Immo dico quod si omnes sensus essent falsi a quibus
accipiuntur tales termini vel quod plus est ad deceptionem, aliqui sensus falsi et aliqui sensus veri, intellectus
circa talia principia non deciperetur, quia semper haberet
apud se terminos qui essent causa veritatis, utpote si
alicui caeco nato essent impressae [*MS om*. miraculose in
somniis] species albedinis et nigredinis et illae remanerent
post in vigilia, intellectus abstrahens ab eis componeret
istam : album non est nigrum, et circa istam non deciperetur intellectus, licet termini accipiantur a sensu
errante, quia ratio formalis terminorum ad quam deven-
tum est, est necessaria causa veritatis hujus negativae.

[*b. De cognitis per experientiam*].   De secundis, scilicet de cognitis per experientiam, dico quod licet experientia non habeatur de omnibus singularibus, sed de
pluribus, neque quod semper, sed quod pluries, tamen
expertus infallibiliter novit quia ita est et semper et in
omnibus, et hoc per istam propositionem qui est quiescentem in anima : Quidquid evenit ut in pluribus ab
aliqua causa non libera, est effectus naturalis illius
causae, quae propositio nota est intellectui licet acce-
pisset terminos ejus a sensu errante.   Quia causa non
libera non potest producere ut in pluribus effectum non
libere ad cujus oppositum ordinatur, vel ad quem ex
sua forma non ordinatur.   Sed causa casualis ordinatur
ad producendum oppositum effectus casualis, vel non
ad illum producendum.   Ergo, nihil est causa casualis
effectus frequenter producti ab eo, et ita si non sit libera
erit causa naturalis.   Iste autem effectus evenit a tali

assents to the proposition "Socrates is white", because it saw the terms united in reality.

Indeed, if the senses from which these terms were received were all false, or what is more deceptive, if some were false and others true, I still maintain that the intellect would not be deceived about such principles, because the terms which are the cause of the truth would always be present to the intellect. And so it would be if the species of whiteness and blackness were impressed miraculously in sleep upon one who was blind from birth and they remained after he awoke. The intellect could abstract from these and form the proposition "White is not black". And it would not be deceived with regard to this proposition even if the terms were derived from erring senses, because the formal meaning of the terms at which the intellect has arrived is the necessary cause of this negative truth.

[*b. Experimental Knowledge*]. As for what is known by experience, I have this to say. Even though a person does not experience every single individual, but only a great many, nor does he experience them at all times, but only frequently, still he knows infallibly that it is always this way and holds for all instances. He knows this in virtue of this proposition reposing in his soul : "Whatever occurs in a great many instances by a cause that is not free, is the natural effect of that cause". This proposition is known to the intellect even if the terms are derived from erring senses, because a cause that does not act freely cannot in most instances produce an effect that is the very opposite of what it is ordained by its form to produce. The chance cause, however, is ordained either to produce or not produce the opposite of the chance effect. Consequently, if the effect occurs frequently it is not produced by chance and its cause therefore will be a natural cause if it is not a free agent. But this effect occurs through such a cause. Therefore, since the latter

causa, ergo illud est causa naturalis effectus frequenter producti ab eo, quia non est casualis.

Iste enim effectus evenit a tali causa ut in pluribus, hoc acceptum est per experientiam, quia inveniendo talem naturam nunc cum tali accidente nunc cum tali inventum est quod quantacumque esset diversitas accidentium, semper istam naturam sequebatur talis effectus, igitur non per aliquod accidens isti naturae sed per naturam ipsam in se sequitur talis effectus.

Sed ulterius notandum quod quandoque accipitur experientia de conclusione, puta quod luna frequenter eclipsatur, et tunc supposita conclusione quia ita est, inquiritur causa talis conclusionis per viam divisionis, et quandoque devenitur ex conclusione experta ad principia nota ex terminis, et tunc ex tali principio noto ex terminis potest conclusio, prius tantum secundum experientiam nota, certius cognosci, scilicet primo genere cognitionis, quia ut deducta ex principio per se noto, sicut istud est per se notum, quod opacum interpositum inter perspicuum et lumen, impedit multiplicationem luminis ad tale perspicuum ; et si inventum fuerit per divisionem quod terra tale est corpus interpositum inter solem et lunam, scietur certissime demonstratione propter quid, quia per causam et non tantum per experientiam, sicut sciebatur ista conclusio ante inventionem principii.

Quandoque autem est experientia de principio ita quod non contingit per viam divisionis invenire ulterius principium notum ex terminis, sed statur in aliquo uno ut in pluribus cujus extrema per experimentum scitum est frequenter uniri, puta quod haec herba talis speciei

is not a chance cause, it is the natural cause of the effect it frequently produces.

That such an effect occurs frequently through such a cause is a fact gathered from experience. For once we find such a nature associated at one time with this accident and at another with that, we have discovered that despite the accidental differences, such an effect invariably follows from this nature. Hence, such an effect is not the result of what is merely incidental to such a nature but is rather the effect of this nature as such.

It should be noted further that at times we experience [the truth] of a conclusion, such as : "The moon is frequently eclipsed". Then, granting the validity of this conclusion because it is a fact, we proceed by the method of division to discover the reason for this. And sometimes, beginning with a conclusion thus experienced, a person arrives at self-evident principles. In such a case, the conclusion which at first was known only by experience now is known by reason of such a principle with even greater certainty, namely that characteristic of the first kind of knowledge, for it has been deduced from a self-evident principle. Thus for instance, it is a self-evident principle that when an opaque body is placed between a visible object and the source of light, the transmission of light to such an object is prevented. Now, if a person discovers by way of division that the earth is such an opaque body interposed between sun and moon, our conclusion will no longer be known merely by experience as was the case before we discovered this principle. It will be now known most certainly by a demonstration of the reasoned fact,[13] for it is known through its cause.

Sometimes, however, we experience a principle in such a way that it is impossible to discover by further division any self-evident principle from which it could be derived. Instead we must be satisfied with a principle whose terms are known by experience to be frequently united, for

est calida nec invenitur medium aliud prius per quod demonstretur passio de subjecto propter quid, sed statur in isto sicut primo noto propter experientias, licet tunc certitudo et infallibilitas [*read* incertitudo et fallibilitas] removeantur per istam propositionem : effectus ut in pluribus alicujus causae non liberae, est naturalis effectus ejus ; tamen iste est ultimus gradus cognitionis scientificae et forte ibi non habetur cognitio actualis unionis extremorum sed aptitudinalis. Si enim passio est alia res absoluta a subjecto, posset sine contradictione separari a subjecto, et expertus non haberet cognitionem quia ita est, sed quia ita aptum natum est esse.

[*c. De actibus nostris*]. De tertiis cognitionibus, scilicet de actibus nostris, dico quod est certitudo de multis eorum sicut de primis et per se notis, quod patet IV *Metaphysicae*,* ubi dicit Philosophus de rationibus dicentium omnia apparentia esse vera, quod illae rationes quaerunt utrum nunc vigilemus an dormiamus, possunt autem idem omnes dubitationes tales omnium enim rationum hii dignificant esse, et subdit, rationem quaerunt quorum non est ratio ; demonstrationis enim principii non est demonstratio. Ergo per ipsum ibi nos vigilare est per se notum, sicut principium demonstrationis.

Nec obstat quod est contingens, quia sicut dictum est alias ; ordo est in contingentibus, quod aliqua est prima et immediata, vel esset processus in infinitum in contingentibus, vel aliquod contingens sequeretur ex causa necessaria, quorum utrumque est impossibile. Et sicut

---

* IV, cap. vi (1011^a, 6–13).

example, that a certain species of herb is hot. Neither do we find any other prior means of demonstrating just why this attribute belongs to this particular subject, but must content ourselves with this as a first principle known from experience. Now even though the uncertainty and fallibility in such a case may be removed by the proposition "What occurs in most instances by means of a cause that is not free is the natural effect of such a cause", still this is the very lowest degree of scientific knowledge —and perhaps we have here no knowledge of the actual union of the terms but only a knowledge of what is apt to be the case. For if an attribute is an absolute entity other than the subject, it could be separated from its subject without involving any contradiction. Hence, the person whose knowledge is based on experience would not know whether such a thing is actually so or not, but only that by its nature is it apt to be so.

[*c. Knowledge of Our Own Acts*]. Regarding the third type of knowledge, viz. of our acts, I say that we are as certain of many of these as we are of the first and self-evident propositions, as is clear from *Metaphysics*, BK. IV.* There the Philosopher says to the arguments of those who say that all that appears is true that they look for proofs of whether we are now awake or asleep. "All these doubts, however, amount to the same thing, for they all think that there is a reason for everything." And he adds : "They seek the reason for things of which there is no reason, for there is no demonstration of a principle of demonstration". According to him, then, the fact that we are awake is as self-evident as a principle of demonstration.

That such a thing is contingent matters not, for as we have pointed out elsewhere, there is an order among contingent propositions.[14] Some proposition is first and immediate. Otherwise, we should have an infinite regress in contingent propositions or something contingent would follow from a necessary cause, both of

est certitudo de vigilare, sicut de per se noto, ita etiam de multis aliis actibus qui sunt in potestae nostra, (ut me intelligere, me audire,)et de aliis, qui sunt actus perfecti. Licet enim non sit certitudo quod videam album extra positum, vel in tali subjecto, vel in tali distantia, quia potest fieri illusio in medio vel organo, et multis aliis viis, tamen certitudo est quod video etiamsi illusio fiat in organo, quae maxime illusio videtur, puta quando actus fit in ipso organo non ab objecto praesente, qualis natus est fieri ab objecto praesente, et ita si potentia haberet actionem suam posita tali positione vere esset illud ibi quod visio dicitur, sive sit actio sive sit passio sive utrumque. Si autem illusio fieret non in organo proprio sed in aliquo proximo quod videtur organum, sicut si non fieret illusio in concursu nervorum, sed in ipso oculo fieret impressio speciei qualis nata est fieri ab albo, adhuc visus videret quia talis species, vel quod natum est videri in ea, videretur quia habet sufficientem distantiam respectu organi visus quod est in concursu nervorum istorum, sicut apparet per Augustinum XI *De Trinitate*, cap. ii,* quod reliquiae visorum remanentes in oculo oculis clausis videntur. Et per Philosophum *De sensu et sensato,*† quod ignis qui generatur ex elevatione oculi violenta et multiplicatur usque ad palpebram clausam, videtur. Istae verae sunt visiones licet non perfectissimae, quia hic sunt sufficientes distantiae specierum ad organum principale visus.

(Nota : notitia principii est immutabilis a veritate in falsitatem, non aliter, quia simpliciter corruptibilis est ;

---

* XI, cap. ii (Migne, P.L., XLII, 987).
† cap. ii (437^a, 23–24).

which are impossible. And just as our certitude of being awake is like that of self-evident propositions, the same is true of many other acts in our power such as "I understand", or "I hear", and other such acts which are being performed.

For even though there is no certitude that I see white located outside, either in such a subject or at such a distance (for an illusion can be caused in the medium or in the organ or in a number of other ways), still for all that there is certitude that I see even when the illusion is in the organ itself, which seems to be the greatest of all illusions (for instance, when the same kind of act takes place in the organ without any object present as naturally should take place only when such an object is present). In such a case, if the faculty should act, that which is called vision would truly be present whether vision be action or passion or both. But if the illusion were not caused in the organ proper but in something near which seems to be the organ, for instance, if the illusion did not take place in the bundle of nerves but in the eye, a species similar to that which naturally results from an object would be impressed. In such a case there would still be an act of vision, for we would see such a species or what is to be seen therein because it is sufficiently distant from the organ of sight in the bundle of those nerves. This is evident from Augustine in *De Trinitate*, BK. XI, c. ii,* because after-images of vision are seen when the eye is closed. It is also evident from the Philosopher in *De sensu et sensato*,† because the flash of fire produced by violently elevating the eye and transmitted as far as the closed eyelid is seen. Although these are not the most perfect, they are true visions, for in this case a sufficient distance intervenes between the species and the principal organ of vision.

(Note [15] : Knowledge of a principle is immutable in the sense that it cannot change from truth to falsity. It is not unchangeable in the other sense, for it is simply

sic species intelligibilis, non phantasma, est debilis, sed immutabilis a vera repraesentatione in falsem ; sed objectum licet corruptibile tamen est immutabile a vera entitate in falsam, et ideo est conformativum notitiae sibi seu causativum notitiae sive veritati in essendo, quia entitas vera immutabilis in falsam virtualiter continet notitiam veram immutabiliter, id est, conformem entitati verae.) (Nota : secundum Augustinum verum neces-sarium sive immutabile est supra mentem, intellige : in ratione veritatis evidentis, quia hanc de se causat in mente, non autem secundum ejus evidentiam subest menti ut possit apparere vera vel falsa, sicut subest verum probabile menti, ut ipsa possit facere illud apparere verum vel falsum, quaerendo rationes hinc inde per quas probetur et improbetur. Sic intelligendum est quod mens non judicat de vero immutabili, sed de aliis, quia dictatio quod hoc sit verum, quae est actus judicandi, est in potestate mentis respectu probabilis, non autem respectu necessarii, nec tamen minus perfecte asserit de necessario quod ipsum sit verum ; et haec assertio apud Aristotelem potest dici judicium, sed Augustinus vult judicium esse in potestate judicantis, non quod statim necessario determinetur ab alio. Sic patet quomodo de conclusione necessaria mens judicat quia non est statim ex se ; ideo non determinat ex se ad evidentiam sui ipsi menti. Potest etiam mens rationes sophisticas adducere

perishable. Thus the intelligible species, not the image, is weak. Nevertheless, it is unable to change from a true to a false representation. But the object, although perishable, cannot change from something true to something false. As a result, it is able to conform knowledge to itself or to cause knowledge or truth by being what it is, for a true entity, unable to become something false, virtually contains true knowledge immutably, that is, knowledge conformed to true entity.) (Note [16] : According to Augustine, necessary or immutable truth is "above the mind"—understand "taken precisely as evident truth". For what is necessarily and immutably true causes this evident knowledge of itself in the mind, As evident, such a truth is not subject to the mind so that it could appear either true or false in the way that a probable truth is subject to the mind inasmuch as it is in the power of the mind to make it appear true or false by looking here or there for reasons that prove or disprove it. In this way we must understand the statement that the mind judges about other things and not about immutable truth. For it is only in the case of something probable and not in the case of something necessary that the assertion of its truth—an act of judgment—lies within the power of the mind. But this does not mean that the mind asserts the truth of a necessary proposition in a less perfect manner. According to Aristotle, the latter can be called a "judgment", whereas Augustine understands judgment as something that is in the power of the one judging and not as something that is immediately and necessarily determined by a factor beyond one's control. And so it is patent how the mind "judges" about a necessary conclusion that is not immediately evident of itself and therefore does not force itself upon the mind as something evident. The mind can even bring up sophistical reasons against the conclusion in question and on the basis of these reasons refuse its assent. But this it cannot do with something that is

contra eam per quas dissentiat. Non sic contra primum
notum, IV *Metaphysicae* * :   In mentem venire, etc.)
[d. *De cognitis quae subsunt sensibus*]. Sed quomodo
habetur certitudo eorum quae subsunt actibus sensus,
puta quod aliquid extra est album, vel calidum, quale
apparet? Respondeo : aut circa tale cognitum eadem
opposita apparent diversis sensibus aut non, sed omnes
sensus cognoscentes illud, habent idem judicium de eo.
Si secundo modo, tunc certitudo habetur de veritate talis
cogniti per sensus et per istam propositionem praece-
dentem :   Quod evenit in pluribus ab aliquo illud est
causa naturalis ejus, si non sit causa libera. Ergo cum
ab isto praesente ut in pluribus evenit talis immutatio
sensus sequitur quod immutatio vel species genita sit
effectus naturalis talis causae, et ita tale extra erit album,
vel calidum, vel tale aliquid quale natum est praesentari
per speciem genitam ab ipso ut in pluribus.

Si autem diversi sensus habeant diversa judicia de
aliquo viso extra, puta visus dicit baculum esse fractum
cujus pars est in aqua et pars est in aere, visus semper
dicit solem esse minoris quantitatis quam est, et omne
visum a remotis esse minus quam sit, in talibus est certitudo quid verum sit et quis sensus erret per propositionem
quiescentem in anima certiorem omni judicio sensus, et
per actus plurium sensuum concurrentes, ita quod semper
aliqua propositio rectificat mentem vel intellectum de
actibus sensus quis sit verus et quis falsus, in qua propositione intellectus non dependet a sensu, sicut a causa,
sed sicut ab occasione. Exemplum : intellectus habet
istam propositionem quiescentem : Nullum durius frangi-
tur in actu alicujus mollis sibi cedentis. Haec est ita per

---

* IV, cap. iii (1005^b, 15 ff.).

first known [viz. a primary principle] according to *Metaphysics*, BK. IV).*

[*d. Certitude of Sense Knowledge*]. But how can a person be certain of those things which fall under the acts of the senses, for instance, that something outside is white or hot in the way that it appears to be ? I reply : Regarding such an object, either the same things appear opposite to different senses or they do not appear so but rather all the senses knowing such an object judge the same about it. If the latter be the case, then we have certitude of this thing perceived by the senses in virtue of the aforementioned principle, viz. "What occurs in most instances by means of something that is not a free cause is the natural effect of this thing". Therefore, if the same change repeatedly occurs in the majority of cases when such an object is presented, it follows that the transformation or image produced is the natural effect of such a cause, and thus the external thing will be white or hot or such as it naturally appears to be according to the image so frequently produced.

But if the judgment of different senses differs in regard to what is seen outside ; for instance, if sight says that the staff which is partly in the water and partly in the air is broken, or if sight says, as it invariably does, that the sun is smaller in size than it really is, or in general, that everything seen from a distance is smaller than it is in reality, in all such instances we are still certain of what is true and know which sense is in error. This we know by reason of some proposition in the soul more certain than any sense judgment together with the concurrent testimony of several of the senses. For there is always some proposition to set the mind or intellect aright regarding which acts of the senses are true and which false—a proposition, note, which the senses do not cause but merely occasion in the intellect. For instance, the intellect has this proposition reposing in it : "The harder object is not broken by the touch of something soft which

se nota ex terminis quod etiamsi essent accepti a sensibus
errantibus, non potest intellectus dubitare de illa. Immo,
oppositum includit contradictionem. Sed quod baculus
sit durior aqua, et aqua sibi cedat, hoc dicit uterque
sensus tam visus quam tactus. Sequitur, ergo baculum
non est fractus sicut sensus judicat ipsum fractum, et ita
quis sensus erret et quis non circa fractionem baculi,
intellectus judicat per certius omni actu sensus. Similiter, ex alia parte quod quantum applicatum quanto
omnino est aequale sibi, hoc est notum intellectui quantumcumque notitia terminorum accipiatur a sensu
errante. Sed quod idem quantum possit applicari viso
propinquo et remoto, hoc dicit tam visus quam tactus.
Ergo, quantum visum sive a prope sive a remotis est
aequale ; ergo visus dicens hoc esse minus errat. Haec
conclusio concluditur ex principiis per se notis et ex
actibus duorum sensuum cognoscentium ut in pluribus
esse ita, et ita ubicumque ratio judicat sensum errare,
hoc judicat non per aliquam notitiam praecise acquisitam
a sensibus ut causa, sed per aliquam notitiam occasio-
natam a sensu in qua non fallitur etiam si omnes sensus
fallantur, et per aliquam aliam notitiam acquisitam a
sensu vel a sensibus ut in pluribus quae sciuntur esse vera
quae sciuntur esse vera per propositionem saepe allega-
tam, scilicet : Quod in pluribus evenit, etc.

[*Tertius articulus. Solutio ipsius Henrici*]. Quantum ad
tertium articulum ex istis est respondendum ad illas
rationes tres.
    Ad primam : ad illud de mutatione objecti, ante-
cedens est falsum ; non enim sensibilia sunt in continuo
motu. Immo permanent eadem in aliqua duratione, nec

gives way before it". So evident is this proposition upon analysis of its terms that the intellect could not call it in doubt, even if its terms were derived from erroneous senses. Indeed, the opposite of this proposition includes a contradiction. Now both sight and touch attest that the stick is harder than the water and that the water gives way before the stick. It follows therefore that the stick is not broken as the sense of sight judges. Hence, in the case of the "broken staff" the intellect judges by something more certain than any testimony of the sense. And so too with the other cases. Even though the terms be derived from erring senses, the intellect knows that the measure used to measure remains perfectly equal to itself. Now the sense of sight as well as that of touch tell us that the identical measure can be applied to a nearby object of vision and to a distant object. Therefore, the actual size of the object is equal whether seen from near by or from afar. Sight errs, consequently, when it declares the size to be less. This conclusion is inferred from self-evident principles and from the repeated testimony of its truth by two senses. And so when reason judges that the senses err, it does so in virtue of two kinds of knowledge. The first is a knowledge for which the intellect requires the sense only as an occasion and not as a cause—a knowledge in which it would not be deceived even if all the senses were deceived. The other is a knowledge acquired by the oft-repeated testimony of one or more senses which are known to be true by reason of the proposition so frequently quoted, viz. "Whatever occurs in most instances, etc.".

[*Article III. Reply to Henry's Arguments*]. In this third article, we must answer the three arguments [of Henry] [17] in the light of what has been said.

As for the *first argument* (viz. that based on the change in the object) the antecedent is false. For sensible things are not in continual motion ; indeed, they remain the same for some time. Neither is this the opinion of

est opinio Augustini, sed error Heracliti et discipuli sui Cratyli, qui nolebant loqui sed movere digitum ut dicitur IV *Metaphysicae*.* Et consequentia non valet, dato quod antecedens esset verum quia adhuc secundum Aristotelem, posset haberi certa cognito de hoc dato quod omnia continue moverentur.

Non sequitur etiam : si objectum est mutabile, igitur quod gignitur ab eo non est repraesentativum alicujus sub ratione immutabilis, quia mutabilitas in objecto non est ratio gignendi, sed natura ipsius objecti, quod est mutabile, vel quae natura est immutabilis. Genitum igitur ab ipso repraesentat naturam per se. Igitur si natura, unde natura habeat aliquam immutabilem habitudinem ad aliquid, illud aliud per suum exemplar et natura ipsa per suum exemplar repraesentatur ut immutabiliter unita, et ita per duo exemplaria generata a duobus mutabilibus, non inquantum mutabilia, sed in quantum naturae, potest haberi notitia immutabilitatis unionis eorum.

(Quamvis non in quantum mutabile significat, si tamen est mutabile, quomodo ejus ad aliud est habitudo immutabilis ? Respondeo : habitudo est immutabilis sic quia inter extrema non potest esse opposita habitudo, nec non esse ista positis extremis, sed per destructionem extremi vel extremorum destruitur. Contra : Quomodo propositio necessaria affirmatur si identitas extremorum potest destrui ? Respondeo : quando res non est, non est identitas ejus realis ; sed tunc si est in intellectu, est identitas ut est objectum intellectum, et necessaria secundum quid, quia in tali esse extrema non possunt esse sine tali identitate. Tamen illa potest non esse sicut

---

* IV, cap. vi (1011^a, 4-13).

Augustine. It is rather the error of Heraclitus and his disciple Cratylus, who did not even wish to speak but only move his finger, as *Metaphysics*, BK. IV,* relates. But even if the antecedent were true, the consequence would still be invalid, for as Aristotle pointed out, we could still be certain of this truth, viz. that all things are in continuous motion.

Likewise, it does not follow that just because an object is mutable, therefore the knowledge produced does not represent anything under an immutable aspect. For it is not precisely this *mutability* in the object that causes the knowledge ; it is the *nature* of this mutable object that does so, and this nature is immutable. Hence, the knowledge produced by it represents the nature itself. And if it is the nature, this nature may have an immutable relation to something, and then both this nature and the other thing to which it is related, each by its own exemplar, are represented as immutably united. And so by means of two terms produced by two mutable things (though not in so far as they are changeable, but in so far as they are natures) it is possible to have a knowledge of their immutable union.

(Even [18] though something mutable is not signified in so far as it is mutable, how is it that its relation to another thing is immutable ? I reply that the relation is immutable in this sense, that the opposite relation could not exist between the extremes ; neither could this relation be non-existent, given these extremes. By the destruction of one or both extremes, however, this relation is also destroyed. To the contrary : How can we assert that the proposition is necessary if the identity of the extremes could be destroyed? I reply : When a thing is non-existent, it has no real identity, but in such a case, if it is in the mind it has an identity inasmuch as it is an object known, and this identity is necessary only in a qualified sense inasmuch as the extremes cannot exist in thought without possessing this identity. Neverthe-

extremum potest esse non intellectum. Ergo, propositio necessaria in intellectu nostro secundum quid, quia immutabilis in falsam. Sed simpliciter necessaria non nisi in intellectu divino, sicut nec extrema habent identitatem simpliciter necessario in aliquo esse, nisi in illo esse intellecto.)

Patet etiam quod repraesentatum in se mutabile, potest repraesentare aliquid sub ratione immutabilis, quia essentia Dei sub ratione immutabilis repraesentabitur intellectui per aliquid omnino mutabile sive illud sit species sive actus. Hoc patet per simile, quia per finitum potest repraesentari aliquid sub ratione infiniti.

Ad secundum, dico quod in anima potest intelligi duplex mutabilitas, una ab affirmatione in negationem, et econverso, puta ab ignorantia ad scientiam, vel a non intellectione ad intellectionem. Alia quasi a contrario in contrarium, puta a rectitudine in deceptionem, vel econverso. Ad quaecumque autem objecta est mutabilis anima prima mutabilitate, et per nihil formaliter in ea existens tollitur ab ea talis immutabilitas. Sed non est mutabilis secunda mutabilitate, nisi circa illa complexa quae non habent evidentiam ex terminis. Circa illa vero quae sunt evidentia ex terminis, mutari non potest secunda mutabilitate, quia ipsi termini apprehensi sunt causa necessaria et evidens conformitatis compositionis factae ad ipsos terminos. Ergo si anima est mutabilis a rectitudine in errorem absolute, non sequitur quod per nihil aliud a se potest rectificari. Saltem

less, this identity need not exist, even as the term need not be known. Therefore, the proposition in the mind is necessary only in a qualified sense inasmuch as it cannot become false. But it would only be necessary in an unqualified sense in the divine intellect, for the terms have an identity that is simply necessary in no other form of existence save that which they possess by being known by God.)

It is also evident that something can be represented under an immutable aspect even if that which does the representing is something mutable in itself. For the essence of God is represented to the intellect as something immutable by means of something that is radically changeable, whether the latter be the species or the act of knowing. This is evident from a similar case, for something can be represented as infinite through what is finite.

As to the *second*, this changeability of the soul can be understood in a twofold sense : one from affirmation to negation and vice versa, such as from a state of ignorance to a state of knowledge or from a lack of understanding to understanding ; the other from one contrary as it were to another, such as from being right to being deceived, or vice versa. The soul, however, is changeable with regard to any object only in the first sense of mutability, and there is nothing which exists formally in the soul that will remove this kind of mutability. But the soul is not mutable in the second sense except in regard to such propositions as are not evident from their terms. But with those propositions that are evident from their terms, the soul cannot be altered in the second way for the terms which are apprehended are themselves the necessary and evident cause of the conformity of the judgment involving the aforesaid terms. Therefore, even if the soul is mutable in the sense that absolutely speaking it can pass from the state of being correct to a state of error, it does not follow that it can be set aright only by something other than itself. At least it can be set aright

rectificari potest circa illa objecta circa quae non potest intellectus errare apprehensis terminis.

Ad tertium, dico quod si aliquam apparentiam haberet, magis concluderet contra opinionem illam quae negat speciem intelligibilem, quae est opinio ponentis istam opinionem hic, quia illa species quae potest repraesentare sensibile tamquam objectum in somniis esset phantasma, non species intelligibilis. Igitur si intellectus solo phantasmate utatur per quod objectum est sibi praesens et non aliqua specie intelligibili, non videtur quod per aliquod in quo objectum sibi relucet posset discernere verum a verisimili ; sed ponendo speciem in intellectu, non valet ratio, quia intellectus non potest uti illa pro se ut pro objecto, quia non contingit uti illa in dormiendo.

Si objicis : si phantasma potest repraesentare se ut objectum, igitur intellectus per illum errorem virtutis phantasticae potest errare vel saltem potest ligari ne possit operari, ut patet in somniis et phreneticis, potest dici quod etsi legetur quando est talis error virtute phantastica, non tamen tunc errat intellectus, quia tunc non habet aliquem actum.

Sed quomodo sciet vel erit tunc intellectus certus quando non errat virtus phantastica quam tamen non errare requiritur ad hoc quod intellectus non erret ? Respondeo : ista veritas quiescit in intellectu quod potentia non errat circa objectum proportionatum nisi indisposita, et notum est intellectui virtutem phantasticam non esse indispositam in vigilia tali indispositione

in regard to those objects about which the intellect cannot err once the terms are grasped.

To the *third argument*, I say that if it held at all, it would rather be valid against that opinion which denies the intelligible species—the view of the man who has advanced the opposing theory [viz. Henry of Ghent].[19] For the species which is able to represent the sensible in dreams as though it were an object would be the sense image or phantasm and not the intelligible species. Therefore, if the intellect were to use the sense image alone so that the object would be present to the mind through the sense image and not in virtue of any intelligible species, there seems to be no way of distinguishing between what is true and what merely appears to be true by means of something in which the object itself appears. But if we assume the existence of a species in the intellect, the argument does not hold, because the intellect is unable to use such a species as though it were an object in itself for the simple reason that it is not able to use such a species in sleep.

You may object that if the sense image can represent itself as object, then it follows that the intellect could err by reason of this error in the faculty of the imagination, or at least, as is the case in dreams or with madmen, the intellect could be so bound that it could not operate. It can be said in reply that if the intellect is bound when there is such an error due to the imaginative faculty, then the intellect does not err for the simple reason that it does not act.

But how will one know or how will the intellect ever be certain that the imagination does not err when the latter faculty must be free of error if the intellect is not to err? I reply that the following truth reposes in the mind. "A faculty does not err in regard to an object that is properly proportioned to it unless the said faculty is indisposed". Now it is known to the intellect that the imaginative faculty is not indisposed during a waking

quae facit phantasma repraesentare se tamquam objectum, quia per se notum est intellectui quod intelligens vigilat, ita quod virtus phantastica non est ligata in vigilia sicut in somniis.

Sed adhuc instatur contra certitudinem dictam de actibus hoc modo : Videtur mihi quod videam vel audiam ubi tamen nec video nec audio. Igitur, de hoc non est certitudo. Respondeo : Aliud est contra negantem aliquam propositionem ostendere eam esse veram ; aliud est alicui admittenti eam ostendere quomodo sit vera. Exemplum : IV *Metaphysicae*,* contra negantem primum principium non inducit Philosophus istud inconveniens, quod opiniones contrariae simul essent in anima. Hoc ipsi concederent sicut praemissam, sed inducit eis alia inconvenientia manifestiora eis, licet non in se ; sed recipientibus primum principium ostendit quomodo sit notum, quia ita notum est quod oppositum ejus non possit venire in mentem, quod probat quia tunc possent opiniones contrariae simul stare, talis conclusio est ibi magis inconveniens quam hypothesis.

Ita hic, si concedis nullam esse per se notam nolo disputare tecum quia constat quod protervus [*MS* protervis] et non es persuasus, sicut patet in actibus tuis, quomodo objicit Philosophus IV *Metaphysicae*,† somnians enim de aliquo quasi in proximo consequendo sive obtinendo et postea evigilans non prosequeris illud sicut prosequeris vel prosequereris, si ita esses proximus in vigilando ad illud consequendum.

Si autem admittis aliquam propositionem esse per se notam, et circa quamcumque potest potentia indisposita errare, sicut patet in somniis, ergo ad hoc ut aliqua cog-

---

* IV, cap. iii (1005^b, 25 ff.). † IV, cap. v (1010^b, 10).

state to such an extent that the sense image would represent itself as an object, for it is self-evident to the intellect that when it knows, it is awake, and that, consequently, the imagination is not bound in a waking state as it is in sleep.

But there is still another objection to the aforementioned certitude about our actions. It runs as follows. I seem to see and to hear, whereas in reality I neither see nor hear ; consequently, I have no certainty on this point. I reply that it is one thing to show someone who denies a given proposition that it is true and quite another to indicate to someone who admits the given proposition how it is true. For example in *Metaphysics*, BK. IV,* the Philosopher does not adduce the inconsistency that "contrary opinions would be present in the soul at one and the same time" against those who deny the first principle [viz. of contradiction], for they indeed would concede this as a premise. Instead he brings out other inconsistencies which are more manifest to them though they are not more evident in themselves. But he does show those who grant this first principle how this principle is known. For it is known in such a way that its opposite could not even enter the mind. This he proves from the fact that otherwise contrary opinions could exist simultaneously in the mind. Such a conclusion is, in this case, even more inconsistent than the hypothesis.

So it is in our case. If you hold that nothing is self-evident, I will not argue with you for it is clear that you are a quibbler and are not to be convinced. This is apparent from your actions, as the Philosopher indicates in *Metaphysics*, BK. IV,† for if you dream of obtaining or going after some nearby object, after you awake you no longer seek it as you would do, or would have done, had you been that close to getting it while awake.

If, however, you admit that some proposition is self-evident and that a power indisposed can err with regard to anything, as is clear in the case of dreams, then from

noscatur per se esse nota, oportet quod possit cognosci quando potentia est disposita et quando non. Et per consequens potest haberi notitia de actibus nostris, quod potentia est ita disposita quod illa est per se nota quae apparet sibi per se nota.

Dico tunc ad formam hujus cavillationis, quod sicut apparet somnianti se videre, ita posset sibi apparere oppositum unius principii per se noti speculabilis, et tamen non sequitur quin illud principium sit per se notum et ita non sequitur quin sit per se notum audienti quod audiat, quia circa utrumque potest potentia indisposita errare ; non autem disposita. Et quando sit disposita et quando non, hoc est per se notum ; alias non posset cognosci aliquam aliam esse per se notam, quia non posset cognosci quae foret per se nota, utrum illa cui intellectus sit dispositus vel cui sic assentiret.

[*Articulus Quartus. Contra conclusionem Henrici*]. Circa quartum articulum contra conclusionem opinionis arguo sic. Quaero quid intelligit per veritatem certam et sinceram, aut veritatem infallibilem absque dubitatione, scilicet, et deceptione, et probatum est prius et declaratum in articulo secundo et tertio, quod illa potest haberi ex puris naturalibus. Aut intelligit de veritate quae est passio entis, et tunc cum ens possit naturaliter intelligi, ergo et verum ut est passio ejus, et si verum igitur et veritas per abstractionem quasi, quia quaecumque forma potest intelligi ut in subjecto, potest intelligi ut in se et in abstracto a subjecto. Aut alio modo intelligit per veritatem conformitatem ad exemplar, et si ad creatum, patet propositum. Si autem ad exemplar

the fact that something can be recognised as self-evident it follows that a person can tell when a faculty is disposed and when it is not. Consequently, in regard to our actions it is possible to know that a faculty is so disposed that what appears to be self-evident is actually so.

As to the form of this sophistical argument, then, I say this. Just it appears to the dreamer that he sees, so also the opposite of some self-evident speculative principle might appear to him. But from this it still does not follow that such a principle is not self-evident. Likewise it does not follow that it is not self-evident to the hearer that he hears. For if a power that is indisposed can err with regard to either truth, a power that is disposed cannot. And it is self-evident when it is disposed and when it is not. Otherwise, nothing else would be recognised as self-evident, for one could never tell what would be self-evident, or whether this is something to which the intellect is disposed or to which it would assent in this way.

[*Article IV. Concerning Henry's Conclusion*]. In the fourth article I argue against the conclusion of [Henry's] view [20] as follows : What, I ask, is meant by certain and unadulterated truth? Either it means infallible truth, that is, a truth which excludes all doubt and deception. And in this case, we have proved and declared already in the second and third articles that such truth is possible on purely natural grounds. Or by such truth he means truth as an attribute of "being". In which case, since we can know "being" we can also know its attribute "true". And if we know "true" we can also know truth by a kind of abstraction. For any form that can be recognised in a subject can also be known in itself and in the abstract apart from the subject. Or truth is to be understood in still another way, as truth of conformity to an exemplar. If the exemplar in question is taken to be created, we have what we seek to prove. If conformity to an uncreated exemplar is meant, why such

increatum, conformitas ad illud non potest intelligi nisi in illo exemplari cognito, quia relatio non est cognoscibilis nisi cognito extremo ; ergo falsum est quod ponitur exemplar aeternum esse rationem cognoscendi et non cognitum.

Praeterea secundo sic : Intellectus simplex, omne quod intelligit confuse, potest cognoscere definitive, inquirendo definitionem illius cogniti per viam divisionis. Haec cognitio definitiva videtur perfectissima pertinens ad intellectum simplicem. Ex tali autem cognitione perfectissima terminorum, potest intellectus perfectissime intelligere principium et ex principio conclusionem, et in hoc compleri videtur notitia intellectualis ita quod non videtur cognitio veritatis necessaria ultra veritates praedictas.

Item tertio, aut lux aeterna quam dicis necessariam ad habendum sinceram veritatem, causat aliquid prius naturaliter actu aut non. Si sic, aut igitur in objecto aut in intellectu. Non in objecto, quia objectum in quantum habet esse in intellectu, non habet esse reale, sed tantum intentionale. Igitur non est capax alicujus accidentis realis. Sed in intellectu, igitur lux increata non immutat ad cognoscendum sinceram veritatem nisi mediante effectu suo, et ita aeque perfecte videtur opinio communis ponere notitiam in lumine increato, sicut ista positio ; quia ponit esse videri in intellectu agente qui est effectus luminis increatae et perfectior quam esset illud lumen accidentale creatum. Si autem nihil causat ante actum, aut ergo sola lux causat actum, aut lux cum

conformity cannot be recognised unless the exemplar itself is known, for unless the term of a relation is known the relation itself cannot be known. Consequently, it is false to assume that an eternal exemplar is the reason why we know something when this exemplar itself remains unknown.

Secondly, I argue further that simple intelligence [21] can know by way of definition all that it knows in a confused manner by the simple expedient of discovering the definition of the thing known by way of division. This definitive knowledge seems to be the most perfect kind of knowledge that pertains to simple intelligence. From this most perfect knowledge of the terms, however, the intellect can understand the principle most perfectly ; and from the principle, the conclusion. Intellectual knowledge seems to be complete with this, so that no further knowledge of truth over and above the aforementioned truths seems necessary.

In the third place, either the Eternal Light, which you say is necessary in order to have unadulterated truth, causes something naturally prior to the act or not. If it does, then this thing is produced either in the object or in the intellect. But it cannot be produced in the object, because the object, in so far as it exists in the intellect, has no real existence but only intentional existence. Therefore, it is incapable of any real accident. If this thing is produced in the intellect, then the Eternal Light transforms [the mind] to know pure truth only through the medium of its effect. If this be the case, then it seems that common opinion attributes knowledge to the Uncreated Light to the same extent as does this, for the common view assumes that knowledge is seen in the active intellect, which is the effect of the Uncreated Light, and indeed is a more perfect effect than this accidental created Light would be.[22] If this Uncreated Light does not cause anything prior to the act, then either the Light alone causes the act [of knowledge], or the Light

intellectu et objecto. Si sola lux, ergo intellectus agens
nullam habet operationem in cognitione sincerae veritatis, quod videtur inconveniens, quia ista operatio est
nobilissima intellectus nostri. Igitur intellectus agens qui
est nobilissimus in anima, concurreret aliquo modo ad
istam actionem. [Non in libro Scoti] [24] (et iterum actus
intelligendi non magis diceretur unius hominis quam
alterius, et sic superflueret intellectus agens quod non
est dicendum, cum ejus sit omnia facere sicut possibilis
omnia fieri. Similiter etiam secundum Philosophum
III *De anima* : Intellectus agens correspondet in ratione
activi, possibili in ratione passivi ; ergo quidquid
recipit possibilis ad illud, aliquo modo se habet active
intellectus agens).

Et hoc etiam inconveniens quod illatum est ibi, concluditur ex opinione praedicta per aliam viam, quia
secundum sic opinantem, agens utens instrumento non
potest habere actionem excedentem actionem instrumenti. Ergo cum virtus intellectus agentis non possit
in cognitionem sincerae veritatis, [*MS om.* lux aeterna
utenti intellectu agente non poterit in cognitionem vel in
actionem istius cognitionis sincerae veritatis,] ita quod
intellectus agens habeat ibi rationem instrumenti. Si
dicas quod lux increata cum intellectu et objecto causet
istam veritatem sinceram, haec est opinio communis
quae ponit lucem aeternam sicut causam remotam
causare omnem certam veritatem, vel erit ista opinio
inconveniens, vel non discordabit a communi opinione.

[*Articulus Quintus. Solutio Quaestionis*]. Ad quaestionem
igitur dico quod propter verba Augustini, debet con-
cedere quod veritates infallibiles videntur in regulis
aeternis, ubi potest li in accipi objective, et hoc quadrupliciter : vel sicut in objecto proximo, vel sicut in

with the intellect and object do so. If the Light does so alone, then the active intellect has no function whatsoever in knowing pure truth. But this seems inconsistent because the latter is the most noble function of our intellect. The active intellect, then, which is the most noble [faculty of knowledge] [23] in our soul, must concur in some way in this action. [24]

And the inconsistency here inferred also follows from the aforesaid opinion in another way. For according to the one who holds this opinion, any agent using an instrument is incapable of performing an action which exceeds the action of the instrument. Therefore, since the power of the active intellect could not arrive at the knowledge of pure truth, the Eternal Light using the active intellect could not produce this knowledge or have anything to do with the act whereby pure truth is known and still have the active intellect function as an instrument. And if you say that the Uncreated Light causes this unadulterated truth together with the intellect and the object, this is the common opinion which assumes that the Uncreated Light acting as the remote cause produces all certain truth. Consequently, either this opinion [of Henry] is inconsistent or it is not at variance with the common view.

[*Article V. Solution of the Question*].[25] As to the question, then, I say that because of what Augustine has said, one should concede that infallible truths are seen in the eternal rules, where the term "in" can be taken in the sense of "in an object". There are four ways in which this could be done : (1) either as in a proximate object, or (2) as in that which contains the proximate object, or (3) as that in virtue of which the

continente objectum proximum, vel sicut in eo virtute
cujus objectum proximum movet, vel sicut in objecto
remoto.

[Prima Via]. Ad intellectum primi, dico quod omnia
intelligibilia actu intellectus divini habent esse intelligibile, et in eis omnes veritates de eis relucent, ita
quod intellectus intelligens ea, et virtute eorum intelligens necessaria veritates de eis, videt in eis sicut in
objectis istas veritates necessarias. Illa autem inquantum sunt objecta secundaria intellectus divini, sunt
veritates quia conformes suo exemplari, intellectu scilicet
divino ; et sunt lux quia manifestae ; et sunt immuta-
biles ibi et necessariae. Sed aeternae sunt secundum
quid, quia aeternitas est conditio existentis, et illa non
habent existentiam nisi secundum quid. Sic igitur
primo possumus dici videre in luce aeterna, hoc est in
objecto secundario intellectus divini, quod est veritas et
lux aeterna modo exposito.

[Secunda Via]. Secundus modus patet similiter, quia
intellectus divinus continet istas veritates quasi liber,
sicut illa auctoritas Augustini dicit De Trinitate xiv,
cap. xv * : quod istae regulae scriptae, scriptae sunt in
libro lucis aeternae, id est, in intellectu divino inquantum
continet istas veritates et licet ille liber non videatur,
videntur tamen illae veritates quae sunt scriptae in libro
illo primo, et eatenus posset dici intellectus noster videre
veritates in luce aeterna, hoc est, in libro illo sicut in
continente objectum [26] (et hoc secundum secundum
modum vel in illis veritatibus quae sunt lux aeterna
secundum quid, sicut in objectis videmus secundum
primum modum).

Et alter istorum modorum videtur esse de intellectu

---

* xiv, cap. xv (Migne, P.L., xlii, 1052).

proximate object moves [the intellect], or (4) as in a remote object.

[The First Way]. In explanation of the first, I say that all the intelligibles have an intelligible being in virtue of the act of the divine intellect. In these intelligibles all the truths that can be affirmed about them are visible so that the intellect knowing these intelligibles and in virtue thereof understanding the necessary truths about them, sees these truths in them as in an object. Now these intelligibles inasmuch as they are secondary objects of the divine intellect are "truths" because they are conformed to their exemplar, viz. the divine intellect. Likewise, they are a "light" because they are manifest. And there they are immutable and necessary. But they are eternal only in a qualified sense, because eternity is characteristic of something really existing, and these intelligibles "exist" only in a qualified sense. This then is the first way in which we can be said to see in the Eternal Light, i.e. as in the secondary object of the divine intellect, which object is truth and eternal light in the sense explained.

[The Second Way]. The second way is also clear, because the divine intellect contains these truths like a book, as Augustine testifies in *De Trinitate*, BK. XIV, c. XV * : "These rules are written in the book of Eternal Light", that is, in the divine intellect inasmuch as it contains these truths. And although this book itself is not seen, nevertheless those truths are seen which are written in this book. And to this extent, our intellect could be said to see truths in the Eternal Light, i.e. to see things which are in that book as in something which contains the object.[26]

And Augustine's statement in *De Trinitate*, BK. XII,

Augustini xii *De Trinitate*, cap. xiv,* quod ratio quadrati corporis manet incorrumptibilis et immutabilis, etc. Non autem manet talis nisi ut est objectum secundarium intellectus divini.

Sed contra primum modum est dubium. Si enim non videmus istas veritates ut sunt in intellectu divino, quia non videmus divinum intellectum, quomodo dicemur videre in luce increata ex hoc quod videmus in tali luce aeterna secundum quid, quae habet esse in luce increata sicut in intellectu cognoscente.

[Tertia Via]. Huic respondet tertius modus, qui talis est : illa ut sunt objectum secundarium intellectus divini non habent esse nisi secundum quid ; operatio autem aliqua vera realis non competit alicui praecise enti secundum quid virtute sui, sed si aliquo modo competit sibi, hoc oportet esse virtute alicujus cui competit esse simpliciter. Igitur istis objectis secundariis non competit movere intellectum praecise nisi virtute esse intellectus divini quod est esse simpliciter, et per quod ista habent esse secundum quid. Sic ergo in luce aeterna secundum quid, sicut in objecto proximo videmus ; sed in luce aeterna increata videmus secundum tertium modum sicut in causa proxima cujus virtute objectum proximum movet.

Juxta hoc etiam potest dici quod quantum ad tertium modum videmus in luce aeterna sicut in causa objecti in se. Nam intellectus divinus producit ista actu suo in esse intelligibili, et actu suo dat huic objecto esse tale et illi tale, et per consequens dat eis talem rationem objecti per quas rationes post movent intellectum ad cognitionem

---

* xii, cap. xiv (Migne, P.L., xlii, 1011).

c. xiv,* that the meaning of "square body" remains incorruptible and immutable, and so on, can be understood seemingly in either of these two ways. For the meaning of a square body remains incorruptible and immutable only inasmuch as it is a secondary object of the divine intellect.

But there is a doubt about this first way. We do not see these truths as they are in the divine intellect, because we do not see the divine intellect itself. How then can we be said to see things in the Uncreated Light—things, which exist indeed in the Uncreated Light as objects known by that intellect, but which we see only in something which is the eternal light in a qualified sense.[27] To this the third way gives the following answer.

[The Third Way]. These intelligibles in so far as they are secondary objects of the divine intellect have existence only in a qualified sense. But something that exists only in a qualified sense, to the precise extent that it "exists" in this way, is incapable of any truly real operation.[28] If such an operation pertains to it at all, it does so only in virtue of something which exists in an unqualified sense. Therefore, these secondary objects do not enjoy the power to move the intellect, to speak precisely, except by virtue of the existence of the divine intellect, which exists in an unqualified sense and through which the intelligibles have existence in a qualified sense. And so we see in the eternal light in a qualified sense as in the proximate object. But according to this third way we see in the Uncreated Light as in the immediate cause by virtue of which the proximate object moves [the intellect].

We can also be said to see in the Eternal Light in this third way inasmuch as this Light is the cause of the object itself. For the divine intellect produces this intelligible in existence and by its act gives to this object one type of being and to another a second type of being. Consequently, the divine intellect gives them such intelligible content as they possess as objects of knowledge. Now

certam, et quod proprie posset dici intellectum nostrum videre in luce, quia lux est causa objecti. Apparet per simile : quia proprie dicimur intelligere in lumine intellectus agentis, cum tamen illud lumen non sit nisi causa activa, vel faciens objectum in actu suo, vel virtute cujus objectum movet, vel utrumque.

Ista igitur duplex causalitas intellectus divini, quod est vera lux increata, videlicet quae producit objecta secundaria in esse intelligibili, et quod est illud virtute cujus secundaria etiam objecta producta movent actualiter intellectum, potest quasi integrare unum tertium modum vel membrum propter quod dicamur vere videre in luce aeterna.

Et si objiciatur contra istos duos modos integrantes tertium membrum de causa, quia tunc magis videtur quod diceremur videre in Deo volente, vel in Deo ut voluntas est, quia voluntas divina est immediatum principium cujuslibet actus ad extra, respondeo : intellectus divinus inquantum aliquo modo prior actu voluntatis divinae producit ista objecta in esse intelligibili, et ita respectu istorum videtur esse causa mere naturalis, quia Deus non est causa libera respectu alicujus nisi quod praesupponit ante se aliquo modo voluntatem sive actum volun- tatis, et sicut intellectus ut prior actu voluntatis producit objecta in esse intelligibili, ita ut prior causa videtur cooperari illis intelligibilibus ad effectum eorum natura- lem, scilicet ut apprehensa et composita causent appre- hensionis conformitatem ad se. Videtur ergo quod contradictionem includit intellectum aliquem talem compositionem formare et compositionem non esse con-

it is through their intelligible content that they afterward move the intellect to certain knowledge. And, properly speaking, it could be said that our intellect sees in the Light, because the Light is the cause of the object. This is clear from a simile : for we are said to understand properly in the light of the active intellect, although this light is nothing more than the active cause (i.e., that which makes the [potential] object actual, or that in virtue of which the object moves, or both).

The fact then that the divine intellect, the true Uncreated Light, has a twofold causality (viz. that it produces objects in intelligible being and that it is also that in virtue of which the secondary objects produced actually move the intellect)—this fact can supply as it were a third type or mode of interpretation as to how we can be said to see truly in the Eternal Light.

But suppose someone should object to these two ways of supplying a third interpretation on the following grounds. We should rather be said to see in God willing or in God in so far as He is will, for the divine will is the immediate principle of every act directed towards something outside Himself.

I reply that the divine intellect, as far as it is in some way prior to the act of the divine will,[29] produces these objects in intelligible being, and thus the intellect seems to be a purely natural cause in their regard. For God is not a free cause of anything unless volition as an elicited act somehow precedes the thing in question. Now, inasmuch as the intellect produces objects in intelligible being prior to the act of the will, it would seem to co-operate as a prior cause with these intelligibles in the production of their natural effect—which effect consists in this : Once these intelligibles are grasped and formulated in a proposition they cause the conformity of what is grasped [viz. the proposition] to themselves [as terms]. Consequently, it seems to involve a contradiction that an intellect should form such a proposition and still not

formem terminis, licet possibile sit illos terminos non componere vel non concipere. Quia licet Deus voluntarie coagat ad hoc quod intellectus terminos componat vel non componat, tamen cum composuerit, ut illa compositio sit conformis terminis, hoc videtur necessario sequi rationem terminorum quam habent ex intellectu Dei causante illos terminos in esse intelligibili naturaliter.

Et ex isto apparet qualiter non est necessaria specialis illustratio ad videndum in regulis aeternis, quia Augustinus non ponit in eis videri nisi vera quae sunt necessaria ex vi terminorum, et in talibus est maxima (naturalitas vel) necessitas tam causae remotae quam proximae respectu effectus, puta tam intellectus divini ad objecta moventia quam illorum objectorum ad veritatem complexionis de eis, et etiam licet non tanta sit (naturalitas vel) necessitas ad perceptionem (alius vel) alicujus veritatis quod oppositum contradictionem includat, tamen (naturalitas vel) necessitas est a parte causae proximae coassistente sibi causa remota, quia termini apprehensi et compositi sunt nati naturaliter causare evidentiam conformitatis compositionis ad terminos etsi ponatur quod Deus coagat terminis ad hunc effectum influentia generali, non tamen necessitate naturali. Sed sive sit influentia generalis sive quod plus est necessitas naturalis influendi terminis ad hunc effectum, patet quod non requiritur illustratio specialis.

Assumptum de intentione Augustini patet per ipsum

have this proposition conform to the terms even though it is possible that the intellect should not grasp the terms or formulate them in a proposition. For even though God freely co-operates with the intellect when it combines or does not combine these terms, still once the terms have been formed into a proposition, the conformity of the latter with the terms seems to follow as a necessary consequence from the very meaning of the terms—a meaning which they have by reason of the fact that the intellect of God has naturally produced these terms in intelligible being.

From all this, it is clear why a special illumination is not required in order to see in the eternal reasons, for Augustine assumes that we see in them only such truths as are necessary in virtue of their terms. Now it is in just such truths that we have the greatest necessity between the effect and both its proximate and remote causes (that is, both on the part of the divine intellect in its relation to the objects which move [our intellect] and on the part of the objects in relation to the truth of the propositions about them). Even though the necessity of perceiving such a truth is not so great that not to perceive it would include a contradiction, still there is a necessity present which arises from the proximate cause [viz. the intelligibility of the terms] assisted by the remote cause [viz. the divine intellect which gives such ideas their intelligibility]. For once the terms are grasped and formed into a proposition, they are naturally able to make evident the conformity that exists between the proposition and its terms even though it be granted that God co-operates with these terms in producing their effect, not by a natural necessity, but by a general [free] influence. But whether it be by a general influence, or what is more, by a natural necessity, that God co-operates with the terms in producing their effect, it is quite clear that no special illumination is required.

The assumption as to what Augustine meant is clearly

IV *De Trinitate*, cap. xxxv,* loquitur de philosophis dicens nonnulli eorum poterunt aciem mentis ultra omnem creaturam levare et lucem incommutabilis veritatis quantulacumque ex parte attingere qui Christianos multos ex sola fide viventes nondum posse derident. Ergo vult quod Christiani credita non viderunt in regulis aeternis, sed philosophi vident in illis necessaria multa. Idem etiam IX *De Trinitate*, cap. vi † : Non qualis uniuscujusque hominis mens, etc., quasi diceret contingentia non videntur ibi, sed necessaria et in eodem IV, capitulo xxxvi ‡ arguit contra istos philosophos, numquid quia verissime disputant aeternis rationibus omnia temporaliter fieri propter ea, poterunt in ipsis rationibus aspicere quot sunt animalium genera, quot semina singulorum in exordiis, etc. Nonne ista omnia non per illam incommutabilem scientiam, sed per locorum ac temporum institutionem quaesierunt et ab aliis experta atque conscripta crediderunt. Ergo intelligit quod per regulas aeternas non cognoscuntur illa contingentia quae tantum per sensus cognoscuntur, vel per historias creduntur, et tamen specialis illustratio magis requiritur in credendis quam in cognitis necessariis. Immo, ibi maxime removetur illustratio specialis et sufficit sola generalis.

Contra : Quid igitur dicit Augustinus XII *De Trinitate*, cap. xiv ** : quod paucorum est mentis acie pervenire ad rationes intelligibiles, et *Octaginta tres quaestionum*, quaestio xlvi †† : nonnisi purae animae ad illas pertingunt. Respondeo : Ista puritas non debet intelligi a vitiis, quia XIV *De Trinitate*, cap. xv,‡‡ vult quod justus videt in regulis aeternis quid justum faciendum sit vel quid in his

* IV, cap. xv (Migne, P.L., XLII, 902).
† IX, cap. vi (Migne, P.L., XLII, 966).
‡ IV, cap. xvi (Migne, P.L., XLII, 902).
** XII, cap. xiv (Migne, P.L., XLII, 1010).
†† q. xlvi (Migne, P.L., XL, 30).
‡‡ XIV, cap. xv (Migne, P.L., XLII, 1052).

justified by what he says of the infidel philosophers in *De Trinitate*, BK. IV, c. xxxv * : "Some of them have been able to see through and beyond all creation and with their mind's eye to reach at least in some degree the light of immutable truth, a thing which they ridicule many Christians, who live meanwhile by faith alone, for not being able to do". He wishes to say, therefore, that Christians do not see in the eternal rules the things they believe and yet the philosophers see many necessary truths therein. And the same with *De Trinitate*, BK. IX, c. vi † : "Not of what sort the mind of one particular man happens to be, etc."—as if he were to say : "It is not contingent but necessary truths that are seen there". And in the same work he argues against those philosophers : "Just because they argue most truly that all that happens in time takes place on account of eternal reasons, are they therefore able to perceive therein how many kinds of animals exist or how many seeds of each there were in the beginning, and so on. . . . Have they not sought all these things not by that unchangeable knowledge, but by the history of places and times, and have they not believed the written experience of others?" Consequently, he means that contingent truths known by the senses alone or believed on the account of others are not known through the eternal rules. And yet special illumination is required even more for what must be believed than for necessary truths. Indeed, this special illumination is least needed in the case of the latter ; general illumination alone suffices.

On the contrary, Why then does Augustine say in *De Trinitate*, BK. XII, c. xiv : "It is only for the few to attain the intelligible reasons with their mind's eye", and in the *Eighty-three Questions*, q. xlvi : "Only the pure of soul reach them"? I reply that he does not mean by this purity a freedom from vices, for in *De Trinitate*, BK. XIV, c. xv, he holds that the unjust man sees in the eternal rules what a just man must do and how he must regard

sentiendum sit. Et IV libro cap. praeallegato,* vult quod plures non vident veritatem in regulis aeternis sine fide. Et quaestione eadem, † vult quod nullus potest esse sapiens sine cognitione idearum, eo modo quo Platonem concederent forsan sapientem esse. Sed ista puritas debet intelligi elevando intellectum ad considerandum veritates ut relucent in se, non tantum ut relucent in phantasmate.

Ubi considerandum est quod res sensibilis extra causat phantasma confusum et unum per accidens in virtute phantantica, repraesentans scilicet rem secundum quantitatem, secundum figuram, et colorem, et alia accidentia sensibilia. Et sicut phantasma repraesentat tantum confuse et per accidens, ita multi percipiunt tantum ens per accidens. Veritates autem primae sunt praecise tales ex propria ratione terminorum in quantum illi termini abstrahuntur ab omnibus per accidens conjunctis cum eis. Non enim haec propositio : Omne totum est majus sua parte, primo vera est ut totum est in lapide vel ligno, sed ut totum abstrahitur ab omnibus quibus conjungitur per accidens. Et ideo intellectus qui numquam intelligit totalitatem nisi in conceptu per accidens, puta in totalitate lapidis vel ligni, numquam intelligit sinceram veritatem hujus principii, quia numquam intelligit praecisam rationem termini per quam est veritas. Paucorum ergo est pertingere ad rationes aeternas, quia paucorum est habere intellectiones per se et multorum est habere conceptus tales per accidens. Sed isti pauci non dicuntur distingui ab aliis proter specialem illustrationem sed vel propter meliora naturalia, quia habent intellectum magis abstrahentem et magis perspicacem, vel propter majorem

---

* IV, cap. xvi (Migne, P.L., XLII, 902).   † loc. cit.

CONCERNING HUMAN KNOWLEDGE

things in their light. And in the fourth book, in the chapter cited above, he maintains that the philosophers saw truth in the eternal reasons even though they lacked faith. And in the same question, he holds that no one can be wise without a knowledge of the ideas in the way, for instance, that they would concede Plato to be wise. But this purity must be understood of the elevation of the intellect to the contemplation of these truths as they are in themselves and not as they appear in the sense image.

Here we must remember that the sensible thing outside causes a confused sense image, something with only an incidental unity in the faculty of imagination, which represents the thing according to its quantity, colour and other sensible accidents. And just as the sense image represents things only confusedly and according to an incidental unity, so many perceive only such incidental combinations. Now, primary truths are primary precisely because their terms are grasped in their proper nature and apart from all that is merely incidental to them. Now this proposition, "The whole is greater than its part", is not primarily true of the whole as realised in a stone or in wood, but of "whole" in the abstract, i.e. apart from everything with which it merely happens to be joined. Consequently, the mind which never conceives totality except in an incidental concept such as the totality of a stone or the totality of wood, never really understands the pure truth of this principle, because it never grasps the precise nature of the terms to which the principle owes its truth. It is only within the power of the few to attain the eternal reasons, because it is only the few that have an understanding of the essentials, whereas the many grasp things merely in incidental concepts such as those mentioned above. But these few are not said to be distinguished from the others by a special illumination, but by better natural powers, since they have a sharper and more abstractive mind, or be-

inquisitionem per quam aeque ingeniosus pervenit ad cognoscendum illas quidditates quae alius non inquirens, non cognoscit.

Et isto modo intelligitur illud Augustini IX *De Trinitate*, cap. vi,* de vidente in monte et vidente inferius aerem nubilosum et superius lucem sinceram. Qui enim tantum intelligit semper conceptus per accidens eo modo quo phantasma repraesentat objecta talia quasi entia per accidens, ipse est quasi in valle circumdatus aere nebuloso. Sed qui separat quidditates intelligendo praecise eas conceptu per se quae tamen relucent in phantasmate cum multis aliis accidentibus adjunctis, ipse habet phantasma inferius quasi aerem nebulosum, et ipse est in monte inquantum cognoscit illam veritatem et videt verum supra ut illam veritatem superiorem in virtute intellectus increati, quae est lux aeterna.

[Quarta Via]. Ultimo modo potest concedi quod cognoscuntur veritates sincerae in luce aeterna sicut in objecto remoto cognito, quia lux increata est primum principium entium speculabilium et ultimus finis rerum practicarum et ideo ab ipso sumuntur principia prima tam speculabilia quam practica. Et ideo cognitio entium tam speculabilium quam practicabilium per principia sumpta a luce aeterna ut cognita est perfectior et prior cognitione sumpta per principia in genere proprio sicut dictum est in quaestione illa de subjecto theologiae, et est eminentior alia quacumque. Et hoc modo cognitio omnium pertinet ad theologum. Hoc modo sincera veritas cognosci dicitur quia per illud cognoscitur quod est tantum veritas non habens aliquid permixtum non veritatis quia per primum ens, a quo cognito sumuntur principia sic cognoscendi ; aliud autem quodcumque a

---

* IX, cap. vi (Migne, P.L., XLII, 966).

cause of greater research which enables one person to know those essences which another equally talented individual does not discover because he does not investigate them.

And in this way we can understand Augustine's statement in *De Trinitate*, BK. IX, c. vi,* regarding the individual on the mountain who sees the pure light above and the mist below. For whoever grasps nothing but incidental notions in the way that the sense image represents such objects, viz. as a kind of accidental aggregate, is like one in a valley surrounded by mist. But by grasping just what things are of themselves, a person separates the essences from the many additional incidental features associated with them in the sense image. Such a one, as it were, has the sense image in the mist beneath him, but he himself is on the mountain to the extent that in virtue of the uncreated intellect, the Eternal Light, he knows this truth and sees what is true from above, as a more universal truth.

[The Fourth Way]. And finally, we can concede that pure truths are known in the Eternal Light as in a remotely known object. For the Uncreated Light is the first source of speculative things and the ultimate end of practical things. The first speculative and practical principles, then, are derived from it. Hence, the knowledge of speculative and practical things by means of principles derived from the Eternal Light, where the latter is known,30 is more perfect and prior to knowledge derived from principles from the respective class of things as such, as has been pointed out in the question on the subject of theology. Such knowledge is more eminent than any other. Now it is in this way that the knowledge of all things pertains to the theologian. In this way pure truth is said to be known, since truth alone without admixture of anything else is known, for it is known through the First Being. And once this Being is known, the principles for knowing in this perfect way are derived

quo sumuntur principia cognoscendi in genere est verum defectivum.

Hoc modo solus Deus cognoscit omnia sincere quia ut dictum est in quaestione de subjecto theologiae,* solus ipse novit omnia praecise per essentiam suam. Omnis autem intellectus moveri potest ab objecto alio ad cognoscendum veritatem aliquam virtute ejus. Et hoc modo cognitio omnium pertinet ad theologum, sicut dictum est in quaestione illa de subjecto theologiae, et est eminentior alia quaecumque. Cognoscere enim triangulum habere tres ut est quaedam participatio Dei et habens talem ordinem in universo quod quasi perfectius exprimit perfectionem Dei, hoc est nobiliori modo cognoscere triangulum habere tres quam per rationem trianguli. Et ita cognoscere quod temperate vivendum est propter beatitudinem ultimam consequendam quae est attingendo essentiam Dei in se, perfectius est cognoscere istud cognoscibile practicum quam per principium aliquod in genere moris, puta per hoc quod honeste vivendum est.

Et isto modo loquitur Augustinus de luce increata ut cognita xv *De Trinitate*, cap. xxvii,† ubi seipsum alloquens ait : Multa vera vidisti et ea quae discrevisti ab ista luce qua tibi lucente vidisti ; attolle oculos ad ipsam lucem et eos in ea infige si potes ; sic enim videbis quomodo distat nativitas Verbi Dei a processione Doni Dei. Et paulo post : Haec et alia oculis tuis interioribus lux ista (monstrabit vel) monstravit. Quae est ergo causa cur acie fixa ipsam videre non poteris nisi utique infirmitas, · etc.

---

* *Opus oxoniense*, prol. q. iii.
† xv, cap. xxvii (Migne, P.L., XLII, 1097).

therefrom. But any other thing from which principles of knowing something in kind are derived is defective truth.

Only God knows all things purely in this perfect way, for as we have said in the question on the subject of theology,* He alone knows all things precisely through His essence. Nevertheless, every intellect can be moved by some object to know that something is true in virtue of Him, and in this way the knowledge of all things pertains to the theologian, as has been said in the question on the subject of theology. For to know that a triangle has three [angles equal to two right angles], in so far as this is a kind of participation of God and that it has such an order in the universe that it expresses more perfectly as it were the perfection of God,[31]—this is a nobler way of knowing a triangle has three [angles, etc.] than to know this truth from the notion of a triangle itself. Similarly, to know that one should live temperately in order to attain the supreme happiness, which consists in attaining the essence of God in Himself, is a more perfect way of knowing this practical truth than to be aware of it through some principle in the class of mores, for instance, through the principle that one is obliged to live uprightly.

And in this manner Augustine speaks of the Uncreated Light as known in *De Trinitate*, BK. xv, c. xxvii,† where addressing himself, he says : "You have seen many things and these you have discerned through that Light in which you saw them shining forth to you. Turn your eyes to the Light itself and fasten them upon it, if you can, for in this way you will see how the nativity of the Word of God differs from the procession of the Gift of God." And a little later : "This and other things this Light has revealed to your inner eyes. What then is the reason with fixed glance you are unable to see the Light itself, if it is not indeed your weakness ? . . ."

[Ad Argumenta Principalia]

Ex dictis patet ad omnes auctoritates Augustini ad oppositum ; et secundum aliquem dictorum modorum "videndi in" exponi possunt auctoritates Augustini quae occurrunt de ista materia.

[*Articulus Sextus. Quomodo rationes Henrici concludunt*]. De sexto articulo videndum est quómodo tres rationes factae pro prima opinione aliquid verum concludunt in quantum accipiuntur ab Augustino, licet non concludant illam conclusionem falsam ad quam inducuntur.

Ubi sciendum est [quod a sensibilibus, sicut a causa per se et principali, non est expectanda sincera veritas ; quia notitia sensus est circa aliquid per accidens, ut dictum fuit, licet actus sensuum aliqui sint certi vel veri ; sed virtute intellectus agentis, qui est participatio lucis increatae, illustrantis super phantasmata, cognoscitur quidditas rei, et ex hoc habetur sinceritas vera. Et per hoc solvitur primum argumentum Henrici ; et secundum intentionem Augustini non plus concludit.

Ad secundam rationem Henrici dico quod anima mutabilis est ab uno actu disparato ad alium, secundum diversitatem objectorum, propter suam illimitationem et immaterialitatem, quia est respectu cujuslibet entis ; similiter ab actu in non actum, quia non semper est in actu ; sed respectu primorum principiorum, quorum veritas nota est ex terminis, et conclusionum evidenter deductarum ex terminis, non est mutabilis a contrario in contrarium, scilicet a vero in falsum. Regulae enim in lumine intellectus agentis intellectum rectificant, et

[Reply to the Arguments at the Beginning]

From all that has been said, it is clear how the citations from Augustine to the contrary are to be interpreted. The texts of Augustine concerning this matter can also be explained in terms of one of the aforementioned ways of seeing.

[*Article VI. To What Extent Henry's Arguments Hold*]. As to the sixth article, we must see how the three reasons adduced in favour of the first opinion in so far as they are taken from Augustine do prove some truth, although they do not establish that false conclusion for which they were advanced.[32]

Here we must recognise [33] that we should not expect pure truth from sensible things as from a primary and essential cause, for sense knowledge has to do with something incidental, as we have pointed out,[34] even though some of the acts of the senses are certain and true. But the essences of things are known in virtue of the active intellect, a participation of the Uncreated Light, which illumines the imagination and in this way true purity [of truth] results. In this fashion, the first argument of Henry is solved. And according to the mind of Augustine, it proves nothing more.

To the second reason of Henry, I say that the soul can change in the sense that it has now one act, now another, accordingly as objects differ. For the soul is not material and is unlimited in the sense that it can know and love anything whatsoever.[35] Likewise, it can be active or inactive, for it is not always in act. But with regard to the first principles the truth of which is known from their terms, or with regard to conclusions evidently deduced from the terms, the soul cannot change from one contrary state to another, i.e. from truth to falsity. For rules [36] known in the light of the agent intellect keep the mind from erring, and even though the intelligible species

ipsa species intelligibilis terminorum, licet in essendo
sit mutabilis, in repraesentando tamen in lumine intellectus agentis immutabiliter repraesentat, et per duas
species intelligibiles cognoscuntur termini primi principii,
et ita illa unio est vera et certa evidenter.

Ad tertium dicendum quod concludit contra eum,
quia non ponit nisi speciem sensibilem vel phantasma ;
non autem concludit de specie intelligibili repraesentante
quidditatem.

Dicendum autem, quod si potentiae sensitivae non
sunt impeditae, species sensibilis veraciter repraesentat
rem ; sed in somno potentiae sensuum exteriorum sunt
ligatae, ideo virtus imaginativa, conservans species
sensibiles, secundum diversitatem fluxus humorum capitis,
apprehendit eas tamquam res quarum sunt similitudines,
quia vim rerum habent, secundum Philosophum, *De
motibus animalium.** Non plus concludit tertia ratio.]

* cap. vii (701^b, 20).

of the terms is mutable in its being, still in representing in the light of the agent intellect, the intelligible species represents things in an immutable way, and the terms of a first principle are known by two intelligible species and consequently the union [of the terms in a proposition] is true and evidently certain.

As for [Henry's] third argument, we must point out that it is telling against his own position, since he admits of no species other than the sense image or sensible species. But the argument is not effective where an intelligible species is held to represent the essence. However, it must be admitted that if the sensitive powers are not impeded, the sensible species truly represents the things. In sleep, however, the powers of the external senses are bound. Wherefore, the imaginative power, conserving the sensible species according to the different movement of humours in the head, apprehends those species as the things themselves of which they are but likenesses, for they have the force of things, according to the Philosopher in *De motibus animalium*.* The third reason proves no more than this.

VI

THE SPIRITUALITY
AND IMMORTALITY OF
THE HUMAN SOUL

Summary of the Argument

[VI. DE SPIRITUALITATE ET IMMORTALITATE ANIMAE
HUMANAE] *

*Quaero utrum possit esse notum per rationem naturalem
resurrectionem generalem hominum esse futuram ?*

[Pro et Contra]

Quod sic :

Desiderium naturale non potest esse frustra, Commentator secundo *Metaphysicae*.† Sed homo habet
desiderium naturale ad semper essendum et istud
desiderium potest esse notum ratione naturali ; ergo,
etc. Probatio minoris : quia non fugitur aliquid naturaliter nisi virtute naturalis desiderii vel amoris ad aliud ;
sed naturaliter homo fugit mortem. Hoc patet per experientiam. Patet etiam per Apostolum ad Corinthios ‡ :
Nolumus expoliari sed supervestiri.

Item, naturaliter notum est quod beatitudo naturaliter
appetitur. Hoc patet ex primo *Ethicorum* ** de beatitudine in generali, et ex decimo †† de beatitudine in
speciali. Sed notum est per rationem naturalem, beatitudinem non posse esse nisi sempiternam ; ergo notum
est per rationem naturalem hominem esse ordinatum ad
perfectionem aliquam sempiternam. Probatio minoris :
Augustinus XIII *De Trinitate*, cap. viii,‡‡ probat illud per
rationem sic : Morientem vita ipsa deserit, si beata ;
aut ergo nolentem deserit aut volentem, aut neutrum.

---

* *Opus oxoniense*, IV, dist. XLIII, q. ii (Assisi 137, f. 259v^b–261r^b ;
cf. Vivès, VOL. XX, 34^a–59^b).
† Averroes, *Metaphysica*, II, com. I.   ‡ II Cor. v. 4.
** *Ethica Nicomachea*, I, cap. vii (1097^b, 1ff.), X, cap. vii–viii
(1177^a, 12ss).   †† X, cap. vii–viii (1177^a, 12ff.).
‡‡ XIII, cap. viii (Migne, P.L., XLII, 1022).

[VI. THE SPIRITUALITY AND IMMORTALITY OF THE
HUMAN SOUL]

I ask : *Can it be known by natural reason that there will be
a general resurrection of mankind ?*

[Pro et Contra]

Proof that it can be known [1] :

[Arg. I]. A natural desire cannot be in vain.† Man,
however, has a natural desire to live forever, and it can
be known by natural reason that such a desire exists.
Therefore, etc. Proof of the minor : Where a natural
aversion for something exists, it is only because of a
natural desire or love for something else. But man has
a natural aversion for death. This is evident both from
experience and from what the Apostle says to the
Corinthians‡ : "We do not wish to be unclothed, but
rather clothed over".

[Arg. II]. Also, it is naturally known that we seek
happiness by our very nature. This is clear from
Nicomachean Ethics, BK. I,** with regard to beatitude in
general and from *Nicomachean Ethics*, BK. X,†† for beatitude
in particular. But from natural reason it is known that
beatitude must be eternal. Hence, it is known from
natural reason that man is ordained to some eternal
perfection. Proof of the minor : Augustine‡‡ proves it
thus : "And if life quits him by his dying, how can a
blessed life remain with him? And when it quits him,
without doubt it either quits him unwillingly, or willingly

Si nolentem, quomodo est vita beata, quae ita est in voluntate, quod non sit in potestate ? Si autem volentem, quomodo beata vita erit quam finire voluit qui habebat ? Si dicas quod neutrum, nec velle, nec nolle, sed nec illa beata est vita quae talis est ut quem beatum facit amore ejus indigna sit.

Item, naturaliter notum est quod tota species non caret fine suo, quin illum in aliquo individuo consequatur. Sed naturaliter notum est beatitudinem esse finem speciei humanae ; ergo et hominem posse consequi illam saltem in aliquo individuo ; sed non potest eam consequi in ista vita propter multas miserias quae concomitantur vitam istam utpote varietas fortunae, infirmitas corporis, imperfectio scientiae et virtutis, et instabilitas et fatigatio in exercendo actus perfectionis, in tantum ut nulla operatio, quantumcumque in principio delectabilis, possit continue esse delectabilis, imo per ipsam fastidiendo delectabile erit cessare ab ipsa ; et notum est per rationem naturalem operationem beatificam non esse fastidiosam, nec potest a sola anima separata haberi, quia in hoc homo non consequeretur finem suum ; ergo habebitur in alia vita a toto conjuncto, et per consequens ad minus videtur per rationem naturalem concludi in quibus homo ad finem suum pertinget.

Item, per rationem naturalem notum est quod omnis species quae est de integritate universi, est perpetua, quia totum integrum est perpetuum ; sed homo est species perfectissima, saltem inter ista inferiora. Nos enim aliquo modo sumus finis omnium, secundo *Physicorum.** Ergo, etc.

---

* II, cap. ii (194ᵃ, 35).

or neither. If unwillingly, how is the life blessed which is so within his will as not to be within his power? And whereas no one is blessed who wills something that he does not have, how much less is he blessed who is quitted against his will, not by honour, nor by possessions, nor by any other thing, but by the blessed life itself, since he will have no life at all. . . . But neither is that a blessed life which is such as to be unworthy of his love whom it makes blessed".

[Arg. III]. Furthermore, it is known naturally that an entire species cannot fail to attain its end. At least the end must be achieved in some individuals. But it is naturally known that beatitude is the end of the human species. Therefore, it is naturally known that at least some individual can attain it. But he cannot attain it in this life because of the many concomitant miseries such as the vicissitudes of fortune, bodily infirmity, imperfect knowledge and virtue, instability and fatigue in the exercise of even the most perfect acts, inasmuch as no operation, be it ever so delightful in the beginning, can continue to be delightful. Furthermore, when such an operation causes what is delightful to become distasteful, it will no longer be performed. Now it is known by natural reason that the beatific vision is not something distasteful. Neither is it something that the soul can possess alone in separation from the body, for in this way *man* would not attain his goal. Consequently, this end will be attained in another life by the whole man, body and soul together. It seems, then, that natural reason can reach this conclusion at least in regard to those ways by which man will attain his end.

[Arg. IV]. Furthermore, by natural reason it is known that every species required for the integrity of the universe, is eternal. For the universe as an integral whole is eternal. Now man is the most perfect species, at least among terrestrial beings, for, *Physics*, BK. II,* "we are in some way the end of all things". Therefore, etc.

Oppositum :

Augustinus, XIII *De Trinitate*, cap. ix,* loquens de vita immortali vel sempiterna dicit : Hac utrum careat humana natura, nec parva questio est. Humanis quippe argumentationibus hanc invenire conantes, vix pauci, magno praediti ingenio, vacantes otio, doctrinisque subtilissimis eruditi, ad indagandam solius animae immortalitatem pervenire potuerunt.

Item, Act. xvii,† dicitur de quibusdam Atheniensibus audientibus Paulum, qui dicebant quoniam novorum daemoniorum videbatur annuntiator esse, quia Jesum et resurrectionem annuntiabat eis ; et tamen illi Athenienses erant philosophi, multum vigentes ratione naturali ; patet de Dionysio converso, qui fuit unus eorum ; ergo istud quod videbatur eis ita remotum a veritate, non videtur esse bene notum per rationem naturalem ; unde omnia quae adducit ibi Paulus, non sunt nisi quaedam persuasiones ut patet ibi.

Item, Act. xxvi,‡ cum diceret Paulus : Si passibilis Christus, si primus ex resurrectione, etc. Festus magna voce dixit : Insanis, Paule.

[Corpus Quaestionis]

[*Pars Prima : Ratio quodammodo a priori*]

Hic manifestum est quod si aliqua ratio ostendat resurrectionem, oportet quod accipiatur ex aliquo, quod est proprium hominis, ita quod non conveniat aliis corruptibilibus. Hoc autem non est materia etiam incorruptibilis, nec forma aliqua destructibilis, quia etsi talis sit in homine, et excellentior omni forma bruti, tamen ex

* XIII, cap. ix (Migne, P.L., XLII, 1023).
† Acts, XVII. 18.   ‡ loc. cit. XXVI. 23–24.

To the contrary :

[Arg. 1]. Augustine, speaking of the life that is eternal and immortal in *De Trinitate* BK. XIII, c. ix,* says : "Whether human nature can receive this . . . is no small question. . . . Assuredly, of those who endeavour to discover it from human reasonings, scarcely a few, and they endowed with great abilities and abounding in leisure, and learned with the most subtle learning, have been able to attain to the investigation of the immortality of the soul alone".

[Arg. II]. Furthermore, in *Acts* xvii,† it is related that certain Athenians listening to Paul said : " 'He seems to be a herald of strange gods', because he proclaimed to them Jesus and the resurrection". Nevertheless, these Athenians were philosophers whose *forte* was the use of natural reason, as is clear from the case of the convert Dionysius, who was one of them. But it does not seem that what appeared to them to be so far from the truth is known adequately by natural reason. Hence, it is evident here that what Paul adduces in this connexion is meant to be nothing more than a kind of persuasive form of argumentation.

[Arg. III]. Furthermore, when Paul said in *Acts* xxvi,‡ "that Christ was to suffer, that he first by his resurrection [from the dead was to proclaim light to the people and to the Gentiles . . .] Festus said with a loud voice, 'Paul, thou art mad !' "

[Body of the Question]

[*Part I. A Kind of* A Priori *Proof*]

This much is clear, if any argument proves the resurrection, it must be one based on something that is proper to man and does not belong to other perishable things. But such a thing would not be matter, not even incorruptible matter.[2] Neither is it some form that can be destroyed. For even if such a form exist in man and

illa non potest sumi ratio sufficiens ad probandum resurrectionem totius ; ergo oportet quod accipiatur a forma specifica hominis vel ab operatione conveniente homini secundum illam formam.

Isto modo procedente ex tribus propositionibus concluditur propositum, et· si omnes illae essent ratione naturali notae, haberemus propositum. Sunt autem istae : "Anima intellectiva est forma specifica hominis" ; secunda, "Anima intellectiva est incorruptibilis" ; ex quibus sequitur quod forma specifica hominis est incorruptibilis. Additur tertia, quod "forma hominis specifica non remanebit perpetuo extra suum totum" ; sequitur ergo quod aliquando redibit totum idem. Ista reditio iterata, vocatur resurrectio secundum Damascenum lib. iv, cap. xix * : Resurrectio secunda est ejus, quod dissolutum est, surrectio. De istis tribus propositionibus, qualiter notae sunt, videamus per ordinem.

[*Propositio I. Anima intellectiva est forma specifica hominis*]. De prima dicitur quod est ratione naturali nota, quod ostenditur dupliciter : uno modo per auctoritates Philosophorum, qui hoc asserebant, et nonnisi tanquam ratione naturali notum ; alio modo adducendo rationes naturales, ex quibus hoc concluditur.

De primo : Aristoteles definit animam ii *De anima*,† quod est actus corporis physici, organici, etc. Et in principio tertii,‡ dicit de parte autem animae, qua cognoscit et sapit, ubi videtur ponere animam intellectivam partem saltem subjectivam animae prius definitae in communi.

Item, omnes philosophi tamquam differentiam ejus propriam communiter posuerunt in definitione hominis

---

* *De fide orthodoxa*, iv, cap. xxvi (Migne, P.G., xciv, 1220).
† ii, cap. i (412ᵃ, 28).   ‡ iii, cap. iv (429ᵃ, 10).

indeed, one even more excellent than any brute form, still this would not provide an adequate argument for the resurrection of man as a whole. Hence, the argument must be based upon that form which is specific to man or upon some operation which man enjoys by reason of this form.

[*Method of Procedure*]. The method used to establish the thesis is to proceed from three propositions. If all three of these can be known by natural reason, the proposed conclusion will follow. The three propositions are these : (1) *The intellective soul is the specific form of man ;* (2) *The intellective soul is incorruptible.* From these two it follows that the specific form of man is incorruptible. To these a third is added : (3) *The specific form of man will not remain forever outside the composite.* Hence it follows that at some time the same composite will be restored. This second return Damascene calls the resurrection* : "The resurrection is the second rising of what has been dissolved". Let us consider these three propositions in order and see to what extent they are evident.

[*First Proposition. The intellective soul is the specific form of man*]. This first proposition is said to be known by natural reason and is proved in two ways. The first proof is based upon the testimony of philosophers who assert this as something known by natural reason alone. The other proceeds from natural arguments which lead to this conclusion.

[Proof based on the testimony of the philosophers]. As to the first, Aristotle defines the soul in the *De anima,* BK. II,† as "the act of the natural organised body", and so on. And in the beginning of BK. III,‡ he speaks of "the part of the soul with which the soul knows and thinks . . .", where he seems to make the intellective soul at least a subjective part,[3] of what he has previously defined as the soul in general.

Furthermore, all philosophers commonly assign "rational" as the difference that properly defines man,

rationale, per rationale intelligentes animam intellectivam esse partem essentialem ejus.

Nec breviter invenitur aliquis philosophus notabilis, qui hoc neget, licet ille maledictus Averroes in fictione sua III *De anima*,* quae tamen non est intelligibilis, nec sibi, nec alii, ponat intellectivam quamdam substantiam separatam mediantibus phantasmatibus conjunctam ; quam conjunctionem nec ipse nec aliquis sequax potuit explicare, nec per illam conjunctionem salvare hominem intelligere. Nam secundum ipsum homo formaliter non esset nisi quoddam animal irrationale excellens, per quandam tamen animam irrationalem et sensitivam excellentiorem aliis animabus.

De secundo : ad propositum non invenitur faciliter ratio a priori neque a posteriori, nisi ex propria operatione hominis, siquidem forma innotescit ex propria operatione, sicut materia ex transmutatione.

[1. *Ratio Inadaequata*]. Ex operatione ergo intelligendi arguitur propositum sic : intelligere est propria operatio hominis ; ergo egreditur a propria forma ; ergo intellectiva est propria forma hominis.

Sed ista ratio patitur instantiam quia intellectus ad intelligere se habet secundum eos tantum passive, et non active ; ergo ista propositio, propria operatio est a propria forma, non probat intellectivam esse propriam formam hominis, siquidem ab ipsa non est ista operatio secundum eos, sed ab objecto intelligibili vel secundum aliquos a phantasmate.

[2. *Ratio Scoti*]. Ideo ex illa opinione, formo

---

* III, com. 5.

meaning by "rational" that the intellective soul is an essential part of man.

In fact, to put it briefly, no philosopher of any note can be found to deny this except that accursed Averroes in his commentary on *De anima*, BK. III,* where his fantastic conception, intelligible neither to himself nor to others, assumes the intellective part of man to be a sort of separate substance united to man through the medium of sense images. But neither he nor his followers to the present day have been able to explain this union. Nor can it be maintained that in virtue of such a union man himself understands, for according to him, man as such is nothing more than a kind of irrational animal which excels the other animals by reason of an irrational sensitive soul that is more excellent than other souls.

[Proof from reason]. As to the second, it is not easy to find either an *a priori* or an *a posteriori* argument, unless it be based on a function proper to man, for the form is known from its proper function, even as matter is known from the existence of change.

[1. *An Unsatisfactory Formulation*]. One argument [4] based on the function of the intellect that is used to establish the proposed conclusion is this. To understand is a function proper to man. Therefore, it has its source in the form proper to man. The intellective form then is that proper to man.

This argument, however, is open to criticism inasmuch as those who propound it admit that the intellect has only a passive and not an active relation to intellection. Hence, this proposition "A function that is proper proceeds from the proper form" really does not prove that the intellective part is the proper form of man, for this operation does not proceed from the form but according to them [5] it is caused by the intelligible object, or according to the view of others it proceeds from the sense image.[6]

[2. *Scotus's Formulation*]. I put this argument, then,

rationem aliter sic : Homo intelligit formaliter et proprie ; ergo anima intellectiva est proprie forma hominis.

Antecedens videtur satis manifestum secundum auctoritates Aristotelis tertio *De anima*,* et primo *Ethicorum*,† quod intelligere est propria operatio hominis. Operatio autem ut distinguitur contra actionem seu factionem formaliter inest operanti, et non est ab ipso in alterum. Consimiliter decimo *Ethicorum* ‡ in intelligere ponit felicitatem hominis, et manifestum est quod illa felicitas inest formaliter homini ; ergo et illa operatio in qua consistit.

Sed tentandum est probare antecedens per rationem contra protervum si neget, et hoc intelligendo in antecedente intelligere proprie dictum per quod intelligo actum cognoscendi transcendentem totum genus sensitivae cognitionis.

Probatur ergo illud antecedens uno modo sic. Homo cognoscit actu cognoscendi, non organico ; ergo intelligit proprie. Consequentia patet ex ratione jam posita, quia intellectio proprie est cognitio transcendens totum genus sensationis ; omnis autem sensatio est cognitio organica ex secundo *De anima*. Antecedens hujus enthymematis probatur, nam organum determinatur ad certum genus sensibilium ex ii *De anima*,** et hoc ideo quia consistit in media proportione extremorum illius generis. Sed aliquam cognitionem experimur in nobis quae non competit nobis secundum tale organum, quia tunc determinaretur praecise ad sensibilia determinati generis, cujus oppositum experimur, quia cognoscimus

---

* iii, cap. iii, passim.
† *Ethica Nicomachea*, i, cap. vii (1098^a, 7).
‡ x, cap. viii (1178^b, 21).
** ii, cap. v–xii, passim (416^b, 32ss ; 424^a, 25–26).

in another form. *Man formally and properly understands ; therefore, the intellective soul is the proper form of man.*

[*a*. Proof of the antecedent]. The antecedent seems to be clear enough according to the testimony of Aristotle in *De anima*, BK. III,* and *Nicomachean Ethics*, BK. I,† since to understand is the proper operation of man. Now an operation, in contradistinction to an act of fashioning something or to an action, is formally in the one who performs the operation and is not produced by the agent in something else. Similarly Aristotle in *Nicomachean Ethics*, BK. X,‡ makes man's happiness consist in understanding. Now it is clear that this felicity is formally in man. Consequently the operation in which this felicity consists must also be in man formally.

Nevertheless, we should try to prove the antecedent by reason lest some contentious individual deny it. Now in the antecedent, I take "to know" or "to understand" in the proper sense of the term as an act of knowledge which transcends every type of sense knowledge.

[*First proof*]. One way of proving this antecedent, then, is this. Man knows by an act of knowledge which is not organic ; hence he knows or understands in the proper sense of the term. The consequence is evident for the reason already given, since intellection properly speaking is a knowledge which transcends all sense knowledge. All sensation, however, is organic knowledge as Aristotle shows in *De anima*, BK. II. There the antecedent of this enthymeme is proved from the fact that every organ is determined to a certain kind of sensible,[7] and this because it consists in a balance between two extremes.[8] But we do experience in ourselves some knowledge which we do not have in virtue of some organ, for if it were organic, this knowledge would be limited precisely to the sensibles of some determined kind, which is the very opposite of what we actually

per talem actum differentiam cujuscumque generis sensibilium ad aliud, quod non est aliquid illius generis ; ergo cognoscimus utrumque extremum. Patet ista consequentia secundum Philosophum sic arguentem II *De anima* * de sensu communi.

Sed hic instatur primo, quia cognitio organica est, quae inest secundum determinatam partem corporis ; illa autem de qua arguitur, quod per illam distinguimus sensibilia a non sensibilibus, inest toti primo, et ideo non est per aliquod organum proprie loquendo ; tamen non transcendit totum genus cognitionis sensitivae secundum perfectionem, quia inest primo toti, et per consequens ita est materiale, sicut illud quod inest toti per partem ; ita enim passio totius est materialis, sicut quod inest toti per partem. Secundo negatur assumptum quod ille actus non inest secundum aliquod organum, quia inest secundum organum phantasiae ; cujus probatio est, quia illo laeso impeditur cognitio. Nec probatio illa de determinatione organi ad certum genus concludit, quia phantasia extendit se ad omnia sensibilia.

Sed prima instantia exclusa est per quoddam ibi tactum, quia per illum actum discernimus totum genus sensibilium ab aliquo extra totum genus illud ; nec illa probatio, quod impeditur iste actus laeso organo phantasiae concludit ; hoc enim est propter ordinem istarum potentiarum in operando, non autem quia intellectio exerceatur mediante isto organo.

Aliter probatur antecedens principale, quia aliqua

---

* *De anima*, III, cap. i (425ª, 30 ff.).

experience. For by such an act we know precisely how one kind of sensible differs from another, and conquently we know both extremes. This consequence is evident from the Philosopher, who uses this argument in *De anima*, BK. II,* in regard to common sense.

But to this some object, *first* of all, that organic knowledge is that which is present in some determinate part of the body, whereas the aforesaid knowledge by which we distinguish sensibles from things that cannot be perceived by the senses, is present in the body as a whole and for this reason is not had in virtue of some organ in the proper sense of the word. For an attribute of the whole is as material as something which exists in one of its parts. Nevertheless, this knowledge does not transcend in perfection the whole class of sense knowledge since it is primarily in the body as a whole and hence is just as material in character as the knowledge in only a part of the whole. *Secondly*, they deny the assumption that this act of knowledge is not present in virtue of some organ because it is there by reason of the organ of the imagination. Proof for this is found in the fact that when this organ is damaged, such knowledge is no longer possible. Neither is the proof from the limitation of the organ to a certain kind of sensible conclusive, because the imagination extends to all sensibles.

The first objection, however, has already been excluded by what was treated above, for through this act of knowledge we discern the difference between the whole class of sensibles and something that is outside the class as a whole. Neither does the argument that this act is impeded by damage done to the imagination prove anything. For this is due to the functional relation that exists between these powers and not because the act of understanding is exercised through the medium of an organ.

[*Second proof*]. Another proof for the principal antecedent is based on the fact that we possess some immaterial

cognitio immaterialis est in nobis ; nulla sensitiva potest
esse immaterialis ; ergo, etc.

Istud vocabulum immateriale est frequens in usu Philosophi in proposito, sed videtur ambiguum. Potest enim
ad propositum tripliciter intelligi ; vel immaterialis, quia
incorporea, hoc modo, quia non per partem corpoream
et organum, et tunc istud est idem cum propositione
jam posita de non organica. Vel alio modo immaterialis,
quia nullo modo extensa, et tunc plus dicit quam non
organica ; etsi enim omnis organica sit extensa, quia
recipitur in extenso, non tamen sola, quia si reciperetur
in toto composito primo, cum illud sit extensum, adhuc
operatio esset extensa. Tertio modo potest intelligi
immaterialitas ejus in comparatione ad objectum, ut
scilicet respiciat objectum sub rationibus immaterialibus,
utpote in quantum abstrahitur.ab hic et nunc et hujusmodi, quae dicuntur conditiones materiales. Si autem
(proferetur vel) probaretur immaterialitas secundo modo,
plus haberetur propositum quam ex probatione ejus
primo modo. Sed non videtur sic posse probari, nisi ex
conditionibus objecti, quod respicit ille actus, nisi forte
ex reflectione, quia experimur nos reflecti super actum
istius cognitionis ; et quantum non est super se reflexivum,
et ideo ab objecto istius actus fit finaliter probatio antecedentis.

Sic : Habemus in nobis aliquam cognitionem objecti
sub illa ratione sub qua non potest esse ejus aliqua cognitio sensitiva ; ergo, etc. Antecedens probatur, quia
experimur in nobis quia cognoscimus actu universale ;

knowledge. No sense knowledge, however, can be immaterial ; therefore, etc.

This word "immaterial" is frequently used by the Philosopher in this connexion, but it appears to be ambiguous. There are three relevant ways in which it can be understood. (*a*) Either this knowledge is immaterial because it is incorporeal in the sense that it is not an operation that involves a corporeal part or organ. In this sense, the present proposition is the same as that previously posited with regard to non-organic knowledge. (*b*) Another way in which this knowledge could be immaterial would be that it is not extended in any way. In this case much more is asserted than the fact that it is not organic. For although everything organic is extended inasmuch as it is received into something extended [viz. the organ], this is not the only reason. It would still be extended if it were received immediately by the composite as a whole, because the composite is itself extended. (*c*) Immateriality can be understood in a third sense, namely with reference to the object, inasmuch as this knowledge considers the object under immaterial aspects, as for instance, abstracting from the "here and now" and such like, which are said to be material conditions. If we would prove this knowledge to be immaterial in the second sense and not merely in the first our proposed conclusion would follow all the more. But it seems that the only way we could do this would be from the conditions which characterise the object of such an act (unless perhaps we could do so on the basis of reflection, since we experience ourselves reflecting on this act of knowledge, for what has quantity is not capable of reflecting upon itself.) At any rate the proof of the antecedent ultimately rests upon the object of this act.

The proof is as follows. We possess some knowledge of an object under an aspect it could not have as an object of sense knowledge ; therefore, etc.—Proof of the antecedent : (i) We experience in ourselves that we

et experimur quia cognoscimus ens, vel qualitatem
[MS quantitatem] sub ratione aliqua communiori quam
sit ratio primi objecti sensibilis, etiam respectu supremae
sensitivae. Experimur etiam quod cognoscimus relationes consequentes naturas rerum, etiam non sensibilium.
Experimur etiam quod distinguimus totum genus sensibilium ab aliquo quod non est illius generis. Experimur
etiam quod cognoscimus relationes rationis, quae sunt
secundae intentiones, scilicet relationem universalis,
generis et speciei et compositionis, et aliarum intentionum
logicalium. Experimur etiam quod cognoscimus actum
illum quo cognoscimus ista, et illud, secundum quod
inest nobis iste actus, quod est per actum reflexum super
actum rectum et susceptivum ejus. Experimur etiam
quod assentimus complexionibus quibusdam sine possibilitate contradicendi vel errandi, utpote primis principiis.
Experimur etiam quod cognoscimus ignotum ex noto per
discursum, ita quod non possumus dissentire evidentiae
discursus, nec conclusionis illatae ; quodcumque istorum
cognoscere est impossibile cuicumque potentiae sensitivae,
ergo, etc.—Si quis autem proterve neget istos actus inesse
homini, nec se experiri istos actus in se, non est ulterius
cum eo disputandum, sed dicendum est sibi quod est
brutum ; sicut cum dicente, non video colorem ibi, non
est disputandum, sed dicendum sibi, tu indiges sensu quia
caecus es. Ita quod quodam sensu, id est, perceptione
interiori, experimur istos actus in nobis ; et ideo si quis
istos neget, dicendum est eum non esse hominem, quia
non habet istam visionem quam alii experiuntur.—
Assumptum, scilicet quod nullus istorum actuum potest
inesse secundum aliquam potentiam sensitivam, probatur,
quia actu universale cognoscitur sub tanta indifferentia

know the actual universal. (ii) We experience that we know being or quality under a more general notion than that characteristic of the primary object of even the highest sense faculty. (iii) We experience that we also know relations that follow from the nature of things, even when the latter are not capable of being perceived by the senses. (iv) We experience that we distinguish the whole class of sensible objects from what is not such. (v) We experience that we know conceptual relations, which are second intentions, such as that of the universal, the genus, the species, the judgment and other logical intentions. (vi) We also experience that we know the very act whereby we know these things and we experience that this act exists within us. This we do by an act of reflection upon the direct act and its recipient. (vii) We experience that we assent to propositions such as the first principles without a possibility of error or contradiction. (viii) We also experience that we learn the unknown from the known by means of discursive reasoning, so that we are unable to refuse our assent to the evidence of the reasoning process or to the conclusion that is inferred. But the knowledge of any of these cannot be attributed to any sensitive faculty; therefore, etc.—Should a contentious individual deny that such acts are present in man or that he experiences these acts in himself, a person ought not to argue with him any further, but he ought to be told that he is a brute animal. It is the same with one who says : "I do not see colour here". We should not argue with such a one but simply tell him : "You need senses because you are blind". And so by a certain "sense", namely internal perception, we experience these acts within ourselves. Hence, if someone were to deny their existence we would have to say that he is not a man because he lacks this interior vision which others experience.—The assumption that a sense faculty is not the source of any of these acts [viz. (i) to (viii)] is proved as follows : The actual universal has such an indifference

sub quanta ipsum sic cognitum est simul dicibile de
omnibus singularibus in quibus salvatur ; sic non cognoscit sensus. Sed de secundo est evidentius, quia nulla
potentia potest cognoscere aliquid sub ratione universa-
liori ratione sui proprii objecti ; sicut visus non cognoscit
aliquid sub ratione indifferenti ad colorem et ad sonum ;
ergo cognitio illa est alicujus sub ratione communiori
quocumque posito objecto, etiam supremi sensus non
potest esse aliqua sensatio. Quartum probat idem, quia
nulla sensatio potest esse distinctive primi objecti sensibilis, i.e. communissimi, ab eo quod non est tale, quia nec
potest esse utriusque extremi. De relationibus conse-
quentibus alia non sensibilia inter se vel insensibilia ad
sensibilia, patet per idem quia sensus non potest in istos
et multo magis patet de relationibus istis, quae dicuntur
rationis, quia sensus non potest moveri ad cognoscendum
aliquid quod non includitur in objecto sensibili ut sensibili ; habitudo rationis non includitur in aliquo ut
existens est ; sensus autem existentis est ut existens est,
et per hoc posset probari primum etiam de actu universali, quia universali in actu repugnat esse existens ut
existens est. Aliud de reflexione super actum et potentiam, probatur per hoc quod quantum non est reflexivum
supra se. Alia duo de compositione et assensione com-
positioni, et de discurrere et assentire evidentiae discursus
probantur ex relatione rationis, quia ista non sunt sine
relatione rationis.

Consequentia primi enthymematis probatur sic. Si
talis actus sit in nobis formaliter cum non sit substantia

about it that what is known in this way can be predicated simultaneously of all the singulars of which it is characteristic ; no sense faculty, however, knows things in this way. The same is even more evident as regards the second, for no faculty can know something under an aspect more universal than that of its proper object, even as vision perceives nothing under some aspect common to colour and to sound. Consequently, a knowledge of something in even more general terms than that characteristic of the first object of even the highest sense cannot be a sensation. The same holds true of the fourth, for no sensation can distinguish between the most universal of all sensible objects and that which is not sensible, because it cannot perceive both extremes. This is also true of the relations which exist between things imperceptible to the senses or between such things and those which can be perceived by the senses, for the sense faculty has no ability to perceive such relationships. And this is all the more true of those relations which are purely conceptual, since the senses can be moved to perceive only what is included in a sensible object as such. But conceptual relations are not included in any existing thing as such, whereas the senses have to do with existing things as existing. The same argument could be applied to the actual universal, for it is absurd that the actual universal should exist as such. The other, regarding our ability to reflect upon the act and the faculty, is proved from the fact that anything that has quantity cannot reflect upon itself. As for the other two (viz. the act of judgment and the assent to the same or the act of reasoning and the assent given to the evidence for the same), what was said of conceptual relations proves these acts do not proceed from a sense faculty, for neither of these two exist without a conceptual relation.

[*b*. Proof of the consequent]. The consequence of the first enthymeme [9] is proved as follows :

[*First proof*]. If we formally possess such an act, since

nostra, quia quandoque inest et quandoque non inest, ergo oportet dare illi aliquod receptivum proprium ; non autem aliquod extensum, sive sit pars organica sive totum compositum, quia tunc illa operatio esset extensa ; nec posset esse talis qualis dicta est, circa objecta talia qualia dicta sunt ; ergo oportet quod insit secundum aliquid non extensum ; et quod illud sit formaliter in nobis, illud non potest esse nisi anima intellectiva, quia quaecumque alia forma est extensa.

Vel aliter potest probari consequentia ista eundo ad conditionem objecti istius actus, quia quaelibet forma inferior intellectiva, si habet operationem, habet praecise respectu objecti sub rationibus oppositis istis rationibus dictis ; ergo si habemus operationem circa objectum sub istis rationibus, illa non inerit nobis secundum aliquam formam aliam ab intellectiva ; ergo inest nobis secundum intellectivam ; ergo intellectiva formaliter inest nobis, aliter non essemus formaliter operantes secundum illam operationem.

Ex secunda operatione humana, scilicet voluntate, potest probari idem, quia homo est dominus actuum suorum, ita quod in potestate ejus est per voluntatem determinare se ad hoc vel ejus oppositum, sicut dictum est distinctione xxii, secundi vel xxiii,* q. iii, et hoc est notum non tantum ex fide sed etiam per rationem naturalem. Ista autem indeterminatio non potest esse in aliquo appetitu sensitivo seu organico vel extenso quia quilibet appetitus organicus vel materialis determinatur ad certum genus appetibilium sibi conveniens, ita quod illud apprehensum non potest non convenire nec appetitus nec appetere ; ergo voluntas, qua sic indeterminate volumus est appetitus non alicujus talis formae, scilicet

---

* *Opus oxoniense*, ii, dist. xxv, q. unica (Vivès ed.).

it is not our substance as such—for it is not always present in us—it follows, therefore, that this act needs a proper subject. Now the latter cannot be something extended, whether it be a part of the organism or the whole composite, for then this operation itself would be extended and would lack the prescribed characteristics. Neither would it be concerned with such objects as have been described above. Hence, it is necessary that this act be in us in virtue of something unextended and that the latter be formally in us. Now this can be nothing else than the intellective soul, for every other form is extended.

[*Second proof*]. Another way to prove this consequence would be to consider the condition of the object of this act, for if any form inferior to the intellective form functions, it is always with reference to an object having characteristics the very opposite of those cited above.[10] Therefore, if we have an operation which regards an object under the aforementioned aspects, this will not be present in us in virtue of any form other than the intellective. Hence, it is by reason of this form that it is present in us, and consequently the intellective form itself is formally in us, for otherwise we would not formally function in this way.

[*Third proof*]. We can prove the same from the second operation characteristic of man, namely volition, for man is master of his acts to such an extent that it is within his power to determine himself at will to this or to its opposite, as has been said in BK. II, dist. XXII or XXIII, q. iii.* And this is something known by natural reason and not merely by faith. Such a lack of determination, however, cannot exist in any organic or extended appetite, because every organic or material appetite is determined to a certain class of suitable objects so that what is apprehended cannot be unsuitable nor can the appetite fail to seek it. The will, therefore, by which we can will in such an indeterminate way, is not the appetite of a

materialis, et per consequens alicujus excedentis omnem talem formem hujusmodi ponimus intellectivam, et tunc si appetitus ille sit formaliter in nobis, quia et appetere, sequitur quod forma illa sit forma nostra.

[*Propositio II. Anima intellectiva est immortalis*]. De secunda propositione principali, quae est, quod anima intellectiva est immortalis, proceditur sicut de prima. Primo adducendo auctoritates Philosophorum qui hoc senserunt.

Aristoteles II *De anima** dicit quod intellectus separatur a caeteris, sicut perpetuum a corruptibili. Si dicatur quod separatur quantum ad operationem ; contra— ex hoc sequitur propositum, quia si potest separari secundum operationem et secundum esse secundum ipsum I *De anima.*†

Item, III *De anima* ‡ ponitur differentia inter sensum et intellectum, quod excellens sensibile corrumpit sensum, et propter hoc post sensationem talis minus sentit minus sensibile ; non sic de intellectu. Imo postquam intellexerit summa intelligibilia, magis intelligit inferiora ; ergo intellectus non debilitatur in operando, et tunc ultra sequitur, quod sit incorruptibilis in essendo.

Item, XII *Metaphysicae*, cap. i,** moventes causae velut prius existentes, quae autem ut ratio, id est, forma substantalis supple cum causato ut toto ; quando enim sanatur homo, tunc et sanitas est. Si autem posterius aliquid manet, perscrutandum est ; in quibusdam enim

---

material form, and in consequence it belongs to something which excels every such form. But this is just what we assume the intellective form to be. And therefore, if this appetite is formally in us inasmuch as its act is in us, it follows that this form is our form.

[*Second Proposition* : *The intellective soul is immortal*]. The method of dealing with the second proposition, viz. that the intellective soul is immortal, is the same as that used with the first. The testimony of those philosophers who held this is adduced first.

[*Arguments for immortality* : [11] Arg. 1]. Aristotle, in *De anima*, BK. II,* says that the "intellect differs from the rest as what is eternal differs from what is perishable". And if someone objects that it is something different and apart only in so far as its operations are concerned, the proposed conclusion still follows, for according to Aristotle in *De anima*, BK. I,† if it can be set apart by reason of its operations it can also exist apart.

[Arg. II]. Furthermore, in *De anima*, BK. III,‡ he says that the senses differ from the intellect, because something that stimulates the sense excessively tends to impair it so that afterwards even an object that does not stimulate the sense so strongly is less capable of being perceived, whereas such is not the case with the intellect. Quite the contrary, once the highest intelligibles have been grasped what is less intelligible becomes even better known. The intellect consequently is not weakened in function, and from this it follows further, the intellect is imperishable in its being.

[Arg. III]. Also, in *Metaphysics*, BK. XII, c. i,** he says : "The causes that produce motion, for instance, exist previously whereas those which are the essence; that is, the substantial form, exist simultaneously (*Add* 'with the effect considered as a whole'). For when a man is healthy, then health also exists. . . . But we must inquire whether anything remains afterwards. For in some cases there is nothing to prevent this, for instance

nihil prohibet, ut si anima est talis, non omnis, sed intellectus, etc. Vult ergo dicere quod intellectus est forma manens post compositum, sed non ante.

Item, XVIII *De animalibus*,* relinquitur solum intellectum de foris advenire. Ergo non accipit esse per generationem, sed a causa extrinseca ; et per consequens non potest accipere non esse per corruptionem, nec per aliquam causam inferiorem corruptivam, quia ejus esse non subest alicui tali causae, cum sit a causa superiori immediate.

Item, ex dictis Philosophi formantur aliquae rationes ; est unum principium apud eum, quod naturale desiderium non est frustra ; nunc autem in anima est desiderium naturale ad semper esse.

Item, VII *Metaphysicae*,† vult quod materia est, qua res potest esse et non esse. Ergo illud quod non habet materiam secundum eum non habet potentiam non essendi ; intellectiva non habet materiam secundum eum, quia est forma simplex.

Item, III *Ethicorum* ‡ vult quod fortis debet se exponere morti pro republica et idem vult IX *Ethicorum*,** et loquitur secundum judicium rationis naturalis ; ergo secundum rationem naturalem potest cognosci immortalitas animae. Probatio istius consequentiae, quia nullus propter quodcumque bonum virtutis vel in se, vel in alio vel communitatis debet appetere vel potest omnino non esse suum, quia secundum Augustinum III *De libero arbitrio*,†† Non esse non potest appeti. Nunc autem si anima non esset immortalis, moriens acciperet totaliter non esse.

---

* *De generatione animalium*, II, cap. iii (736^b, 28).
† VII, cap. xv (1039^b, 29).
‡ *Ethica Nicomachea*, III, cap. vii (1117^b, 8).
** IX, cap. viii (1169^a, 20).
†† III, cap. viii (Migne, P.L., XXXII, 1282).

the soul may be of this sort—not all the soul, but the intellect". Hence, what Aristotle wishes to say is that the intellect is the form which exists after the composite ceases to exist, even though this form does not exist prior to the composite.

[Arg. IV]. Also, he says in his work *De generatione animalium* * : "It remains for the intellect alone to enter from the outside". Hence, the intellect does not receive existence by way of generation but rather from an extrinsic cause ; consequently, it cannot cease to exist by perishing. Neither can any inferior cause corrupt the soul since its existence does not come under the power of any such cause, for it owes its existence directly to a higher cause.

[Arg. V]. Also, some arguments can be constructed from the dicta of the Philosopher. One of his principles is that a natural desire is not in vain.[12] Now the soul has a natural desire to exist forever.

[Arg. VI]. Also, in *Metaphysics*, BK. VII,† he has this to say : "Matter is that in virtue of which a thing can exist or not exist". Therefore, according to him, whatever has no matter lacks the capacity to be non-existent. Now the intellective soul, according to him, is devoid of matter since it is a simple form.

[Arg. VII]. Also, in *Nicomachean Ethics*, BK. III,‡ he says that a brave man must expose himself to death for the state. And this he appears to repeat in BK. IX of the same work.** Now he speaks according to the dictates of natural reason. Consequently, the immortality of the soul can be known by natural reason. Proof of this consequence : No-one is obliged or is even able to seek his complete non-existence for the sake of some virtuous good whether that good be something in himself or in another or a good of the community, for according to Augustine a person cannot desire non-existence.†† If the soul were not immortal, however, the one who is dying would be accepting complete non-existence.

Item, arguit unus Doctor quasi ex verbis Philosophi sic : Quod corrumpitur aut corrumpitur per contrarium, aut per defectum alicujus necessario requisiti ad esse ejus. Sed anima intellectiva non habet contrarium, nec esse corporis est simpliciter necessarium ad ejus esse, quia habet proprium esse per se, et idem in corpore et extra corpus ; nec est differentia nisi quod in corpore communicat illud corpori [*MS* corrumpitur] ; extra corpus non communicat.

Item, simplex non potest separari a seipso ; anima est simplex ; ergo non potest separari a seipsa et per consequens nec a suo esse separari potest quia non per aliam formam a se habet esse. Secus est de composito, quod habet esse per formam, quae forma potest separari a materia, et ita esse compositi destrui.

Sed oppositum videtur Philosophus sensisse, quia in fine, VII *Metaphysicae*,* ex intentione vult quod omnes partes, quae possunt separatae manere a toto, sunt elementa, id est, partes materiales, sicut ipse ibi accipit elementa ; et praeter tales necesse est ponere in toto aliquam formam, quae totum est illud quod est, quae non possit manere separata a parte materiali, toto non manente. Ergo si concessit animam intellectivam esse formam hominis, ut patet ex probatione propositionis praecedentis, non ponit eam manere separatam a materia, toto non manente.

Item, principium videtur apud eum quod illud quod incipit esse, desinit esse. Unde I *De caelo et mundo*,† contra Platonem videtur habere pro incom-

---

* VII, cap. xvii (1041^b, 12 ff.).
† I, cap. x (279^b, 31–32) ; cap. xii (282^b, 4).

[Arg. viii]. Also, one teacher [13] argues as it were from the words of the Philosopher as follows : What perishes, perishes by reason of its contrary or because it lacks some necessary prerequisite for its existence. The intellective soul, however, has no contrary. Neither is the existence of the body a necessary prerequisite for the soul's existence, since the soul possesses its own proper *per se* existence. The latter is the same whether the soul is in the body or out of it. The only difference is that when the soul is in the body, it communicates its existence to the body, whereas when it is outside it does not do so.

[Arg. ix]. Also, what is simple cannot be separated from itself. The soul is simple ; therefore, it cannot be separated from itself, nor can it, in consequence, be separated from its existence, for it does not have its existence in virtue of some form other than itself. It is otherwise with something composite which has existence in virtue of the form. This form can be separated from matter, thus destroying the existence of the composite.

[*Arguments against immortality* : Arg. i]. The Philosopher, however, seems to take the opposite view, for at the end of *Metaphysics*, bk. vii,* he expresses the opinion that the only parts which could be separated from the whole are the elements, i.e. the material parts, for in this sense he understands elements here. In addition to these elements it is necessary to assume the existence of some form in the whole which is the totality of that which exists. This form could not exist in separation from the material part once the whole no longer exists. Hence, if he grants that the intellective soul is the form of man, as is evident from the proof of the preceding proposition, he does not admit that it exists in separation from matter, once the whole no longer exists.

[Arg. ii]. Likewise, it seems to be one of his principles that what begins to exist ceases to exist. Hence, in his work *De caelo et mundo*,† against Plato, he seems to consider it impossible that anything could have come into

possibili, quod aliquid inceperit, et tamen sit perpetuum et incorruptibile ; et III *Physicorum*, cap. de infinito,* cujus est principium, ejus est finis.

[*Opino Scoti*]. Potest dici quod licet ad istam secundam propositionem probandam sint rationes probabiles, non tamen demonstrativae, imo nec necessariae.

Et quod adducebatur pro ea secundum primam viam de auctoritatibus philosophorum, dupliciter potest solvi. Uno modo quod dubium est quid Philosophus circa hoc senserit. Varie enim loquitur in diversis locis, et habuit diversa principia, ex quorum aliquibus videtur sequi unum oppositum, ex aliis aliud. Unde probabile est, quod in ista conclusione semper fuerit dubius, et nunc magis videbatur accedere ad unam partem, nunc ad aliam, juxta quod tractabat materiam consonam uni parti magis quam alteri.

Est et alia responsio realior quod non omnia dicta a philosophis assertive, erant eis probata per rationem necessariam naturalem ; sed frequenter non habebant nisi quasdam probabiles persuasiones, vel vulgarem opinionem philosophorum praecedentium. Unde dicit Philosophus II *Caeli et mundi* † in cap. de duabus quaest. difficilibus, tentandum est dicere quod videtur esse dignum, reputantes promptitudinem magis imputari verecundiae, quam audaciae, si quis propter philosophiam stare, et parvas sufficientias diligit, de quibus habemus maximas dubitationes. Unde parvae sufficientiae frequenter suffecerunt philosophis, ubi non poterant ad majorem pervenire, ne contradicerent principiis philosophiae. Et in eodem cap. de [aliis] astris dicunt Aegypti

---

* III, cap. iv (203^b, 9).
† II, cap. xii (291^b, 25–29 ; 292^a, 6 ff.).

existence and still be eternal and imperishable. And in the *Physics* he says* : "Whatever has a beginning has an end".

[*Scotus's Opinion*]. It can be stated that although there are probable reasons for this second proposition, these are not demonstrative, nor for that matter are they even necessary reasons.[14]

[*Reply to the arguments for immortality*]. The testimonies of the philosophers—the first way used to prove the proposition—can be solved in two ways. First of all, it is doubtful what the Philosopher really held on this point, for he speaks differently in different places and has different principles, from some of which one thing seems to follow whereas from others the very opposite can be inferred. Wherefore, it is probable that he was always doubtful about this conclusion and at one time seems to be drawn to one side and at other times to the other depending on whether the subject matter he was treating at the moment was more in accord with the one or with the other.

Another answer, and one more in accord with facts, is that not all the statements by the philosophers were established by proofs both necessary and evident to natural reason. Frequently, what they gave was nothing more than rather persuasive probable arguments or what was commonly held by earlier philosophers. For this reason, the Philosopher in *De caelo et mundo*, BK. II,† in the chapter on the two difficult questions, says : "We must now attempt to state the probable solution, for we regard the zeal of one whose thirst after philosophy leads him to accept even slight indications where it is very difficult to see one's way, as a proof rather of modesty than of over-confidence". Hence, in those matters where they could find nothing better without contradicting the principles of philosophy, "slight indications" frequently had to suffice for the philosophers. As he says in the same chapter : "Accounts of other stars are given by the

et Babylonii, a quibus multas credulitates habemus de unoquoque astrorum. Unde philosophi quandoque acquiescunt propter persuasiones probabiles, quandoque propter assertiones principiorum suorum praeter rationem necessariam. Et ista responsio sufficeret ad omnes auctoritates, licet essent expressae [*MS* nullae], quod non concludunt propositum. Tamen responderi potest per ordinem.

Ad primum, quod non intelligit istam separationem, nisi praecise in hoc quod intellectus non utitur corpore in operando, et propter hoc est incorruptibilis in operando, loquendo de illa corruptione, qua virtus organica corrumpitur propter corruptionem organi ; et ista sola corruptio competit potentiae organicae. Secundum Philosophum I *De anima*,* si senex acciperet oculum juvenis, videret utique sicut juvenis ; ergo ipsa potentia visiva non est debilitata sive corrupta quantum ad operationem ; sed [ad] organum tantum ; nec tamen ex ista incorruptione intellectus, quia scil. non habet organum, per cujus corruptionem possit corrumpi in operando, sequitur quod sit simpliciter incorruptibilis in operando, quïa tunc sequeretur quod in essendo esset incorruptibilis, sicut tunc argutum est ; sed tantum sequitur quod non est corruptibilis in operando, illo modo quo potentia organica ; tamen poneretur simpliciter corruptibilis, juxta illud Philosophi III *De anima*.† Intellectus corrumpitur in nobis quodam interiori corrupto. Et hoc pro tanto, quia poneretur principium operandi toti composito operationem propriam ejus ;

---

* I, cap. iv (408^b, 18–30).
† III, cap. v (430^a, 23) ; I, cap. i (403^a, 7–10).

Egyptians and Babylonians . . . from whom many of our beliefs about particular stars are derived". There-fore, the philosophers agreed to things sometimes because of probable persuasive reasons, at other times because they had asserted as principles, propositions which were not necessary truths. And this reply would suffice for all the testimonies cited above ; even if they clearly asserted the proposed conclusion, they still do not establish it. Nevertheless, these arguments can be answered in order as follows.

[To 1]. To the first : Aristotle understands this separation to mean nothing more than that the intellect does not use the body in performing its operation, and for this reason it is incorruptible as to function. This is to be understood in the sense that it is unlike an organic power which perishes precisely because the organ decays. This type of decay pertains exclusively to an organic faculty. For according to the Philosopher in *De anima*,* BK. I, if an old man were given the eye of a young man, he would indeed see as well as the youth. Hence, the faculty of vision grows weak or decays only from the standpoint of its organ and not in so far as its operation directly is concerned. From the fact that the intellect, however, is incapable of decay in the sense that it has no organ by which it could perish, it does not follow that the intellect is imperishable as to function in an unqualified sense, for then it would indeed follow that it is also imperishable in being as the argument maintains. What does follow is this. So far as its ability to operate alone is concerned, the intellect is incapable of dissolution in the same sense that an organic power is corruptible. Absolutely speaking, however, the intellect is assumed to be perishable according to the Philosopher's statement in *De anima*, BK. III,† that the intellect perishes in us once the interior sense perishes. And this is just what one would have to maintain if he assumed the soul to be a prin-ciple which has an operation proper to the composite

sed compositum est corruptibile, ergo et principium operativum ejus. Quod autem sit principium operandi toti, et quod operatio ejus sit operatio totius, videtur Aristoteles dicere I *De anima.**

Ad aliud dico, quod excellens sensibile corrumpit sensum per accidens, quia corrumpit organum, quia solvit illam mediam proportionem, in qua consistit bona dispositio organi ; et per oppositum intellectus, quia non habet organum, non corrumpitur ab excellenti objecto ; sed ex hoc non sequitur quod sit incorruptibilis nisi probetur quod non dependeat in essendo a toto quod est corruptibile.

Ad tertium de XII *Metaphysicae* dicitur quod Aristoteles posuit illud sub dubio, quia dicit forsan. Sed non dicit forsan ad istud quod intellectus manet posterius, id est, post totum ; sed dicit non omnis anima, sed intellectus ; et sequitur : Omne namque impossibile forsan, ubi dubitabat an possibile sit omnem animam manere post compositum. Sed de intellectu non dubitat non dependeat in essendo a toto quod est corruptibile. Si ergo expresse hoc asserat, potest dici quod tamen non fuit per rationem necessariam sibi demonstratum, sed per rationes probabiles persuasum.

Ad aliud, valde dubium est, quid ipse senserit de inceptione animae intellectivae. Si enim non posuit Deum aliquid immediate de novo agere, sed tantummodo motu sempiterno movere coelum, et hoc ut agens remotum, a quo agente separato poneret ipse intellectivam de novo produci ? Si enim dicas, quod ab aliqua

---

* I, cap. v, passim.

as a whole. The composite, however, is perishable. Consequently, its operative principle is also perishable. That the soul is the operative principle of the whole composite and that its operation is also that of the whole is just what Aristotle seems to say in *De anima*, BK. I.*

[To II]. To the next, I say that an excessively stimulating object damages the senses only incidentally inasmuch as it damages the organ by disrupting that balance which constitutes the quality of being properly disposed. On the other hand, since the intellect has no organ, it is not damaged by a more highly intelligible object. But from this it does not follow that the intellect is imperishable unless it first be proved that it does not depend for existence on a composite being that can perish.

[To III]. To the third argument based on *Metaphysics*, BK. XII, some reply that Aristotle assumes this as something doubtful since he uses the word "perhaps".—However, he does not say "perhaps" when he speaks of the intellect persisting after the whole, but says : "Not all the soul, but the intellect". Only afterward does he add : "For it is *perhaps* impossible that all [the parts of the soul . . .]", where he doubts whether it is possible for the entire soul to outlive the composite. Nevertheless, he has no doubts that the intellect does not depend for its existence on the whole composite which is perishable.

If Aristotle expressly asserts this, then it can be said that he was convinced of this because of probable reasons and not because it was anything demonstrated to him by necessary reasons.

[To IV]. As for the other, it is very doubtful what Aristotle held in regard to the origin of the intellective soul. For if he assumed that God does not immediately produce anything new, but merely moves the heaven with an eternal movement and this only as a remote agent, then by what separate [15] agent did Aristotle assume the soul was produced from without ? If you

Intelligentia, duplex est inconveniens. Unum quia ipsa non potest creare substantiam ex prima distinctione hujus quarti.* Aliud, quia illa non magis potest aliquid novum producere immediate, quam Deus secundum principia Philosophi de immutabilitate agentis, et ideo sempiternitate in agendo. Nec potest ipse, ut videtur, secundum principia sua ponere intellectivam esse terminum agentis naturalis quia ut videtur ex XII *Metaphysicae*,† ponit eam incorruptibilem et nulla forma quae est terminus agentis naturalis, est simpliciter incorruptibilis. Potest dici quod ponit eam immediate accipere esse et novum esse a Deo quia quod acciperet esse satis sequitur ex principiis ejus cum non ponat eam perpetuo praecessisse sine corpore, nec prius fuisse in alio corpore ; nec est probabile secundum rationem a quo possit recipere tale esse, nullo praesupposito, nisi a Deo.

Sed contra : ergo concederet creationem. Respondeo, non sequitur, quia non posuit aliam productionem compositi, et animae intellectivae, sicut nec ignis et formae ignis ; sed illam animationem corporis organici ponit esse productionem per accidens ipsius animae. Nos autem ponimus duas productiones ; unam a non esse animae ad esse ejus, et ista est creatio ; aliam a non animatione corporis ad animationem ejus, et illa est productio corporis animati, et per mutationem proprie dictam. Qui

---

* *Opus oxoniense*, IV, dist. I, q. i, n. 28.
† XII, cap. iii (1070ᵃ, 25–28).

say it was by one of the Intelligences, then we encounter a double difficulty ; one, because an Intelligence cannot create a substance (as I prove in BK. IV, dist. i) * ; the other, because such a being cannot immediately produce anything new any more than God could, for according to the Philosopher's principles regarding the immutability of the agent it follows that the action of such a being is eternal. Neither do we see any way in which Aristotle could claim that the intellective soul is the effect of some natural agent [16] without violating his principles, because he seems to assume the soul to be imperishable in *Metaphysics*, BK. XII.† And no form that is the effect of a natural agent is imperishable in an unqualified sense.

But it can be said that he assumed the soul received existence immediately from God and that this existence was something new. For it would follow readily enough from his principles that it would have received existence, since Aristotle assumed no eternal bodiless pre-existence ; neither did he hold that the soul existed previously in some other body ; nor does it seem possible according to reason that a soul which presupposes no material principle could have received its existence from anyone other than God.

To the contrary : If this explanation were true, Aristotle would have admitted creation.—I reply that this does not follow, for he did not assume a production of the intellective soul distinct from the production of the composite, just as he did not assume one production for fire and another for the fire form. What he posited was the animation of the organic body and this incidentally involved the production of its soul. Now we admit two types of production, one from the soul's non-existence to existence and this we call creation, the other is the passage of the body from an inanimate to an animate state and this is the production of a living body by a change in the proper sense of the word. If anyone, therefore, were to assume merely the second type of production

igitur, poneret tantum secundam, nullam creationem poneret, et ita Aristoteles.

Sed licet vites secundum eum creationem, quomodo tamen potest salvare agens immutabile aliquid novum producere ? Respondeo, nullo modo nisi propter novitatem passi receptivi ; quod enim effectus totaliter et praecise dependens a causa activa, esset novus, reduceretur secundum Aristotelem in aliquam variationem ipsius causae efficientis ; sed quod effectus dependens ab agente et receptivo sit novus, potest reduci in novitatem ipsius passi, sine novitate agentis et ita diceretur hic quod Deus de necessitate naturali, transmutat corpus organicum ad animationem, quam cito corpus est susceptivum istius animationis et a causis naturalibus fit aliquando de novo istud susceptivum, et ideo tunc nova est mutatio ad animationem ab ipso Deo.

Sed quare reducenda est ista novitas in Deum, sicut in causa agentem ? Dico quod, quia sicut est primum agens et ideo secundum Aristotelem est semper agens aliqua actione in passum semper eodem modo se habens, ita si aliquod passum potest esse novum et susceptivum alicujus formae, quae non potest subesse causalitati alicujus causae secundae, Deus est immediata causa illius et tamen de novo, quia omni potentiae passivae in ente oportet ponere aliam activam correspondentem, et ideo si passivae novae non correspondet alia activa creata, correspondebit sibi immediate divina.

Ad aliud de desiderio naturali respondebitur, respondendo ad rationes principales, quia prima ratio principalis et secunda et tertia procedunt ex hoc.

Ad aliud de VII *Metaphysicae*,* de materia, vera est illa

---

* VII, cap. xv (1039^b, 29).

he would not thereby postulate a creation. And this was the case with Aristotle.

But even if you avoid asserting a creation according to Aristotle, how is it possible to save the idea that something new is produced by an agent that is immutable ?—I reply that the only way is to explain what is new in terms of something in the patient or recipient of the action. According to Aristotle, if a new effect depended solely upon the active cause, some variation in the efficient cause itself would be required. But a new effect that depends upon both the recipient and the agent can be accounted for in terms of something new in the recipient alone and not in the agent. And thus we could say that in the present instance God by a natural necessity changed an organic body into a living substance just as soon as the body was capable of receiving life. And natural causes will determine just when the latter becomes ready to receive it, and hence at this moment God produces this new change so that it comes to life.

But why must this new entity be attributed to God as to its [immediate] efficient cause ?—I reply that the reason is this. Just as God, the first agent, is continually operating by some action on a patient which remains constantly in the same condition according to Aristotle, so likewise if something is capable of receiving some new form which cannot be caused by any secondary cause, God must be its immediate cause ; and yet for all that something new comes into existence. For it is necessary to postulate some active potency that corresponds to every passive potency. Now if there is no such created cause corresponding to the new passive potency, then its immediate corresponding cause will be divine.

[To v]. The other argument about the natural desire will be answered in the reply to the initial arguments,[17] for the first three proceed from this notion.

[To vi]. As for the argument about matter in *Metaphysics*, bk. vii,* this description of matter holds not merely

descriptio materiae non tantum intelligendo quod materia est, qua res cujus ipsa est pars potest esse et non esse ; sed res, sive cujus ipsa est pars, sive quae recipitur in ipsa ; alioquin forma ignis non posset non esse, quia materia non est pars formae ignis.

Ad aliud de forti fit magna altercatio, an secundum rectam rationem debet sic se exponere. Potest tamen dici sicut Philosophus respondet in ix* quod bonum maximum tribuit sibi in exercendo illum magnum actum virtutis, et hoc bono privaret se, imo vitiose viveret, si illo actu praetermisso tunc, salvaret suum esse per quantumcumque ; melius est autem simpliciter maximum bonum et momentaneum quam remissum bonum virtitis vel vita vitiosa per magnum tempus. Unde ex illo probatur evidenter, quod bonum commune secundum rectam rationem est magis diligendum quam bonum proprium, quia totum bonum proprium debet homo exponere destructioni simpliciter, etiamsi nesciat animam immortalem, propter boni communis salvationem, et illud magis diligitur simpliciter, propter cujus salutem esse alterius contemnitur.

Ad illas rationes Doctorum. Si intelligit animam habere per se esse idem in toto, et extra totum, prout per se esse distinguitur contra in esse accidentis ; hoc modo forma ignis, si esset sine materia, haberet per se esse et tunc posset concedi quod forma ignis esset incorruptibilis. Si autem intelligat de esse per se, quod convenit composito in genere substantiae, sic falsum est quod anima sine corpore habet per se esse, quia tunc esse ejus non esset alteri communicabile, quia in divinis etiam per se esse isto modo acceptum est incommunicabile. Unde omni

---

* *Ethica Nicomachea,* ix, cap. viii (1169ᵃ, 15–17).

in the sense that a thing which has matter as one of its parts is able to exist and not exist, but also that a thing composed of matter or received into matter is able to exist and not exist. Otherwise the form of fire could not be non-existent, for matter is not a part of the fire form.

[To vii]. To the other about the brave man, there is a great dispute whether according to right reason one must expose himself to death in this way. Be that as it may, one could solve this objection the way the Philosopher does.* One could say that by performing such a great act of virtue, this individual has obtained the highest good, whereas if he had saved his life by omitting this act, he would have deprived himself of this good and what is more, his life would be morally evil. Absolutely speaking it is better to have this greatest good even momentarily than to be without it or to have a long, but a morally evil, life. Wherefore, evident proof is had from this that according to right reason the common good is to be preferred to one's individual good, because even if a man is unaware that his soul is immortal, he is still bound to expose his entire personal good to destruction in order to save the common good. And that must be loved all the more, absolutely speaking, to save which the existence of another is regarded as of little account.

[To viii]. As for the arguments of certain teachers, if the meaning is that the soul has the same *per se* existence [18] in the composite as it has outside the composite, where *per se* existence is understood as contrasted with the existence characteristic of an accident, then' the fire form, if it were to exist apart from matter, would also have *per se* existence, and then we could admit that the fire form is imperishable. But if by *per se* existence is meant that characteristic of the composite in the line of substance, then it is false to say that the soul has *per se* existence outside the body. For were such the case, it could not communicate its being to another, for even in what is divine, *per se* being in this sense is incommunicable.

modo deficit quod anima habet per se esse sine corpore, quia in secundo intellectu antecedens est falsum et in primo consequentia non valet, nisi addas ibi, quod naturaliter sine miraculo habet per se esse primo modo ; sed haec propositio credita est, et non per rationem naturalem nota.

Ad aliud, non omnis corruptio est per separationem alterius ab altero ; accipiendo enim esse angeli, si illud ponatur secundum aliquos aliud ab essentia, illud non est separabile a seipso, et tamen est destructibile per successionem oppositi ad ipsum esse.

[*Propositio III. Anima non remanebit perpetuo extra suum totum*]. De tertia propositione dicitur eam posse probari ex hoc, quod pars extra totum est imperfecta ; forma autem tam nobilis non remanebit perpetuo imperfecta ; ergo nec separata a toto.

Item, nullum violentum est perpetuum secundum Aristotelem I *De caelo et mundo*.* Separatio autem animae a corpore est violenta, quia contra inclinationem naturalem animae ; secundum Philosophum, quia inclinatur naturaliter ad perfeciendum corpus.

[*Opinio Scoti*]. De ista propositione videtur quod Philosophus, si posuisset animam immortalem, magis posuisset eam perpetuo manere sine corpore quam in corpore, quia omne compositum ex contrariis est corruptibile.

Nec rationes istae probant. Prima non, nam illa major, "Pars extra totum est imperfecta," non est vera nisi de

---

* II, cap. iii (286^a, 18).

Hence, there is no way in which the soul has *per se* existence without the body, for if we take the term in the second sense the antecedent of the argument is false, whereas if we take it in the first sense, the consequence is invalid, unless you add that it has this existence naturally and without a miracle. But this latter is something we believe, but it is not known by natural reason.

[To ix]. To the other, not all destruction is the result of separating one thing from another. Take the being of an angel, and let it be assumed as some do that its existence is distinct from its essence.[19] Such a being is not separable from itself and nevertheless it can be destroyed if its existence is succeeded by the opposite of existence.

[*Third Proposition : The human soul will not remain outside the body forever.* Arg. 1]. They say that the third proposition can be proved from this that a part which exists outside the whole is imperfect.[20] This form [viz. the soul], however, is so noble that it will not remain forever imperfect ; therefore it will not exist apart from the composite forever.

[Arg. ii]. Likewise, according to Aristotle in his work *De caelo et mundo*,* nothing unnatural is eternal. But the separation of the soul from the body is unnatural, because it is contrary to the natural inclination of the soul. For according to the Philosopher the soul has a natural inclination to perfect the body.

[*Scotus's Opinion*]. So far as this proposition is concerned, it seems that if the Philosopher had assumed the soul to be immortal, he would have held that it continued to exist outside the body rather than in the body, for everything composed can be destroyed by its contraries.

[Reply to the arguments]. Neither do the reasons given above prove the proposition.

[To 1]. The first does not because this major : "The part without the whole is imperfect", is true only of that part which receives some perfection when it is in the

parte quae recipit aliquam perfectionem in toto ; anima
autem non recipit perfectionem sed communicat ; et sic
potest formari ratio ad oppositum, quia non repugnat
alicui aeque perfecto in se manere, licet alteri non com-
municet suam perfectionem ; hoc apparet de causa
efficiente, cui non repugnat quantumcumque manere
sine suo effectu ; sed anima manet aeque perfecta in esse
suo proprio, sive conjuncta sive separata ; in hoc tamen
habens differentiam, quod separata non communicat
esse suum alteri.

Per hoc ad aliud, quia inclinatio naturalis est duplex :
una ad actum primum et est imperfecti ad perfectionem,
et concomitatur potentiam essentialem ad actum secundum. Et est alia inclinatio ad actum secundum et est
perfecti ad perfectionem communicandum et concomitatur potentiam accidentalem. De prima verum est,
quod oppositum ejus est violentum, et non perpetuum,
quia ponit imperfectionem perpetuam, quam Philosophus
habuit pro inconvenienti, quia posuit in universo causas
ablativas aliquando cujuslibet imperfectionis. Sed
secunda inclinatio, etsi perpetuo suspendatur, nullum
violentum proprie dicitur, quia nec imperfectio ; nunc
autem inclinatio animae ad corpus tantum est secundo
modo. Vel potest dici secundum Avicennam, quod
appetitus animae satiatus est per hoc quod semel perfecit
corpus, quia illa conjunctio est ad hoc, ut anima mediante
corpore, acquirat suas perfectiones per sensus, quas non
posset acquirere sine sensibus, et per consequens nec sine

composite. Now the soul does not receive perfection but communicates perfection. Consequently, one could twist this argument in favour of the opposite view. For there is nothing absurd about a thing existing apart, even though it does not communicate its perfection to another, so long as it is equally perfect existing in this way. This is clear from the [similar] case of an efficient cause. For it is not repugnant that such a cause should exist without causing an effect. Now the soul, so far as its own being is concerned, is equally perfect whether it is separated from or joined to a body. There is, of course, this difference. As separated, the soul does not communicate its being to another.

[To 11]. This also answers the other argument, since there are two kinds of natural inclinations One regards the primary act or actualisation, and this is the natural inclination of the imperfect for its perfection and is something that accompanies an essential potency in relation to its second act. But there is another inclination towards a second act where the latter is a perfection to be communicated and this is the natural inclination that accompanies an accidental potency. Of the first, it is true that the opposite of the natural inclination is something unnatural and not eternal, because it would imply eternal imperfection, which the Philosopher regards as something improper inasmuch as he has postulated that causes exist in the universe which will in time do away with any imperfection. The second inclination, however, even though it would be forever suspended, implies nothing unnatural in the proper sense of the term since no imperfection is involved. Now the inclination that the soul has for the body is of the second type. Or it can be said with Avicenna that once the soul has perfected the body, this desire of the soul has been sated, since the purpose of this union is that the soul through the medium of the body may acquire those of its perfections which it could not acquire without the senses or without a body.

corpore ; semel autem conjuncta, acquisivit quantum illa simpliciter appetit acquirere illo modo.

Dico ergo quod istarum trium propositionum ex quibus formatur ratio ad resurrectionem quodammodo a priori quia sumptae sunt a forma hominis resuscitandi, prima est naturaliter nota et error ei oppositus qui proprius est et solius Averrois, pessimus est, non tantum contra veritatem theologiae, sed etiam contra veritatem philosophiae ; destruit enim scientiam quia omnes actus intelligendi, ut distinctos ab actibus sentiendi, et omnes actus electionis, ut distinctos ab actibus appetitus sensitivi ; et ita omnes virtutes quae non generantur sine electionibus factis secundum rectam rationem et per consequens talis errans esset a communitate hominum, ratione utentium exterminandus.

Sed aliae duae non sunt sufficienter notae ratione naturali, licet ad eas sint quaedam persuasiones probabiles. Ad secundam quidem plures et probabiliores ; unde et illam videtur magis expresse sensisse Philosophus. Ad tertiam autem pauciores, et per consequens conclusio sequens ex istis non est sufficienter per istam viam nota ratione naturali.

[Pars Secunda : Rationes a posteriori]

Secunda via ad eam est a posterioribus, quarum aliquae probabiles tactae sunt in rationibus principalibus, utpote de beatitudine hominis. Ad hoc etiam additur de justitia Dei retribuentis ; nunc autem in

But if at any time the soul was joined to the body, then it has acquired the perfections that it simply desired to acquire in this way.

[*Evaluation of the* a priori *proof*]. Of the three propositions used to construct a kind of *a priori* argument in the sense that the proof is based on the nature of the form of man that is to be restored, I say that the first is known by natural reason and that the contrary error, which is proper to Averroes only, is of the very worst kind. Not only is it opposed to theological truth but to philosophical truth as well. For it destroys knowledge itself inasmuch as it denies any act of knowledge distinct from sensation or any act of choice distinct from sense appetite and hence does away with all those virtues which require an act of choice in accord with right reason. One who errs in this way, consequently, should be banished from the company of men who use natural reason.

The other two propositions, however, are not known adequately from natural reason even though there are a number of probable persuasive arguments in their favour.[21] The reasons for the second, indeed are more numerous as well as more highly probable. For this reason, the Philosopher appears to have held this doctrine more expressly.[22] For the third, however, the reasons are fewer. The conclusion, then, which follows from these three propositions is not sufficiently known *a priori* by natural reason.

[*Part II. The* A Posteriori *Proofs*]

The second way to prove the resurrection is by *a posteriori* arguments. Some probable arguments of this kind were mentioned in the initial arguments, for instance, those concerning the happiness of man. To the latter this argument based on the justice of a rewarding God is added. In the present life the virtuous suffer

vita ista virtuosi majores patiuntur poenas, quam vitiosi. Et istud argumentum videtur Apostolus tangere ad I Cor. xv * : Si in hac vita tantum sperantes sumus in Christo, miserabiliores sumus omnibus hominibus, etc.

Sed istae rationes a posteriori minus concludunt, quam illa a priori accepta a propria forma hominis ; non enim apparet per rationem naturalem, quod unus est rector omnium hominum secundum leges justitiae retributivae et punitivae. Et esto quod sic diceretur quod unicuique in bono actu suo sit retributio sufficiens, sicut dicit Augustinus † : Jussisti, Domine et ita est, ut sit sibi poena omnis peccator, ita quod ipsum peccatum est prima poena peccati. Unde patet quod Sancti arguentes a posteriori ad propositum, non intendunt facere, nisi quasdam persuasiones probabiles, sicut Gregorius lib. xiv, ‡ positis ad hoc quibusdam persuasionibus dicit : Qui propter istas rationes noluerit credere, propter fidem credat. Consimiliter doctrina Pauli Act. xvii et xxvi ** et I ad Cor. xv †† per exemplum de grano cadente, et per resurrectionem Christi : Si Christus resurrexit et mortui resurgent, et per retributionem justam. Hujusmodi non sunt, nisi persuasiones probabiles, vel tantum ex praemissis creditis. Patet discurrendo per singula.

[*Pars Tertia : Solutio Quaestionis*]

Breviter ergo potest teneri quod nec a priori puta nec per rationem principii intrinseci in homine, nec a

---

* i Cor. xv, 19.
† *Confessiones*, i, cap. xii (Migne, P.L., xxxii, 670).
‡ *Moralia in Job*, xiv, cap. xl (Migne, P.L., lxxv, 1077).
** Acts, xvii. 31 ; xxvi. 23.   †† i Cor. xv.

more punishments than those who are wicked. It is this line of argument that the Apostle seems to have in mind in the first letter to the Corinthians * : "If with this life only in view we have had hope in Christ, we are of all men the most to be pitied, etc".

[*Evaluation of the* a posteriori *arguments*]. These *a posteriori* arguments, however, are even less conclusive than the *a priori* proof based on the proper form of man, since it is not clear from natural reason that there is one ruler who governs all men according to the laws of retributive and punitive justice.[23] It could also be said that the good act is itself sufficient reward for anyone, as Augustine says in the *Confessions*, BK. 1 † : "For it is even as Thou hast appointed, that every inordinate desire should bring its own punishment", so that sin itself is the first punishment of sin.

It is clear then that when the saints argued *a posteriori* for the proposed conclusion, they did not intend to give anything more than probable persuasive proofs. Gregory, for instance, having put down certain such proofs says ‡ : "Whoever does not wish to believe because of these reasons, let him believe because of faith". The same is true of Paul's teachings in the *Acts* ** and in the first epistle to the Corinthians † † where he uses the example of the grain that falls into the earth, or where he argues from the resurrection of Christ that if Christ be risen, the dead will rise again, or where he appeals to the notion of a just reward. Such arguments are nothing else than probable persuasive proofs, or they are reasons derived from premises that are matters of belief, as is evident if we examine them individually.

[*Part III. Solution to the Question*]

To put it briefly, then, we can maintain that natural reason cannot prove that the resurrection is necessary, neither by way of *a priori* reasons such as those based on

posteriori, puta per rationem alicujus operationis vel perfectionis congruentis homini, potest probari necessario resurrectio, innitendo rationi naturali ; ergo hoc tanquam omnino certum, non tenetur nisi per fidem. Imo nec secunda propositio in prima via, sicut dicit Augustinus XIII *De Trinitate,* cap. ix,* tenetur per rationem sed tantum per Evangelium,† dicente Christo : Nolite timere eos qui occidunt corpus, animam autem non possunt occidere...

[Ad Argumenta Principalia]

Ad primum argumentum, aut arguitur praecise de desiderio naturali proprie dicto, et ille non est aliquis actus elicitus, sed sola inclinatio naturae ad aliquid, et tunc planum est, quod non potest probari desiderium naturale ad aliquid, nisi primo probetur possibilitas in natura ad illud, et per consequens e converso arguendo est petitio principii ; aut arguitur de desiderio naturali minus proprie dicto, quod scilicet est actus elicitus, sed concorditer inclinationi naturali, et tunc iterum non potest probari quod aliquod desiderium elicitum sit naturale isto modo, nisi prius probetur quod ad illud sit desiderium naturale primo modo.

Si autem arguas : quod illud naturaliter desideratur, quod apprehensum statim actu elicito desideratur, quia ista pronitas non videtur esse nisi ex inclinatione naturali. Hic uno modo negaretur prima, quia vitiosus statim inclinatur secundum habitum suum ad desiderandum illud quod sibi offertur ; sed quia natura non statim est ex se vitiosa, nec in omnibus, et quilibet statim appetit

---

* XIII, cap. ix (Migne, P.L., XLII, 1023).   † Mt. x. 28.

the notion of the intrinsic principle in man, nor by *a posteriori* arguments, for instance, by reason of some operation or perfection fitting to man. Hence we hold the resurrection to be certain on the basis of faith alone. Furthermore, as Augustine says in *De Trinitate*, BK. XIII, c. ix,* the second proposition used in the first [or *a priori*] proof [viz. of the immortality of the human soul] is not held because reason dictates this, but solely because of the Gospel † where Christ tells us : "Do not be afraid of those who kill the body but cannot kill the soul".

[Reply to the Arguments at the Beginning]

To the *first argument* 24 :   If the argument is based on the notion of natural desire taken in an exact and proper sense, and a natural desire in this sense is not an elicited act but merely an inclination of nature towards something, then it is clear that the existence of such a natural desire for anything can be proved only if we prove first that the nature in question is able to have such a thing. To argue the other way round, therefore, is begging the question.   Or if natural desire is taken in a less proper sense, viz. as an act elicited in conformity with the natural inclination, we are still unable to prove that any elicited desire is natural in this sense without first proving the existence of a natural desire in the proper sense of the term.

But suppose that someone were to argue that whatever is immediately desired, once it is known, is something that is desired naturally, since such proneness seems to arise only from some natural inclination.   One answer to this objection would be to deny the first statement, since a person with bad habits is inclined to desire immediately whatever is in accord with these habits just as soon as such a thing presents itself.   However, if nothing else intervenes, nature of itself is not vicious ; neither is it vicious in everyone.   Consequently, if everyone

illud apprehensum, sequitur quod illud desiderium non est vitiosum ; ergo ista responsio non est generalis. Ideo potest dici quod oporteret ostendere illam apprehensionem esse secundum rectam rationem non erroneam; alioquin si ad apprehensionem erroneam statim omnes appetant actu elicito, non sequitur illud desiderium esse consonum inclinationi naturae ; imo magis oppositum. Non est autem manifestum per rationem naturalem, quod ratio ostendens homini semper esse tanquam appetibile, sit ratio non erronea, quia prius oporteret ostendere quod istud posset competere homini.

Breviter ergo omne medium ex desiderio naturali videtur esse inefficax, quia ad efficaciam ejus oporteret ostendere vel potentiam naturalem in natura ad istud, vel quod apprehensio, quam statim sequitur istud desiderium, si sit actus elicitus, sit apprehensio recta et non erronea ; et horum primum est idem cum conclusione quae concluditur ex desiderio naturali. Secundum autem difficilius vel minus notum ista conclusione. Et ad probationem hujus quod desiderium hominis naturale est ad immortalitatem, quia naturaliter fugit mortem, posset dici quod ista probatio concluderet aeque de quocumque bruto. Et si addatur illud Philosophi II *De generatione* *: Melius est in omnibus semper esse quam non esse, istud est ad oppositum, tum quia aeque concluderet in bruto sicut in homine ; tum quia subdit : Hoc autem in omnibus impossibile existere continue propter longe a principio distare : ideo reliquo modo complevit Deus naturam continuam facere generationem,

---

* *De generatione et corruptione*, II, cap. x (226^b, 25 ff.).

immediately desires such a thing as soon as he knows of it, it would follow that the desire in this case is not vicious. The first answer to this objection, then, is not adequate. Therefore it could be answered like this. We must show that such knowledge is not erroneous but is in accord with right reason. Otherwise, it does not follow that just because everyone, on the basis of an erroneous conception, were immediately to elicit on act of desire, this desire is in accord with an inclination of nature. Indeed, it is rather the opposite that follows. Now it is not clear by natural reason that the argument establishing eternal existence as something desirable is not erroneous, since man must first be shown to be capable of such a thing.

To put it briefly, then, every argument based on natural desire seems to be inconclusive, for to construct an efficacious argument, it would be necessary to show either that nature possesses a natural potency for eternal life, or that the knowledge which immediately gives rise to this desire, where the latter is an elicited act, is not erroneous but in accord with right reason. Now the first of these alternatives is the same as the conclusion to be established.[25] The second is more difficult to prove and is even less evident than the conclusion.

As for the proof that man has a natural desire for immortality because he naturally shuns death, it can be said that this proof applies to the brute animal as well as to man. And should some one bring up the statement of the Philosopher in *De generatione et corruptione*, BK. II* that it is better for everything to exist forever than not to exist forever, this is really an argument for the opposite view ; first of all, because it holds equally well for both brute and man, and secondly, because Aristotle himself adds : "Since it is impossible, however, for all things to exist forever because of their great distance from their source, therefore God adopted the remaining alternative and completes the perfection of nature by making generation continuous". It is just as if Aristotle wished to

quasi dicat, cum desiderium naturale sit ad semper esse, in quibus est hoc impossibile in seipso, est illud sicut possibile est, scilicet in continuatione speciei in diversis individuis ; et ita concederet de homine sicut de alio generabile quod habet naturale desiderium ad semper esse, non in unico individuo, sed in tali successione.

Sed semper videtur stare vis quod fugiens unum oppositum, non fugit illud nisi propter amorem alterius. Concedi potest quod ex hoc sequitur quod cum fugiat mortem pro nunc, amat vitam pro nunc, et sic de quolibet nunc signato. Sed non sequitur, ergo pro infinito.

Ad illud Apostoli : respondeo nolumus nos inspirati sive certificati per fidem, et utique nolumus naturaliter sic, quod istud nolle est secundum inclinationem naturalem, sed non est notum ratione naturali quod istud nolle est secundum inclinationem naturalem.

Ad secundum, concedo quod verum est beatitudinem non solum in universali, sed etiam in speciali appeti naturaliter ab homine, sicut inferius patebit dist. XLIX.* Sed non est notum naturali ratione quod ipsa in particulari, quae scilicet consistit in illo in quo nos credimus eam consistere, appetatur naturaliter ab homine autem ; enim oporteret esse notum per rationem naturalem, quod esset ille actus nobis conveniens tanquam finis. Cum ergo probas per Philosophum quod beatitudo non tantum in generali ex i *Ethicorum*, † sed etiam in speciali ex x ‡ appetitur naturaliter, respondeo : illa ratio beatitudinis quam Philosophus reputat specialem, quod scilicet consistat in speculatione altissimarum causarum perfectissima, est valde universalis ; in speciali autem

---

* *Opus oxoniense*, IV, dist. XLIX, q. ix, nn. 2–3 (Vivès, VOL. XXI, 318).
† *Ethica Nicomachea*, I, cap. vii (1097^b, 1ff.).
‡ x, cap. vii–viii (117^a, 12ff.).

say that since there is a natural desire to exist forever, in those beings incapable of such existence there is a desire for such continued existence as is possible, viz. through the continuity of the species in diverse individuals. And so one could grant that just like the other beings that can be generated, man too has a natural desire to exist forever—not indeed in a single individual, but in a continual succession of individuals.

As for the principle that one flees from one thing only because he loves its opposite, however, it appears that this is always valid. We can admit that it follows from this principle that if one shuns death now, he loves life now, and the same can be said at any given moment. But from this it does not follow that he loves to live forever.

To that argument from the Apostle, I reply that we who do not wish [to be unclothed or who are averse to dying] are we who are made certain or inspired by faith. We are indeed naturally averse to dying inasmuch as such an aversion is in accord with an inclination of nature. But it is not known to natural reason that this aversion is in accord with an inclination of nature.

To the *second argument* : I concede that it is true man naturally seeks happiness not only in general but also in particular, as will be made clear in distinction XLIX.* But it is not known by natural reason that man naturally desires that particular beatitude which consists in what we believe it to consist,26 for it would be necessary to know by natural reason that such an act pertains to us as an end. Consequently, when you prove by the Philosopher that not only is beatitude in general desired naturally (from *Nicomachean Ethics*, BK. I)† but also beatitude in particular (from BK. x),‡ I reply that the beatitude which the Philosopher considered particular, namely the beatitude which consisted in the most perfect speculation about the highest causes, is in fact a knowledge through universals.27 By descending to particulars, then, Aristotle

descendendo, ipse non videtur processisse ultra speculatio-
tionem perfectissimam in vita ista. Unde inquisita ista
beatitudine hominis subdit : Oportet et corpus sanum
esse, et cibum, et famulatum esse, non tamen aesti-
mandum multum magnis indigere, felicem. Ergo
felicitas illa specialis quam nos ponimus speculationem
homini possibilem longe perfectior est quacumque possibili in vita ista, illa non est naturaliter nota esse finis
noster nec naturaliter notum est eam naturaliter appeti
a nobis tanquam finem.

Cum probas per rationem Augustini beatitudinem non
posse esse nisi sempiternam, dabitur istud ab illo qui
tenet beatitudinem humanam posse haberi in vita ista,
quod volens amittit eam, quia debet secundum rectam
rationem velle conditionem naturae suae. Recta autem
ratio ostendit isti non habenti fidem, ut videtur sibi,
quod conditio naturae suae est mortalitas tam animae
quam corporis, et ideo debet velle sicut et vitam amit-
tere, ita vitam beatam. Et cum dicis, non est vita beata
quae non erat amata ab habente, verum est, si non
esset amata pro tunc quando est possibilis, et conveniens illi amanti, sed sic esse convenientem pro semper
non est notum per rationem naturalem.

Ad aliud conceditur quod notum est homini ipsum
posse consequi finem suum in aliquo individuo, et per
consequens, beatitudinem in illo gradu in quo notum
est beatitudinem esse finem hominis. Et cum dicis hoc
impossibile esse in vita ista, dico quod ista impossibilitas
non est nota per rationem naturalem. Cum adducis
infortuna, infirmitatem, imperfectionem virtutis et
scientiae, respondetur quod haec omnia repugnant
perfectae felicitati, qualem notum est competere Intelli-
gentiae, sed non qualem notum est posse competere
homini.

did not seem to go beyond the most perfect speculation possible in this life. Hence, having inquired into
the nature of this happiness of man, Aristotle adds [28] :
"To be happy it is necessary for man that his body be
healthy, that he have food, companionship, that he does
not crave too much or want too much". Since we assume
that man is capable of a speculation far more perfect than
anything possible in this life, the special happiness
which we postulate is not known naturally to be
our end, neither is it known naturally that we seek it
as an end.

When you argue from Augustine's proof that happiness
cannot be anything but eternal, a person who holds that
human happiness is possible in this life will reply that he
does wish to lose it. For according to right reason, he
must wish whatever is the lot of his nature. But to a
person who has no faith, right reason seemingly reveals
the lot of our nature to be mortal both in body and soul.
Therefore, he must wish to lose life and therefore to lose
the happy life. And when you say that such a life is not
happy which had not been loved by the one who possessed
it, this is true only if such a life had not been loved at a
time when it was both possible and fitting to have it. But
it is not known by natural reason that to be happy forever
is something in accord with our nature.

As for the other [or *third* argument], we grant that man
knows he can attain his end in some individual, and
consequently, that he knows he can attain happiness in
the degree recognised to be man's end. When you
say that such happiness is not possible in this life, I reply
that this impossibility is not known by natural reason.
When you adduce the misfortune, bodily infirmity,
inperfection of virtue and knowledge, the answer is that
these are inconsistent with the type of perfect happiness
known to be characteristic of an Intelligence [29] but they
are not inconsistent with the happiness known to be
within the reach of man.

Ad quartum, diceretur quod ista species perpetuabitur in universo per continuam successionem individuorum quam poneret Philosophus per generationem continuam, non autem continuabitur per vitam alicujus, nec aliquorum in specie. Ex his apparet quantae sunt gratiae referendae nostre Creatori qui nos per fidem certissimos reddidit in his, quae pertinent ad finem nostrum, et ad perpetuitatem sempiternam ad quae ingeniosissimi et eruditissimi per rationem naturalem quasi nihil poterant attingere, juxta illud quod adductum est de Augustino xiii *De Trinitate* cap. ix* : Quod vix pauci, etc. Si fides adsit quae est in eis quibus dedit filios Dei fieri, nulla quaestio est quia ipse suos credentes in hoc certissimos reddit.

* xiii, cap. ix (Migne, P.L., xlii, 1023).

To the *fourth*, it might be said that in the universe it is the species that will go on forever through the continuous succession of individuals.   It is this which the Philosopher postulated by his doctrine of continuous generation.   But it is   not the life of any single individual or individuals within the species that will continue to exist.

From all this it is apparent how much thanks must be given to our Creator, who through faith has made us most certain of those things which pertain to our end and to eternal life—things about which the most learned and ingenious men can know almost nothing according to Augustine's statement in *De Trinitate*, BK. XIII, c. ix * : "Scarcely a few, etc".[30]   "But if faith be there—that faith which is to be found in those to whom [Jesus] has given the power to become the sons of God—there is no question about it," [31] for of this He has made those who believe in Him most certain.

NOTES

NOTES

SECTION I

[1] The MSS read either *phicos* or *phycos*. The text is faulty here as it is in so many other instances. Scotus's meaning, however, seems clear enough.

[2] *In quid* and *in quale* are two basic modes of predication. They refer primarily to the five predicables of Porphyry, namely, the genus, species, specific difference, property, and accident, though Scotus extends the idea of *in quid* and *in quale* predication to the transcendental order. Briefly, the difference between the two is this. To predicate *in quid* means to predicate either the entire essence (i.e. the species) or at least the determinable part of the essence (e.g. the genus). The term is derived from *quiddity* or essence and such predication represents an answer to the question : What is it ? (*Quid est ?*). To predicate *in quale* means to predicate a further determination or qualification of the essence. This qualification (*quale*) may be either essential (e.g. a specific difference) or non-essential (e.g. a property or accident). Since the specific difference is really a part of the essence or quiddity, Scotus sometimes speaks of it as being predicated *in quale quid* or *in quale substantiale* in order to distinguish it from properties or accidents which are said to be predicated either *in quale accidentale* or simply *in quale*. To predicate something *in quid*, says Scotus, it is not enough that the predicate be an essential note but that it be predicated *per modum subsistentis*, which from the viewpoint of grammar means that it must be predicated as a *noun*, not as an adjective or participle or adverb. Predication *in quale*, whether it be an essential qualification or not, is always predicated *per modum denominantis*, which from the viewpoint of grammar means it is predicated as a modifier. "Substance", "whiteness", "rationality", "rational animal", "life", "truth", "goodness", if used as predicates, would be predicated *in quid*, whereas "substantial", "white", "rational", "living", "true",

165

"good", if used as predicates, would be predicated *in quale*. "Being" (*ens*) can be used either as a noun or as a participle. In the first case it is predicated *in quid* and is equivalent to "a being" or "a thing" with a singular and plural. In the second case, if used as a predicate, it is predicated *in quale* or *denominative*. Used as a participle, "being" always requires a subject which it modifies.

3 *Ultimate differences* are denominative terms that are irreducibly simple. In regard to concepts that designate real things or some real aspects of real things (*first intentions*), Scotus distinguishes those which are irreducibly simple and those which are not. *Irreducibly simple concepts* (*conceptus simpliciter simplices*) are such as cannot be reduced or broken down into two more simple concepts that are first intentions, one of which is determinable and the other determining. The concept of "man", for instance, can be reduced to "animal" and "rational". "Animal" in turn can be broken down into "sentient " and "organism". This process, according to Scotus, cannot go on indefinitely. Otherwise nothing would be known. Ultimately we arrive at intelligible elements or notions that are incapable of further analysis and hence are irreducibly simple. Restricting ourselves to real concepts, that is "first intentions", we can say, according to Scotus, that there is but one irreducible simple concept that is determinable or quidditative, and that this is "thing" or "being" used as a noun. But there will be as many irreducibly simple differential, determining, or qualifying concepts as there are different concepts, where *different* is taken in the technical Aristotelian sense. (Things *differ*, according to the Stagirite, only if they have something in common ; otherwise they are simply *diverse*. Cf. *Metaphysica*, x, cap. iii, 1054^b, 23-30). Since Scotus gives as examples of concepts that are not irreducibly simple that of the individual, the species and the genus, and since even such concepts must contain an ultimate difference, it seems that we can distinguish three types of ultimate differences, according to him : (1) the *haecceitas* or individuating difference ; (2) certain kinds of specific differences ; (3) transcendental differences, such as those which limit or contract "being" to the ultimate genera

or categories, or such notions as "infinite", "necessary", "accidental", etc. According to Scotus, not every specific difference should be considered to be irreducibly simple. Since we are speaking of first intentions we must take into consideration the nature of the reality designated by the concept. Consider the notion "living body". According to Scotus, "living" is derived from and connotes the life principle which is a form or substance really distinct from the body which has its own *forma corporeitatis*. Since the life principle can be designated by a determinable or non-differential notion (e.g. "substance", "thing", "a being") Scotus does not consider the term "living", as applied to an organism or man, as an irreducibly simple concept. Such a specific difference is not ultimate, though further analysis will eventually yield a specific difference that is irreducibly simple (Cf. *Opus oxoniense*, II, d. III, q. vi, n. 12 ; I, d. III, q. iii, n. 15 ; II, d. xxv, q. i, n. 16).

4 Attributes or properties (*propria* or *passiones*) are those qualifications which are necessarily connected with their respective subject yet do not enter into its essential definition. "Being" has two types or attributes, those which are simply coextensive, such as "one", "true", "good", and those which are coextensive in disjunction such as "infinite-finite", "simple-composed", "necessary-contingent", etc.

5 The *primacy of commonness*, or better, of common predication, which Scotus ascribes to being, simply means that "being" conceived quidditatively or as a noun is predicable of anything that can be grasped by a concept that is not irreducibly simple. The *virtual primacy* that Scotus attributes to "being" in reference to its attributes and ultimate differences does not mean that the formal concept or *ratio* "being" contains these notions in such a way that the latter can be abstracted from the former by an act of intellectual abstraction or analysis as some have claimed. It simply means that these other notions or *rationes* are predicable by a necessary or *per se* predication of some subject that can be designated as "a being" or "a thing". According to scholastic usage, if the predicate of a necessary or *per se nota* proposition is part of the essential definition of

the subject, the latter is said to "contain the predicate essentially" and the predicate is said to be predicated according to the first mode of *per se* predication. If the predicate, however, is an attribute or property (see above, note 4) it is said to be "contained virtually in the subject " of which it is predicated necessarily and according to the second mode of *per se* predication. Since every modification or qualification presupposes some subject that is modified or qualified, the subject is said to have a natural priority or primacy in regard to the modification or qualification. Applying this to the notion of "being" conceived quidditatively or as a noun, Scotus argues that since "being" is the ultimate subject or determinable element to which every concept not irreducibly simple can be reduced, "being" has a primacy in regard to all such concepts or "primary intelligibles". Since "being" is furthermore the ultimate subject of which the attributes and ultimate differences are predicable, "being" can be said to enjoy a virtual primacy in regard to these notions. Since the latter will express either a property (*proprium*) or an essential determination (specific difference or transcendental modification), Scotus declares that all notions that are ultimate qualifications (such as the attributes like "one", "true", etc., or ultimate differences like "substantial", "infinite", "finite", etc.) are "contained virtually [i.e. as a *proprium*] or essentially [i.e. as a specific difference or transcendental determination] in something else which does include ' being' essentially [i.e. in something which is a primary intelligible]".

⁶ Scotus alludes to the theological teaching that in the Eucharist the substance of bread and wine is no longer present after the act of consecration, though the species or appearances (accidents) remain.

⁷ For the meaning of *irreducibly simple* cf. note 3 above.

⁸ The *simple intellect* or *simple intelligence* is a term applied to the mind or intellect in so far as it is the principle of the act of simple apprehension or intelligence. The scholastics distinguish three acts or functions of the mind or intellect : (1) simple apprehension, whereby the mind grasps the meaning of

something without affirming or denying anything of it ; (2) the act of "composition and division", or immediate judgment, whereby the mind affirms or denies some predicate of some subject ; (3) the act of reasoning or mediate judgment, by which the mind infers one proposition from another or other propositions.

9 Demonstration, according to Aristotle (*Analytica posteriora*, I, cap. xiii) is of two kinds : demonstration of the fact (*demonstratio quia*) and demonstration of the reasoned fact (*demonstratio propter quid*). The first merely establishes that the conclusion of the syllogism is true, but the second additionally indicates the reason why the predicate of the conclusion inheres in the subject. For the middle term of a demonstration of reasoned fact gives the cause or some ontologically prior principle (e.g. the essential definition) that can be considered as the reason or rational explanation why the predicate must be affirmed of the subject. A demonstration of reasoned fact will always be an *a priori* form of demonstration ; an *a posteriori* demonstration, on the contrary, will always be a demonstration of the simple fact.

10 Scotus has previously discussed why God is the subject of theology but not of metaphysics, and to what extent theology verifies the Aristotelian notion of a science.

11 "Its principle", that is, some self-evident or analytical proposition of which it is the subject.

SECTION II

1 For Scotus's reply to these arguments, see pp. 30 ff.

2 The statement of Pseudo-Dionysius that we do not know what God is ; we know only what he is not (Cf. *De caelesti hierarchia*, II. Migne, P.G., III, 141 ; see also St John Damascene, *De fide orthodoxa*, I, iv. Migne P.G., XCIV, 800), was often quoted by the scholastics. This *docta ignorantia* was exaggerated by many. Scotus Eriugena, for instance, suggests that perhaps it might be more correct to say that God is not good, true, just, etc.,

since any term or concept we might derive from the universe of creatures is so radically inadequate to express what God is that it could more truly be denied of God than affirmed of Him (Cf. *De divisione naturae*, I, xiv ff. Migne, P.L., cxxII, 462ff.). Duns Scotus reminds us that this way of speaking cannot be taken too seriously. If our knowledge is purely negative, it is no knowledge of God at all.

3 Henry of Ghent makes use of this distinction in his *Summa*, art. xxii, q. i ad iii ; q. iv.

4 Henry of Ghent, loc. cit., q. iv ; St Thomas, *Summa theologica*, I, q. iii, art. iv ad iii.

5 Henry of Ghent, loc. cit.

6 Ibid.

7 Henry maintains that God is already known in a most general manner in every concept the human intellect forms of a created object as "this being". Consequently, he is forced to hold that we cannot know a creature without at the same time having some knowledge of God. This knowledge of God in creatures, however, must be distinguished from a knowledge of God as He is in Himself. See *Summa*, art. xxii, q. vi.

8 Henry, *Summa*, art. xxiv, q. vi. For Scotus's answer to Henry's arguments, see p. 32.

9 Henry contrasts two radically different notions. By privatively undetermined being, he understands the notion of being that applies to creatures. As creatures actually exist, they are qualified or determinate forms of being. For instance, man is a rational, sentient, organic, material, substantial being. Nevertheless, the mind prescinds from all these determinations to form a simple concept of being, *undetermined* but *determinable*. The concept of being that applies to God, however, negates or denies all determination and therefore is called negatively undetermined being. God, in a word, is not only being in an unqualified and undetermined sense, but His being is incapable of any restriction, limitation or determination. Therefore, being in this sense is *undetermined* and *indeterminable*. Now *determinable* and *indeterminable* beings have nothing positive

in common ; they agree only in what is denied, namely, *determination*. Therefore, our so-called "concept" of being as common to God and creatures is in reality not one concept but two. But because of their similarity, the mind fails to distinguish between the two, even as the eye fails to resolve two distant objects. This dual "concept" is what Henry calls the "analogous concept of being".

10 In scholastic terminology, "indetermination" as applied to God is a *first intention*. It expresses a perfection of a really existent entity, in this case the positive mode of existence, infinity. Indetermination in the second instance, is characteristic not of a real entity, but of our *concept* of being. It is a *second intention*, since it refers not to some condition of reality but to a characteristic of a concept or *ens rationis*.

11 Only what is true can be an object of "knowledge" or *scientia* in the strict Aristotelian or scholastic sense of the term. Hence, "false knowledge" is a contradiction in terms. Similarly certitude, in the technical sense of the term, presupposes that the proposition to which the mind gives its firm assent is a true and not a false statement.

12 The intellect, according to the general view of the scholastics, is a dual faculty comprising the active or agent intellect and the passive or possible intellect. This division is based upon an obscure passage in Aristotle's *De anima* (III, cap. v ; 430ᵃ 18) and underwent a variety of interpretations. With Alexander of Aphrodisias, as well as with some scholastic interpretations of Augustinian illumination, the active intellect is identified with God. With Alfarabi and Avicenna, it is a subordinate intelligence or "angel" somehow connected with the moon. St Thomas considers the active intellect to be a faculty of the soul really distinct from the possible intellect. Scotus also considers it to be a property of the soul but regards it as only formally distinct from, but really identical with, the possible intellect and the soul's substance. The general function of the active intellect is to render the potentially intelligible in the sense image actually intelligible. The additional specific refinements Scotus has given to this general function do not concern us here.

[13] Notions pertaining to the essence of the object (generic, differential or specific notions) are contained "essentially". Colour, for instance, is contained essentially in redness. A notion is regarded as virtually contained in a given object, if the object has the power or *virtus* of producing the notion in the mind. In a broad sense, "virtual" is not opposed to "essential", since the object has the power to produce a concept of what it contains essentially. In addition, however, the object can be said to contain virtually its necessary properties (*propria*) or any effects it is capable of producing. An object such as a golf-ball could produce a simple notion proper of itself as a sphere and also a simple proper notion of a circle, according to Scotus, for the notion of circularity is virtually contained in the notion of sphericity. Such an object, however, could not give rise to a simple proper notion of a triangle or pentagon.

[14] A pure or simple perfection (*perfectio simpliciter*) is one that does not contain in its formal notion any imperfection or limitation. As such it is opposed to mixed perfections (*perfectio secundum quid*) which involve both perfection and imperfection. Knowledge, volition, existence, wisdom and the like are regarded by Scotus as pure perfections. Matter, corporeity, sense knowledge or even knowledge obtained by a reasoning process as contrasted with intuitive knowledge, all involve limitation and imperfection in their very notion.

[15] For this discussion see above, pp. 4–8.

[16] Scotus distinguishes between two types of objects that move the intellect of a creature to knowledge, one natural, the other voluntary or supernatural. The natural motivating object of an intellect causes knowledge automatically or necessarily, as it were, by the very fact that it is what it is and is co-present to that intellect. Now the divine essence is a natural or adequate motivating object of immediate and intuitive knowledge only in regard to the divine intellect itself. For any created intellect, God's essence is a purely voluntary object. The reason, says Scotus, lies in this fact that God's essence cannot be related necessarily or automatically, as it were, to any

creature or part thereof—a corollary of the absolute independence of the First Being. All relationships between God and creatures are contingent and dependent upon the divine will, the ultimate source of all contingency. Consequently, in the beatific vision of God in heaven, says Scotus, it is not the divine essence as such that moves the intellect but rather the divine will. In this sense, God is a voluntary object. But the peculiarity of the beatific vision lies in the fact that the divine will motivates but does not terminate this act of intuition. And this is something unique in the order of objects and follows from the fact that God's will is really identical with God's essence (Cf. *Quodlibet*, q. xiv).

[17] For the distinction between a demonstration of the fact and a demonstration of the reasoned fact see note 9 above. In this particular instance, the demonstration of the fact referred to is an *a posteriori* argument which proceeds from effect (creatures) to cause (God). In such a process, that which is most unlike creatures, and consequently most distinctive of God, is the last to be demonstrated.

[18] See Scotus's proof for the existence of God, pp. 52 ff.

[19] The less universal and more specific the concept, the greater its comprehension or intension. The concept of man, for instance, contains the more universal notions of "animal", "organism", "substance", "being", in its intension.

[20] The scholastics list a number of *loci* from which a dialectitian may draw his arguments. The *locus a minori* assumes that what is within the power of the less perfect, is also within that of the more perfect. Now the intellect, a purely spiritual faculty, is more perfect than the imagination, an organic faculty.

[21] See p. 14.

[22] See p. 14.

[23] For a description of this fallacy see Aristotle's *De sophisticis elenchis*, cap. v (167^b, 1–20).

[24] Intuitive knowledge of God is supernatural. See note 16.

[25] See p. 14.
[26] See pp. 68 ff.
[27] See p. 14.
[28] See p. 17.

SECTION III

[1] For Scotus's reply to these arguments, see p. 76.

[2] This is the solution given by Henry of Ghent, *Summa*, art. xxi, q. i.

[3] See Aristotle, *De caelo*, I, cap. iii (270^a, 12–13) ; cap. xii (281^b, 18 ff.) ; II, cap. iv (287^a, 23–24) ; cap. vi (289^a, 8–9) ; *Metaphysica*, IX, cap. viii (1050^b, 22–24).

[4] See p. 173, note 17.

[5] Cf. *Opus oxoniense*, I, dist. xxxvi, q. unica, n. 5.

[6] Cf. St Thomas, *Summa theologica*, I, q. ii, art. iii corpus, quarta via.

[7] "Natural" is understood in the technical sense of a cause that acts by a necessity of nature and not deliberately or freely. Efficient causes, according to Scotus, fall into two classes : (1) those which possess antecedent rational knowledge and act deliberately ; (2) those which lack such knowledge and act automatically or by a necessity of nature. See *Quaest. in Metaphysicam*, IX, q. xv, n. 4 (Vivès, VOL. VII, 608^b ff.) where he divides all active powers into either *nature* or *will*. Here he proves paradoxically that according to Aristotle's division of rational and irrational powers the intellect is "irrational" in the sense that it acts automatically in the presence of evident truth whereas the will is "rational" in the sense that it can freely choose to love or not to love an object known through reason or intellect.

[8] In an ascending order one progresses by going from the posterior to the prior ; in a descending order, from the prior to the posterior. For instance, in regard to a series of temporally ordered causes where one precedes the other in time, many philosophers (e.g. St Bonaventure) deny the possibility of an

infinite regress into the past (an ascending order) and use this argument to establish a creation in time, yet they admit the possibility of effects of created causes continuing indefinitely into the future (infinite regress in a descending temporal order). Scotus, as his answer to the objection that follows indicates, denies categorically the possibility of an infinite regress in an ascending order only in regard to essentially ordered causes. Inasmuch as such causes must exist simultaneously to produce a given effect, a chain of such causes will be non-temporal in character.

9 According to Aristotle's theory of colour borrowed from Plato (*Timaeus*, 67E), fine particles penetrate and dilate the medium whereas large particles compress it producing white or black colour respectively. Cf. *Metaphysica*, x, cap. vii (1057^b, 8). Hence "dilating" is regarded as a property of anything white, and "white" may be regarded as a *per se* cause of the same.

10 See Aristotle, *Physica*, II, cap. iii (195^a, 27 ff.) ; cap. v (196^b, 24-29) ; *Metaphysica*, v, cap. ii (1013^b, 29ss).

11 See Aristotle, *Metaphysica*, v, cap. xi (1018^b, 9-11).

12 See p. 39.

13 See p. 42.

14 Scotus contrasts "nature" as a necessarily acting cause with a free agent acting with purpose or deliberation. See above, note 7.

15 See pp. 46-7.

16 Cf. Scotus's third conclusion, p. 46.

17 See pp. 47-8.

18 A univocal cause is one whose effect is of the same nature as itself. A father, for instance, is the univocal cause of his son. An equivocal cause, on the contrary, is of a different nature from its effect. For instance the artist is an equivocal cause of his painting. Since the less perfect cannot be the total cause of the more perfect, the total or principal cause, if

equivocal, must be more perfect than its effect. This argument seems to presuppose that efficient causality involves no imperfection and therefore will be found in the most excellent nature. Cf. pp. 42 and 45.

[19] Scotus is not attempting to prove numerical or individual unity at this point but rather a unity of nature. To put it in other words, the triple primacy is characteristic of but one *kind* of being. Whether there is more than one individual of this kind is not discussed here but in the following question on the unicity of God (cf. pp. 82 ff.). Scotus's intention is expressed more clearly in the *De Primo Principio*, chapter iii of which parallels the present question of the *Oxoniense*. He proposes "to demonstrate, if Thou wilt grant it, that some one nature is simply first. However, I say one *nature* for this reason, because in this third chapter the aforesaid three primacies will be shown, not about a unique singular or one in number, but about a unique quiddity or nature. There will, however, be mention of numerical unity later." (*De Primo Principio*, cap. iii ; Roche translation, p. 39).

[20] "Possible" is taken as the contradictory disjunction of "necessary". It designates a being which exists in virtue of another and hence, of itself, is merely possible. Scotus seems to have been influenced by Avicenna's *possibile esse* and *necesse esse*.

[21] See note 14.

[22] Scotus refers to his theory of "natural appetite" in virtue of which appetite every nature seeks its own perfection. This "seeking", however, is not to be understood in the sense of a conscious striving for some known goal but is merely the ontological relation that exists between a thing and whatever can perfect. In this sense, for instance, *matter* seeks or loves *form* and vice versa. In the present case the subject perfected and that which perfects it (viz. the end) are simply identical. Hence, Scotus argues that if we say the First Agent has a "natural love" of itself, this is equivalent to saying that it is its own perfection or it is itself.

[23] See Aristotle, *Physica*, VIII, cap. vi (259^b, 32 ff.) ; *De caelo*, II, cap. iii (286^a, 34 ff.) ; *De generatione et corruptione*, II, cap. x (336^a, 23 ff.) ; *Metaphysica*, XII, cap. vi–vii (1072^a, 9 ff.).

[24] A subject is said to be in contradictory potency to something if it can either have it or not have it. The argument here is this. If thought can either be present or absent so far as the nature itself is concerned, then to think requires some effort on the part of the nature and this would eventually produce weariness.

[25] The first act or actualisation of a being is that it exists with its various faculties or powers. Thus, for instance, so far as man's body is endowed or informed by the human soul, man is in *first act*. When a man actualises his human faculties or powers by acts of seeing, thinking, willing, etc., he is in *second act*. For Scotus, a rational nature achieves its highest perfection by loving the highest good.

[26] *Activum* implies an immanent operation, that is one which is not only initiated by the subject but remains in and perfects that subject. Vital activities such as thought, volition and the like are immanent operations. *Factivum*, on the other hand, implies that the operation is transient, that is, has a term outside the agent. Man's artifacts are produced by a transient activity.

[27] Cf. St Thomas, *Sent.*, I, dist. xxxv, q. i, art. i ad iii ; *Summa theologica*, I, q. xiv, art. ii.

[28] Scotus uses the term *ratio intelligendi* (literally "the reason for knowing"). The allusion here is probably to the notion of an "intelligible species", which in human knowledge is supposed to substitute for the object in such a way as to make universal concepts possible. Even if one were to postulate something analogous to the species in regard to God's knowledge, it would still be identical with His essence and intellect.

[29] Since whatever receives something is perfected by the form received, it would follow that the more perfect knowledge would be perfected by the less perfect.

[30] See *Quaest. in Metaphysicam*, VII, q. xv, n. 9.

31 "Infinity" is regarded here as a degree of intensity which the perfection in question possesses. Scotus distinguishes between intensive and extensive infinity. A thing is said to be extensively infinite if there is no pure perfection (cf. p. 172, note 14) which it does not possess. Nothing, however, is said in regard to the intensity or degree to which such perfections are possessed. Each pure perfection, however, is said to be intensively infinite if it exists in the highest degree possible for that respective perfection. Thus God would not be extensively infinite if He lacked knowledge and love. But His knowledge is intensively infinite if it is a comprehensive knowledge of all that can be known, including His infinitely intelligible nature.

32 Cf. e.g. Aristotle, *Metaphysica*, ii, v (994^a, 1-2).

33 Scotus distinguishes between the omnipotence of God as an article of his Catholic creed (omnipotence in the proper sense of the term) and the infinite power of God (omnipotence in a qualified sense) as demonstrated philosophically by reason unaided by faith (Cf. *Quodlibet*, q. vii ; *Opus oxoniense*, i, dist. xlii, q. unica). In this distinction we see the influence of the philosophy of Alfarabi and Avicenna. The latter, influenced by Plotinus's theory of emanation, maintained that God can create only one being immediately, viz. the highest Intelligence. This creature in turn produces subordinate Intelligences. The creation of the earth as well as the heavenly bodies and their souls is the work of these created Intelligences. Even in this theory, however, God is the ultimate cause of all things that emanate directly or indirectly from Him, and therefore the First Cause in some qualified sense at least is omnipotent. As a theologian, however, Scotus could not subscribe to this view, for according to his theology, he believed that whatever God can do through the medium of the secondary cause He has created He can do directly or immediately if He so willed. But Scotus makes this much of a concession to Arabic philosophy, namely, that in our present state we can only demonstrate that God can create all things either mediately or immediately and in this sense God's power must be infinite intensively. We can give only probable arguments for

omnipotence in the proper sense of the term, according to him, and cannot demonstrate that God could create all possible things immediately.

[34] See, for instance, Aristotle's doctrine (cf. note 23). Also Averroes, *Physica*, VIII, com. 9 ; *Metaphysica*, VII, com. 28 ; IX, com. 41, etc. ; Avicenna, *Metaphysices compendium*, I, pars iv, tr. ii, cap. I, etc.

[35] See, for instance, St Thomas, *Summa theologica*, I, q. xlv, art. v ad iii ; Henry of Ghent, *Summa*, art. xxxv, q. vi ; *Quodlibet* IV, q. xxxvii.

[36] The classical definition of creation is *esse post non-esse*, that is "existence after non-existence". The question arises : How is *post* or "after" to be understood ? The obvious interpretation is to take it in a temporal sense. Avicenna, however, to reconcile the dogma of divine creation and the Aristotelian theory of the eternity of the world understood *post* in an ontological sense, viz. that the nature of a creature considered absolutely or in itself does not imply existence. Since any thing it possesses in addition to its nature is subsequent to that nature, existence can be said to be subsequent or "after" non-existence. Following Avicenna, St Thomas, Scotus and others tend to interpret this definition in an ontological rather than a temporal sense.

[37] See note 28.

[38] See pp. 46 and 73.

[39] See pp. 45–6.

[40] See *Opus oxoniense*, I, dist. iii, q. iii, nn. 10, 24, 28 ; dist. ii, q. vii, n. 42, etc. Briefly, intuition is a simple or non-discursive knowledge of something *as existing*. Abstract knowledge prescinds from actual existence or non-existence.

[41] Cf. St Thomas, *Summa theologica*, I, q. vii. art. i ; *Contra gentiles*, I, cap. xlv, etc.

[42] St Thomas, *Sent.*, II, dist. iii, q. i, art. i ; *Summa theologica*, I, q. I, art. ii. See E. Hocedez's introduction to *Aegidii Romani*

theoremata de esse et essentia (Louvain, 1930), pp. 17 ff., regarding the particular interpretation to which Scotus is referring.

[43] In his analysis of a given entity, Scotus often arranges the various perfections or *rationes* the mind distinguishes therein according to an ontological priority, accordingly as one *ratio* presupposes the other for its existence but not vice versa. To conceive the entity under some prior *ratio* in order to discover what additional attributes are implied in virtue thereof is to conceive it according to a *prior instance of nature.*

[44] St Thomas, *Sent.*, II, dist. xliii, q. i, art. i ; *Summa theologica*, I, q. vii, art. I.

[45] See p. 35.

[46] See pp. 27–8.

[47] See p. 35.

[48] See pp. 53–4.

[49] See p. 35.

[50] That is to say, a kind of one-to-one correspondence exists between the two by reason of certain essential likenesses or similarities.

[51] See p. 35.

[52] Cf. Aristotle, *Physica*, VIII, cap. i (251^a, 8–252^a, 4).

[53] See p. 36.

[54] Magnitude is considered as being finite by nature. Cf. the first argument in the *contra*, p. 36.

Section IV

[1] For Scotus's reply to these arguments, see pp. 92ff.

[2] Cf. Aristotle, *Topica*, II, cap. x (114^b, 33).

[3] Cf. Pseudo-Dionysius, *De divinis nominibus*, cap. v (Migne, P.G., III, 819) ; St Bonaventure, *De mysterio Trinitatis*, q. i, art. i

(Quaracchi, VOL. V, 47^a) ; Aristotle, *Metaphysica*, II, cap. i (993^b, 24–31).

4 Cf. Aristotle, *Topica*, III, cap. 1 (117^a, 16) ; St Augustine, *De libero arbitrio*, III, cap. ix, xi (Migne, P.L., XXXII, 1282, 1288).

5 This argument and its accompanying refutation have been added later by Scotus as some manuscripts indicate.

6 William of Ware, *Sent.* I, dist. ii. q. ii (Muscat ed. in *Antonianum*, II (1927), 344–350). For Scotus's reply, see pp. 91f.

7 *Opus oxoniense*, prol. q. iii, n. 12.

8 The "natural will" and "natural love" according to Scotus are not elicited acts or operations at all. They are merely the ontological relation of perfectibility that exists between whatever can be perfected and that which perfects it (cf. section III, note 22). In this sense, everything may be said to love itself, i.e. its own perfection. Only if the thing is a part can it be said to love the whole more than itself since the whole is the perfection of the part. Similarly, God as the ultimate perfection of rational creatures is loved naturally more than the creature itself.

9 To use as a means something that should be loved as an end is a perversion of love.

10 Beatitude in the technical sense implies that the object exhausts the potentialities of the rational being so that the latter is perfectly satisfied and is at rest in the possession of this object. Such an object is necessary to the happiness of this being and therefore it could not be destroyed without destroying the happiness.

11 Cf. the preceding question, pp. 38 ff.

12 St Bonaventure, *Sent.* I, dist. ii, art. i, q. i ad iv ; William of Ware, *Sent.* I, dist. ii, q. i.

13 See p. 84.

14 See pp. 25–6, the third statement.

15 See p. 83.

16 See p. 83.

[17] See p. 83.

[18] Aristotle, *De caelo*, I, cap. ii (269^a, 19–20).

[19] See p. 83.

[20] St Bonaventure, *Sent.* I, dist. ii, a. i, q. 1 ad ii.

SECTION V

[1] For Scotus's reply to these arguments, see pp. 131, 122 ff.

[2] Henry of Ghent, *Summa*, art. i, q. ii.

[3] Aristotle, *Metaphysica*, III, cap. iv (999^a). See Henry's inter-pretation of this passage, *Summa*, art. i, q. ii.

[4] Scotus summarises the teaching of Henry in *Summa*, art. i, q. iii.

[5] Note added by Scotus, according to the scribe of the Assisi manuscript.

[6] Scotus, following St Augustine, uses the term Academician and sceptic as synonyms. The Academicians or Academics were the adherents of Plato, so called because Plato used to deliver his discourse in the Academy at Athens. The Academy continued after Plato's death and was characterised at different periods of its existence by different philosophical trends. Scepticism, it seems, was introduced by Arcesilas, the founder of the Middle Academy, and later modified by Carneades, who dominated the Third Academy. Cf. St Augustine, *Contra Academicos*.

[7] See p. 100.

[8] A marginal note in the Assisi manuscript indicates that the subsequent passage is not found in Scotus's own copy.

[9] Cf. note 25 of sect. III. Here the objector argues : By life or being alive Augustine means nothing more than that the body has a life principle, viz. the soul, which is its primary or first actualisation. He does not mean that the soul is conscious, that is, that we are in second act.

[10] Note added by Scotus.

[11] Additional note by Scotus.

[12] Cf. Aristotle's definition of the perfect syllogism, which is a syllogism of the first figure. *Analytica priora*, I, cap. ii (24^b, 22 ff.), cap. iv (26^b, 29 ff.).

[13] Cf. note 9 of sect. I.

[14] *Opus oxoniense*, prol. q. iii, n. 13 ; I, dist. viii, q. v, n. 24.

[15] Note added by Scotus.

[16] An additional note of Scotus.

[17] See pp. 100 f.

[18] Note added by Scotus.

[19] Henry of Ghent, *Quodlibet*, IV, qq. vii, viii, xxiii ; v, q. iv.

[20] See pp. 101 f.

[21] The acts of "intelligence" as distinguished from "reasoning" are of two kinds : (*a*) simple apprehension or intelligence whereby the mind grasps the meaning of something without affirming or denying anything of it, and (*b*) the act of "composition and division", that is, the act of judgment, in which the mind affirms or denies some predicate of the subject of the proposition.

[22] The active intellect, according to Scotus, is not really distinct from the soul. Hence, it is a more perfect effect of God than would be the impression or accidental effect produced in the soul by God, the Uncreated Light.

[23] This or some similar qualification must be added, because according to Scotus, the will or faculty of love is more noble than either the active or possible intellect.

[24] The marginal note in the Assisi manuscript, *non in libro Scoti*, indicates that the passage in the Latin text within parentheses is not found in Scotus's own copy.

[25] Cf. p. 97. The elaborate attempt to "save face" for St Augustine in this fifth article not only indicates the esteem in

which Scotus held the saint but it also illustrates the cardinal principle he uses in interpretating other thinkers. "I wish to give the most reasonable interpretation to their words that I possibly can" (*Opus oxoniense*, I, dist. viii, q. v, n. 8). The intricate and subtle explanation that follows is typical of the reasoning that earned Scotus the title *Doctor subtilis*.

[26] According to the scribe of the Assisi manuscript, the subsequent section in parentheses in the Latin text is missing in Scotus's own copy.

[27] Scotus tells us (*Opus oxoniense*, I, dist. xliii, q. unica) that prior to their actual existence, God knows all possible creatures whether they shall ever be given existence or not. Absolutely speaking, these creatures may consequently be said to "have an intelligibility" or *esse intelligibile* ; this, however, is dependent upon the divine intellect so that one can say that God does not know these things because they are intelligible, but rather they are intelligible because God knows them. For in knowing the possible, God gives it a kind of "existence", viz. that characteristic of the content or object of thought. Even though the human intellect in the present life has no immediate intuitive knowledge of God, of the divine intellect or its thought content, it still remains true that the ultimate reason why the notions derived from created objects are intelligible is because God first gave them intelligibility in knowing them. This intelligibility or meaning can be called the "eternal light" in a qualified sense. And all propositions that are evident from the meaning of the terms can be said to be seen in the eternal light.

[28] Only something that exists in the proper sense of the word can be an efficient cause. Consequently, we cannot ascribe any such causality to something that exists only in an improper sense as the content or object of thought. Nevertheless, it is the intelligibility of the object that is said to "move" the intellect to know the thing in question. Scotus argues that we should rather ascribe that causality which meaning has in regard to our intellect to the divine mind or intellect which gave to all created things their meaning or intelligibility.

[29] The priority referred to here is one of nature, not of time. Cf. note 43 of sect. III.

[30] Such knowledge implies a direct vision of God and is not possessed by man in this life.

[31] The triangle is considered the first figure in plane geometry. Thus it is symbolic of the Triune God who is first in the hierarchy of beings.

[32] See pp. 99–100.

[33] According to the scribe of the Assisi manuscript, Scotus's personal copy is left incomplete at this point. What follows is supplied from the Vivès edition, VOL. IX, 207.

[34] See p. 128.

[35] Literally, "It is in respect to every being whatsoever".

[36] That is, principles evident from their terms.

SECTION VI

[1] For Scotus's reply to these arguments, see pp. 158 ff.

[2] The matter of the heavenly spheres was considered to be incorruptible in contradistinction to the corruptible terrestrial matter of the four elements.

[3] Subjective parts are contrasted with essential parts. The latter refer to the order of comprehension or intension ; subjective parts refer to the order of extension or class inclusion. Here the meaning is that the intellective or rational soul is a member or part of what Aristotle designates by the general term of the soul or life principle of man.

[4] Cf., for example, St Thomas, *Summa theologica*, I, q. lxxv, art. ii.

[5] St Thomas maintains that the intellect which is perfected by the act of knowledge pertains to the category of passive potencies. This is the so-called *intellectus possibilis*. Cf. *Summa theologica*, I, q. lxxxv, art. ii. iii ; III, q. ix, art. iii ; *Contra gentiles*, II, cap. lxxxv, xcvi, xcviii. Godfrey of Fontaines goes

even further in denying all activity to the possible intellect. Cf. *Quodlibet*, VI, q. vii ; VIII, q. ii ; IX, q. xix ; XIII, q.v. Cf. also Giles of Rome, *Quodlibet*, III, q. xii, xiii.

[6] Henry of Ghent, *Quodlibet*, V, q. xiv.

[7] Aristotle, *De anima*, II, cap. ii (424^a, 30 ff.) ; see also III, cap. i (425^a, 19).

[8] According to Aristotle, the sensory power consists in "the equipoise of contrary qualities in the organ". (Cf. *De anima*, II, cap. xii, 424^a, 30 s.)

[9] See pp. 138 f., number 2.

[10] See pp. 141 ff.

[11] Cf. Richard of Middleton, *Sent.*, II, dist. xix. art. i, q. l.

[12] Cf. for example, *Ethica Nicomachea*, I, cap. ii (1094^a, 20–21) ; also Averroes, *Metaphysica*, II, com. 1.

[13] Cf. St Thomas, *Summa theologica*, I, q. lxxv, art. vi.

[14] According to Aristotle and the scholastics, a demonstrative proof in the technical sense of the term must have premises that are both necessary and evident propositions. Premises known by faith in revelation are not evident and hence are not technically capable of producing a demonstration. Such premises, though never evident, may be either necessary or contingent propositions. For instance, "God is just" would be considered a necessary proposition inasmuch as it is based on the immutable nature of God and could never be otherwise. On the contrary, "Jesus Christ is the redeemer of mankind" would be considered a contingent proposition because the whole order of redemption like creation depends on the free decrees of God. Now Scotus calls proofs based on necessary though not evident propositions "necessary reasons". The arguments for immortality, however, are based on contingent propositions and hence fail to meet the technical requirements for an Aristotelian demonstration on two counts.

[15] "Separate agent", that is, a pure spirit or Intelligence. Such celestial beings (the angels of the scholastics) were called

"separate substances" inasmuch as they subsisted apart from matter and were not destined by nature to inform or dwell in a corporeal body like the spiritual soul of man.

[16] "Natural agent" is understood here as one which causes generation and corruption.

[17] See pp. 158 ff.

[18] Literally, "existence through itself". Technically, however, *per se* existence or subsistence is used by the scholastics to designate that mode of being characteristic of substance or substantial union in contradistinction to *per accidens* existence characteristic of accidents or incidental aggregates. Scotus's reply to the argument plays upon the ambiguity of the term *per se* existence as applied to a composite substance such as man. Since the component elements of man (body and soul) are not accidents but substances, albeit incomplete as to function at least, each could be said to possess *per se* existence. But the same is true of any material or perishable form. On the other hand, since man as a whole is not an accidental aggregate but a composite substance, the union of soul and body represent a *per se* mode of existence, but one which the soul possesses only as long as it is united to the body.

[19] Cf. St Bonaventure, *Sent.* II, dist. ii, pars prima, art. i, q. iii ; St Thomas, *Summa theologica*, I, q. l, art. ii ad iii.

[20] Confer Henry of Ghent, *Quodlibet*, II, q. iii ; St Thomas, *Contra gentiles*, IV, cap. lxxix.

[21] For Scotus, as for Aristotle and the scholastics generally, a probable or dialectical proof does not have the same connotation as it has for the neo-scholastic. A valid and convincing proof may still lack the technical requirements of an Aristotelian "demonstration" as defined by the Stagirite in the *Analytica posteriora*, I, cap. ii (71^b, 18–25) or by Scotus in *Opus oxoniense*, prol. qq. iii–iv lat., n. 26 (Vivès, VOL. VIII, 183^b) ; III. dist. xxiv, q. unica, n. 13, (XV, 44^b) ; *Reportata parisiensia*, prol. q. i, n. 4 (XXII, 7^b) ; III, dist. xxiv, q. unica, n. 16 (XXIII, 454). If such a probable proof is persuasive, it may even give

subjective or moral certitude in the sense that all prudent fear of error is excluded, and yet it will not produce strictly demonstrative knowledge or *scientia*.

[22] See pp. 145 ff.

[23] Though Scotus claims that natural reason can demonstrate the existence, unicity and infinite perfection of God, he regards the Christian concept of a just and merciful God as a matter of faith. Cf. *De Primo Principio*, cap. iv (ed. Roche p. 146).

[24] See p. 134.

[25] According to Scotus's theory of natural desire, to admit that human nature is capable of immortality is to admit that man has a natural desire for it ; for a natural desire is not a conscious act or elicited volition but is rather the ontological relation that arises between the perfectible and its perfection. Only in a metaphorical sense can this relation be called "desire". Cf. *Reportata parisiensia*, iv, dist. xlix, q. ix, nn. 3–5 ; see also note 22 of sect. iii.

[26] Namely, in the beatific face-to-face vision of God.

[27] Cf. the question on man's natural knowledge of God, especially the fifth statement, p. 28.

[28] *Ethica Nicomachea*, x, cap. viii (1178^b, 35 ff.).

[29] That is, a pure spirit or angel.

[30] Cf. p. 136 for the complete text.

[31] St Augustine, *De Trinitate*, xiii, cap. ix (Migne, P.L., xlii, 1023).

INDEXES

INDEX OF PROPER NAMES

INDEX OF SUBJECTS